D0753009

TECHNOLOGY TRANSFER

TECHNOLOGY TRANSFER

TECHNOLOGY TRANSFER

STRATEGIC MANAGEMENT IN
DEVELOPING COUNTRIES

GOEL COHEN

Sage Publications
New Delhi * Thousand Oaks * London

Copyright © Goel Cohen, 2004

All rights reserved. No part of this book may be reproduced or utilised in any form or by any means, electronic or mechanical, including photocopying, recording or by any information storage or retrieval system, without permission in writing from the publisher.

First published in 2004 by

Sage Publications India Pvt Ltd
B-42, Panchsheel Enclave
New Delhi 110017

Sage Publications Inc
2455 Teller Road
Thousand Oaks, California 91320

Sage Publications Ltd
6 Bonhill Street
London EC2A 4PU

Published by Tejeshwar Singh for Sage Publications India Pvt Ltd, phototypeset in 9.5/11.5 Century 751BT at C&M Digitals(P)Ltd., Chennai and printed at Chaman Enterprises, New Delhi.

Library of Congress Cataloging-in-Publication Data

Cohen, Goel.
Technology transfer: strategic management in developing countries/Goel Cohen.

    p.cm.

    1.Technology—Developing countries—International cooperation
    2. Technology transfer—Developing countries. I. Title.

T49.5.C626   338.9'26'091724—dc21   2003   2003006142

ISBN: 0-7619-9770-9 (US-HB)   81-7829-254-8 (India-HB)

Sage Production Team: Aruna Ramachandran, Abhirami Sriram, Larissa Sayers, Radha Dev Raj and Santosh Rawat

TO ILANA

*For her full support and
interest in this book*

Contents

List of Tables

LIST OF FIGURES

PREFACE

This book was motivated principally by my interest in attempting to bridge the gap between the hard and soft sciences in order to evolve a common interactive framework. During my engineering studies and subsequent experience with lecturing in a technology-oriented university, I observed a limited comprehension of the concept of 'technology' among both engineers and scientists at large. Later, while pursuing degrees in economics and business administration, seemingly simple ideas such as 'technology', 'development' and 'developing countries' were transformed into multifaceted concepts with innumerable implications. This intellectual shift from hard science to soft science, combined with my experience of living in an underdeveloped region where organisations try to use foreign technologies, led me to undertake the study of the theoretical and managerial aspects of technology transfer from a new perspective.[1]

The subject itself internally generates many problematic issues in technology management and development, as in other disciplines. In addition, there were no specific joint engineering–social sources in existence that could be used as a tool in addressing these issues. Moreover, due to the lack of a solid conceptual framework and of practical and comprehensive analysis of the subject, it was incumbent upon me to search through a multitude of writings, mostly mono-dimensional works of either 'commercial–economic' or sophisticated 'technical–engineering' origin. My educational background proved to be an asset in this journey, and led me to unexplored areas in the strategic management of technology transfer as well as various important practical and theoretical considerations. The present volume

---

[1] As a preliminary outcome, a number of papers were published in journals or presented at conferences which have been referred to in this volume with a different spelling, 'Kahen' instead of 'Cohen'.

extensively examines notions of technology, development, technological change and technology transfer and the inextricable linkages among them in order to formulate a simple, practical model. It identifies the major factors responsible for the effectiveness or failure of technology transfer, thus establishing a general approach to the design of successful flows of tools, procedures, know-how, information and human expertise from an advanced country or multinational corporation to the underdeveloped world.

The conditions for effective technological change and knowledge flow are complex, involving not only engineering factors but economic and socio-political factors as well. My target has been to develop a methodology for rigorous modelling that takes account of these complex factors, both quantitative and qualitative. Previous works were found to have overlooked several factors that would appear to be significant; consequently, the literature does not offer an adequately systematic and comprehensive treatment of the subject matter, even at the basic level of understanding technology as a concept. Most earlier works focus on the general and economic aspects of transfer, treating all types of technology alike; specific aspects such as the characteristics of the particular technology in question, the country involved, and even human factors are not considered. The incompleteness of these analyses in this regard has meant that no rigorous attempt could previously be made to devise a formal model of the complex process of technology transfer. Such a model is needed to provide an objective, quantitative basis for technology assessment and judgement. It is the purpose of the present book to meet this need.

Having thus identified the important 'missing' factors, it is clear that a realistic model of the demand side of technology transfer to developing countries should take account of such factors (for instance, the issue of bilateral benefits). Initial analysis led to the elaboration of systematic guidelines that may be used to design a model describing the processes involved in transferring and sustaining a technology; this model would be used at the national or sectoral (that is, strategic) level for technology assessment within the integrated engineering–economic system.

The analytical emphasis of the approach presented here allows for logical and systematic evaluation, and, it is hoped, will help in the selection and effective transfer of a technology. The method will enable organisations and governments to develop or apply specific techniques for strategic assessment, in the strategic planning sense, by quantifying the appropriateness, sustainability and the expected outcomes of candidate technologies. It is recommended that the methodology developed in this book be applied in the assessment of different technologies (such as energy, information, manufacturing or health care technologies) in various organisations, sectors or countries. The volume is also intended to be utilised as a guide by senior managers in order to enhance their ability to think strategically in managing technology transfer—an ability widely recognised as the single most important contributory factor in competence conceptualisation.

September 2003   **Goel Cohen**

Acknowledgements

I would like to express my sincere appreciation to Professor B. McA. Sayers. I thank him for his constructive comments, and for his never-ending support during my experience at the Imperial College of Science, Technology and Medicine, University of London. A special thanks to Catherine Griffiths for her continuous contribution and valuable assistance to me in my work. Among many others, I would like to thank Dr Juan F. Ramil and Dr Jeremy Pitt for their valuable suggestions. I wish also to express my gratitude to Dr A. Mohammadi, who encouraged me to submit this manuscript to Sage. My deepest appreciation to my daughter, Dr Niaz Cohen, and my two sons Afshin and Sina, for their support. Finally, grateful thanks are due to Aruna Ramachandran, a considerate editor with many helpful suggestions, and also to all the people at Sage who have contributed in significant ways to this book.

INTRODUCTION

TRANSFERRING TECHNOLOGY TO DEVELOPING COUNTRIES

This book analyses the process of technology transfer to developing countries in order to provide a basis for the quantifiable modelling of technology assessment, which is regarded as a key element in this process. The book is intended to fill a gap in the existing literature on the subject by presenting a comprehensive and systematic approach to the management of technology transfer. We believe that certain issues need to be clarified if we are to understand technology and the process of its transfer, as also the requirements for successful technology transfer. These issues include: the nature and elements of technology; its relation to science and engineering and its socio-cultural context; technological change and its context in developing countries; the fundamental bases and mechanisms of technological planning systems; the structural and contextual aspects of the processes of technology transfer and development understood within a systematic framework; the internal aspects of the process of transfer, including the key elements involved and their interrelationships, which will throw light on the main factors responsible for the effectiveness of the transfer process; and the mechanism of technology assessment and the process of technology related decision making.

Some preliminary thoughts on these matters are presented here, followed by an outline of the content, scope and objectives of this book.

THE NEED FOR A SYSTEMATIC STUDY FOR QUANTITATIVE MODELLING OF TECHNOLOGY TRANSFER

The importance of technology in supporting and sustaining socio-economic growth and national development has been extensively documented (see, for example, Denison 1962; Gaski 1982; S. Kuznets 1966; Lewis 2000; Malecki 1991; Solow 1957; Thomson 1993; Tisdell & Maitra 1988; Xu 2000). Technology is believed to be one of the major forces underpinning economic growth; accordingly, an efficient technology transfer system would lead to an efficient use of resources. Indeed, industrialisation has been treated as a synonym for economic and socio-cultural development by many scholars, planning authorities, technologists and politicians in developing countries (see, for example, Colman & Nixson 1978; Ming & Xing 1999). Industrialisation was attributed the crucial role in the process of development in the international debate on these issues in the 1960s. Industrialisation in both 'hard' and 'soft' domains is now considered to be the most efficient vehicle for comprehensive development of the underdeveloped world. It is also recognised that the 'engine' of such development is technology transfer. Developing countries thus need Western technology to alleviate their economic difficulties (Erdilek 1984; Rostow 1967).

However, the history of technology transfer has not been one of unqualified success. Many failures have occurred for reasons that have not always been clear. We hope that the present book will help reduce the incidence of such failures. Our target is to point out crucial concepts and provide, or at least indicate, a practical approach that will make it possible for planners to improve the chances of success of a process that is extremely important for many developing countries. The available literature on technology transfer suffers from a lack of systematic study and of comprehensive quantitative/ qualitative modelling aimed at gaining insights into the technology transfer process. We approach our task by identifying important factors that have been overlooked in the literature, and arriving at a realistic and suitable model of the *demand side* of technology transfer to developing countries that takes these various factors into account and establishes how best to handle them. On the basis of this understanding, a general and consistent approach to technology transfer to developing countries is delineated. Following this approach, the necessary methodologies may be developed for building a more comprehensive quantitative model of technology transfer.

It may be noted here that some uncertainty about the concept of 'developing countries' and their characteristics exists in the literature (see, for example, Bhagavan 1990; Gemmell 1990; Harrison 1980a, 1980b; N. Sharif 1999). One group of scholars prefers the term 'industrially developing countries' over 'developing countries' (for example, R. Sen 1984; Wisner 1980), although the concept of 'industrially developing countries' is also ambiguous. At first glance, industrialisation would appear to be the dominant criterion for development. But the term addresses three-quarters of all the countries in the world as the group of 'developing countries'. It is clear that these countries are at quite heterogeneous stages of industrial development and tend also to differ according to their situations and the dynamics of their strategic pathways of development. Indeed, one may identify 'industrially developing countries' within three levels or categories: 'slightly industrialised', 'semi-industrialised', and 'relatively highly industrialised' countries. While many definitions exist (see, for instance, Todaro 1981), for the purposes of our volume, developing countries are operationally defined as all those countries in which the manufacturing industry contributes less than 10 per cent to GDP (following the definition provided by the World Bank [1979]).

TECHNOLOGY AND THE PROBLEMS OF DEVELOPING COUNTRIES

The crucial role of science and technology (S&T) information in techno-economic advancement and in research and development (R&D) is obvious. The academic literature produced in developing countries does not always contain up-to-date science and technology information. Most of these countries rely for such information on literature produced in developed countries (it should be pointed out here that around 60 per cent of the total world output relating to science and technology was produced by only 11 industrially developed countries: UNESCO [1992]). For any candidate technology to be transferred to a given country, it requires to be assessed in terms of both the technological level and the technical capability of that country. Furthermore, the absorption and assimilation of that technology is facilitated by a sub-process of technological adjustment. The stage of techno-economic development reached by a country will therefore influence its ability to absorb technologies: the more advanced it is, the more easily might it be expected to take up and internalise transfers.

Many factors affect the transfer of knowledge and technology to developing countries. The lack of adequate financial and technological resources, low per capita income and gross national product (GNP), and unfair income distribution and the lack of hard currency (Kahen & Sayers 1995b) are the major economic and financial factors influencing the process of transfer in most developing countries. Among numerous other problems are specific political conditions and rigid or ineffective bureaucracies, high rates of illiteracy, riots and other forms of social violence caused by differences in language, religion and caste, political instability, and frequent labour strikes (Eres 1981; Kahen 1994, 1995c, 1996a; Kahen & Sayers 1995c). Transportation, telecommunication and communication systems are poor and cost-oriented (Kahen & Sayers 1994, 1996a). Moreover, unmodernised educational systems in most developing countries result in poor research facilities and academic institutions, and insufficient professional institutions for technologists and researchers; as a result of this, these countries also suffer from the very serious problem of 'brain drain'.

We may consider technology as a set of specialised knowledge; the transfer of this knowledge from one place (that is, where it is generated) to another may be seen as an organised technological flow with its own complexity. As the world becomes increasingly interdependent technologically, the transfer of technology from one country to another plays a key role in *global* development. The transfer of Western technologies to Japan, for example, was extremely successful and has been a predominant factor in securing Japan its current technological position in the world (Kahen 1995b, 1999). The notion of transfer of technology, when the transfers are between industrialised countries, is relatively straightforward, but it is much more fluid when the transfers are to developing countries. Problems involving the mastery of foreign technology do not arise in exchanges between industrialised countries in the same way as for developing countries; in the former case, the balance between transfer and mastery is more easily attained. But for a developing country, the capacity transferred is not predetermined to the same extent; it can range from the mere transfer of production or organisational capacity to the mastery of a complete process (from design through to production).

These differences in the capacity to master technology can raise important political problems. In some developing countries, disappointing outcomes of transfers have been viewed as the result of deliberate actions by technology suppliers (such as the industrialised countries) to maintain monopolies that they may have been losing elsewhere. Such suspicions have resulted in a number of conflicts, exacerbating an already complicated situation (OECD 1981). While the 'technological backwardness' of many developing countries means that transfer of modern technology is essential, technology transfer is more than simply the extra production capacity that is acquired. In fact, technology transfer may be said to begin as a solution to 'someone else's' problems (Mogavero & Shane 1982). The adaptation of 'outside' solutions to someone else's problems can be regarded as the essence of the process of technology transfer, the rationale being to avoid reinventing the wheel, as it were.

At the present time, not only is the process of technology transfer very costly and complicated, but its ultimate success is far more contingent upon a number of fundamental factors (economic and socio-political) than was previously realised. Rosenberg & Frischtak (1985) state that 'among the most important of these factors are the level and direction of *indigenous* technological efforts, as well as numerous aspects of the *institutional* setting in the recipient country' (emphases mine). Thus, it would seem that a complete *system* is required for technology transfer; this system must accommodate the movement from a physical transaction to indigenous technological endowment to technology adoption and development in a host country. It is also clear that good choices of technologies to be transferred depend critically upon the availability of the relevant *information* in the host country.

A SIMPLIFIED DATA ACQUISITION SYSTEM

Many complex factors are involved in the consideration of the social, political, economic and environmental aspects of technology transfer. Some of those factors are not completely defined, or cannot be precisely measured. As a result, much technology evaluation within the process of technology transfer is necessarily subjective in nature. Moreover, since the number of candidate technologies generally far exceeds the number of sectoral or national technological projects that will be selected for implementation, there is need for a consistent approach to technology assessment. Such a process of evaluation would require the availability of a data acquisition system; however, the funds available for data acquisition in developing countries are very limited. Therefore, we need to develop a simplified data acquisition system for the process of assessment of technologies to be transferred to these countries. Such a system should aim to be both realistic and practicable.

In this volume, we focus specifically on the issue of technology assessment within the process of technology transfer, and discuss how such a problem can be formulated and solved, when it manifestly involves ethics, aesthetics, and the representation of values. Our aim is to develop just such an approach and to evaluate its potential contribution to engineering management at national and sectoral levels. We formulate our approach to technology assessment through the provision of conceptual and theoretical frameworks to help understand the transfer of technology.

OBSTACLES TO SUCCESSFUL TECHNOLOGY TRANSFER TO DEVELOPING COUNTRIES

The parameters of development are determined by the pace at which technological changes take place in a particular society (MacLeod & Kumar 1995). While every developing nation seeks new technologies for national development, most also experience social and cultural problems in the use, adaptation and diffusion of these technologies. These problems stem from the fact that technology transfer is a sophisticated process, the structure of which is beyond the control of developing countries. Furthermore, the technological output of technology transfer is so fundamentally alien to poorly developed communities that adverse social impacts are inevitable. Recent experience with agricultural technologies, for example, shows that socio-economic factors are highly influential in determining the success or failure of technological change (Au 2000; Henry 1995; Ross 1999). This evidence is significant, because it suggests that socio-economic factors may constitute a real barrier to change emanating from imported and new technologies, and contradicts the belief that such factors are only temporary obstacles to change. Even colonial history clearly confirms the importance of 'structural factors' in the successful use of transferred technology.

The experience of transfer of technology to India, for instance, illustrates how socio-cultural factors have operated to constrain technological change and innovation (see, for example, Geertz 1963; Morris 1983).

Why does the technology transfer process meet with obstacles? As has been shown, the reason is that factors like knowledge, know-how, science and technology (S&T) and management have become crucial in technological development. These factors are not easily transferred, nor can they be developed or acquired in a short period of time. Today, the transfer of a number of highly sophisticated technological and technical systems poses a major problem for developing countries. Compounding these difficulties is the fact that technological progress is occurring at an unprecedented pace. Further, in this age of intensifying international competition, developing countries have to enter directly into global competition, for which they require investment capabilities, dynamic learning capabilities and organisational-operational capabilities. Indeed, the growing glob-alisation of technology and economy has significantly reduced the actual flows of transfer from the North to the South. Nevertheless, technology transfer continues to be an integral part of the dynamic process of development, and can be facilitated by a long-term inter-action between developed and developing countries (an example is the successful electronic load controllers project in Peru: see Touche Ross [1991]).

Technology development in *developed* countries, on the other hand, may be described as a continuous and organic process. Every new step is incremental and needs to be supported by the material and knowledge base of the country. As we shall show in the second chapter, when technology transfer takes place between two advanced countries, the new technology can easily be integrated with the host country's technological base. A large portion of the new technology's input requirements (equipment, energy, information, parts, operator skill, etc.) can, in principle, be supplied from within the host country. But such smooth linkages rarely exist in a developing country: its material and knowledge bases are normally inadequate to provide the necessary support for the new technology. Supplier and recipient are each constrained or facilitated in turn by the environment and by factors within their own milieus. Thus, a major difference between developed and developing countries lies in the state of their technological/knowledge bases (M. Sharif 1986). While the former tend to be *knowledge-intensive* societies, the latter, by contrast, are characterised by a distinct poverty of knowledge (see Sayers 1995).

However, if the imported technology is only marginally more advanced than the existing technology in the country, it may stimulate a positive response.

Much of the literature on technology transfer has revolved around studying the economic system and the innovative atmosphere of industrialised countries. It is by no means obvious that such a background provides the right kind of perspective to help us understand the process of technological change and innovation in developing countries. Developing countries differ from industrialised societies in terms of their technological capability, organisational and managerial systems, communication and telecommunication systems, economic characteristics (for instance, market size, degree of tariff protection, level of personal income, market and information distortions), availability of skills, political stability and value systems among many other factors.

Substantial differences also exist in the calibre of technology management functions between developed and developing countries. This is partly due to the widening gap between their respective science and technology capabilities, but it is also because of differences in some related functions, such as innovation and technology transfer, technology development, technology assessment, technology substitution, technology production and technological R&D.

Developing countries need to find and import suitable technologies that can provide both for the fulfilment of fundamental needs and for the promotion of technical capabilities for development. The lack of necessary resources (such as human skills, technical knowledge, information networks and foreign exchange) in these countries, however, delays the progress towards acceptable living standards. Therefore, the strategy of technological planning in these countries should be to emphasise the selection and transfer of the most appropriate technologies. The logic behind such a strategy is to utilise the transferred technology so as to improve their total capabilities, as well as to achieve the most rapid pace of techno-economic and social development possible.

Considerable attention has already been devoted in the literature on technology transfer to the subject of 'appropriate technology'. This term has been interpreted in different ways, mostly as 'labour-intensive' and 'low level' technology. However, in the light of the comprehensive analysis undertaken in this book (see chapter five), we extend the concept of appropriateness to include machine-intensive, and even advanced and knowledge-based (for example, see Kahen & Sayers [1997] on 'expert systems') or soft, technologies.

Traditional notions of 'appropriate technology' inevitably limit the process of technology selection, and imply that the choice of a technology is made from only a single subset of the technologies available to a country. However, we should recognise that the appropriateness of a technology is not an intrinsic quality of any technology, but is derived from the surroundings (technological, techno-economic, national aggregated capability, socio-cultural, political, environmental, legal, anthropocentric) in which it is to be utilised, and from the specific purpose of its application in a given country. Therefore, the selection of technology should be made by matching the characteristics of various technologies (from primitive to high and advanced) to the environment in which they would be utilised, and to the purpose of such utilisation.

'Choice' of technology and technological 'change' serve different roles at different stages in a country's development process. Technological change refers to the organic process of growth of technology that occurs once a country is well on the path of development. Choice of technology, on the other hand, is a process that is more relevant to developing countries looking for the right technologies to catalyse growth in terms of their own strategic priorities. This means that the choice of technology for transfer is governed by the position of the country in terms of its stage of development; consequently, the technology that is to be transferred must be identified and evaluated in accordance with that position. Various approaches to technology assessment have been delineated, mostly with reference to the micro level and applicable to developing countries (see, for example, Bennett et al. 1999; K. Chen 1979; Kahen 1997a, 2001b, 2001c; Panerai & Attinger 1985; Panerai & Pena Mohr 1989; Porter et al. 1980; Vincent et al. 1985). Although many different perspectives on technology assessment are available with reference to industrialised countries, choice of technology in developing countries remains dominated by economic assessment. We lack a comprehensive, multidimensional approach to technology assessment with reference to the process of technology transfer to developing nations.

One of the most important obstacles to technological efficiency in developing countries is 'institutional' or 'behavioural' in nature. However, current practices relating to technology selection within the process of technology transfer continue to suffer from the following major shortcomings:

1. The process of technology evaluation mostly considers technologies at the micro or firm level.
2. The process of technology evaluation is limited to the financial assessment (that is, a monetary cost–benefit analysis) of the project, isolated from the socio-cultural, technical and regional environments.
3. Economic, social, environmental and anthropocentric factors are often excluded. This is mainly because these factors are complex and mostly require subjective judgements (this shortcoming has occasioned a major focus of the present research: devising an appropriate model to solve this problem).
4. Guidelines for subjective and approximate assessment of complex and non-quantifiable factors are lacking. In some cases, although subjective judgements and non-quantifiable factors such as those involving equity issues and special commitments are included, they are not systematically and consistently accounted for in the technological evaluation process.
5. There is a lack or shortage of data and information; moreover, the available data have a low degree of accuracy and are not reliable.
6. Existing priority setting techniques rely heavily upon the accuracy of quantitative data input, and are not capable of systematically incorporating subjective and imprecise data and information into the evaluation process.

The present volume is directed towards minimising these shortcomings in the technology transfer selection process, with the aim of maximising the contribution and effectiveness of the transferred technology within the national production system of any given country.

An Outline of the Book

In more specific terms, we might say this book has the following objectives:

1. understanding the actual context in which technological change and innovation take place;
2. clarifying the nature of technology from first principles, that is, opening up the 'black box', in order to conceptualise the essence of

the technology transfer process and address it as a realistic system highlighting the interrelationships among its major components;

3. arriving at a systematic understanding of the major factors responsible for effective and sustainable transfer of technology;

4. defining an effective system for technological planning and decision making and exploring its relationship with the national developmental policy-making authority; and

5. establishing a rigorous, contextual methodology in order to facilitate the development of a comprehensive quantitative model for technology assessment applicable in any given developing country.

The first chapter focuses on the process of technological change and its relationship with the innovation process in industrialised nations, and compares this with the situation of developing countries. This chapter presents a conceptual analysis of the nature of technological change in both industrialised and developing countries. Aspects of the process of change which reveal its complexity are highlighted in order to achieve a proper understanding of the technology transfer process. This chapter also contains a theoretical discussion of the fundamental differences between the two techno-economic systems whose technological practices lead to two different processes: *innovation* in the industrialised world and *technological change* based on the transfer of foreign technology in developing countries. The purpose of this analysis is to identify the philosophy, objectives and foundations of technological practice and of technology development in developing countries. These insights will allow us eventually to establish the direction in which the foreign technology, that is, the technology that has been transferred, should move within the developing country context.

Chapter two critically reviews the concept of technology as a paradigm. This examination will facilitate our understanding of the technological situation of developing countries, as also the characteristics of the process of technological development within their socio-economic systems. Of the specific objectives enumerated earlier, the second and the third will be considered in this chapter, in which an attempt is made to recognise the elements and components that comprise technology in order to identify an appropriate socio-economic framework for its study. This framework will then provide a basis for developing a comprehensive picture of the process of technology transfer to developing countries. The conceptual results of these investigations will help identify the contextual prerequisites for a successful process of technology transfer.

In chapter three, the process of technology transfer will be analysed systematically. This analysis lays the foundations for a comprehensive theoretical approach, involving both 'engineering' and 'economic' perspectives. Based on this systematic approach, institutional infrastructures for technology transfer and industrial development within the national planning system will also be investigated. Chapter four discusses the pyramid of technology transfer, along with the major stages in the process of transfer and the different types of technological capability required to cope with the initial domination of foreign-imported technology.

Chapter five addresses the concept of appropriateness and identifies a group of key-role factors as likely to be responsible for the effectiveness of any technology transfer project. These major components are also considered within an effective technology transfer system. This discussion will enhance the development of our proposed comprehensive approach, addressed in chapter six. On the basis of such an approach, we arrive at the relevant criteria and theoretical bases for technology assessment. This approach enables us to identify strengths and weaknesses systematically and to develop a set of appropriate assessment criteria. In the light of this knowledge, it will be possible to develop a generic integrated model for technology assessment in any given developing country.

Chapter seven briefly describes the effects of the globalisation process and the WTO's policies on the process of technology transfer to developing countries. This chapter outlines the objectives underlying the strategic shift from local presence to the global market, and the implications of this shift for international technology transfers. We discuss how the post-WTO era and the phenomenon of global competition have influenced technology policy and decision making in developing countries. In conclusion, chapter seven discusses the strategic adjustment processes of the subsystems involved in the general system of technology transfer introduced in chapter four.

OBJECTIVES AND SCOPE

Our ultimate goal is to develop a comprehensive managerial methodology (that is, a new approach) that will help decision-makers conduct effective evaluation and selection of technologies for transfer. In terms of its scope, the present book includes the following major tasks:

1. It identifies the essential elements of technology transfer within a comprehensive framework.
2. It indicates the fundamental qualitative and quantitative dimensions of an effective technology transfer system.
3. It identifies factors having high relevancy to the technology assessment and selection processes.
4. It systematically develops a conceptual methodology in order to facilitate the incorporation of qualitative data into priority setting within technology transfer assessment models. This will be a key point in the application of any tool in the technology selection process.

We expect that the methodology developed in this book can be integrated in the current technology management system (particularly at the strategic or macro level). The analytical approach suggested here may be used as a tool for the disciplined and systematic formulation of judgements in the management of technology transfers.

Existing analytical approaches to technology evaluation and selection, such as engineering–economic analysis, cost–benefit analysis and optimisation techniques have limited applicability to real technology evaluation, where many of the variables and factors that need to be evaluated are imprecise, ill-defined and non-quantifiable. Consequently, there is a need for the development or integration of appropriate analytical technique(s), following the systematic approach provided in this book.

In other words, the assessment and selection of technology in the process of technology transfer to developing countries is a typical, multi-attribute, decision-making problem that requires decision-makers to evaluate several related factors simultaneously. To do this, an appropriate analytical approach is needed that can help decision-makers set down the relative order of preference of candidate technologies. A simple but powerful ranking procedure can provide an initial listing of candidate technologies or technological projects. Such a list is what strategic managers and decision-makers (that is, government authorities, or executive boards within a sector or an organisation) need to make a final selection.

This book is written for all those concerned with deploying technology in both public and private sectors. We anticipate that academics, the concerned authorities, company managers and researchers will find the approach offered here interesting and of value. This book would also help students in departments of management, engineering, economics, international studies, planning and development, and environmental science, acquire the skills necessary to understand the essence of technology transfer as well as its strategic and managerial aspects. It will be useful to students enrolled in MBA courses, and also to technology managers in industry who would like to update their knowledge of new ideas and approaches.

1

TECHNOLOGY GROWTH

INNOVATION, CHANGE AND DEVELOPMENT

A medium of socio-economic change and a principal catalyst of development, technology induces changes in all aspects of human life around the world. In general, technology refers to the capabilities of human society to transform nature (that is, resources) into useful products for human consumption (Storper & Walker 1989). Technology as such is a man-made phenomenon that affects people, knowledge, human institutions and the environment, as well as economic, industrial and social systems. Not only does technology facilitate human activities, it provides its own structure for the generation of human ambition and the satisfaction of the human hunger for unlimited knowledge. Technology is thus fundamental to 'development', a dynamic process that brings about socio-economic change as well as the growth of human knowledge leading to further technological progress and new cycles of growth.

Technology in both developed and developing countries[1] brings benefits as well as disbenefits; it is continuously updated and improved to meet the new needs and challenges facing contemporary societies (M. Sharif 1988). It is now universally recognised that technological change is vital to socio-economic growth. Nobel laureate economist Robert Solow (1957) concluded that much of the

---

[1]See the discussion pertaining to the definition of 'developing countries' in the Introduction to this volume.

increase in American standards of living was due to technological progress, technological change having caused 87.5 per cent of the increase in output per capita from 1909 to 1949. In support of this idea, Mansfield (1989) contends that 'the rate of technological change is perhaps the most important single determinant of a nation's rate of economic growth'. The accelerating rate of technological progress indicates that there may be no part of the future economy that will not be affected by either existing or emerging technologies.

Recent years have witnessed a renewed interest in activities that generate technological change in industrialised countries.[2] These activities feature centrally in the new trade and growth theories (see Balassa 1986; Bell & Pavitt 1993a, 1993b; Cant 1989; Fagerberg 1987, 1988; Grossman & Helpman 1990; Krugman 1986; Romer 1990; N. Sharif 1999; Tharakan 1984). In developing countries, on the other hand, one sees considerable progress and increasing efficiency in different technologies (Bell et al. 1984; Enos 1991; Havrylyshyn & Civan 1985; Katz 1984; Kim & Kim 2000; Mayer-Stamer et al. 1991; Minami 1994; Ouma-onyango 1999; Pack 1987). This is the result of continuous adaptation, improvement and development, and a tendency towards technology-intensive industries (such as fully computerised manufacturing systems).

Technological change in developing countries has both an external as well as an internal origin (Katz 1987). This is because it is based on technical knowledge and information from both foreign and local sources. Two points should be made in this regard: (*a*) foreign technological knowledge often comes 'embodied' in imported machinery and equipment; and (*b*) imported technology also flows in as 'blueprints', patents, instruction manuals, and other such 'disembodied' technical documents, frequently forming part and parcel of licensing agreements and technical assistance contracts.

---

[2]A terminological distinction is sometimes drawn between 'technological' and 'technical' change. *Technological* change in developing countries is viewed as a means of achieving development and productivity growth. It is construed as a learning process, and as a principal source of techno-economic development. *Technical* change, on the other hand, may be thought of as a complex, evolutionary cultural process that builds cumulatively on itself through technological change and continuous learning. It encompasses complex feedback mechanisms enabling improvement of current techniques and bringing about the generation of new ones. Therefore, many scholars regard technological change and technical change as mutually dependent phenomena. In this volume, despite the fine distinction between the two processes just described, the terms 'technical' and 'technological' are used interchangeably because of their close relationship.

These points about the transfer of technology suggest how technology might be systematically conceived. For instance, technology can be categorised into four main forms as follows:

1. technology as general theoretical and practical understanding of how to do things (know-how or information);
2. technology as objects (goods or tools);
3. technology as installed techniques of production (processes); and
4. technology as the personal know-how and abilities of workers (skills).

This classification, however, still leaves a gap. There is another form of technology: technology as 'organisational framework and managerial systems'. Technological change, and consequently development, may be said to occur in all of these dimensions. Each country has its own internal potential and a unique absorptive capacity with respect to each of these dimensions. This capacity, which is related to specific industries or technologies, emerges from the resources and institutions, including socio-cultural ones, that make up a country's technological capabilities.

TECHNOLOGY AND TECHNOLOGICAL DEVELOPMENT

Technology is the magic word in today's ideological lexicon. Not only developed nations but even developing countries may be seen as societies permeated by technology: new technology, key technology, high technology, up-to-date technology, leading-edge technology, state-of-the-art technology. While experts understand the nuances of these phrases, they have become part of the everyday language of people who have little knowledge of science and technology. This suggests how significant the notion of technology has become in our consciousness. But if one accepts the critical importance of technological change in socio-economic and industrial development, this leads onward to further questions. It is essential to point out that no one can reasonably view technology and technological growth as constituting purely positive and healthy developments. It is frequently believed, in developing countries, that technology will lead automatically to improved welfare; but the evidence shows that there is no such automatic route. The experience of developed countries proves that each developmental attempt cannot be expected to lead to the promotion or improvement of welfare and the advancement of human beings. As a result, researchers (such as Tisdell 1988) have been led to address crucial questions concerning misunderstandings about technology and development interactions. These questions can be summarised as follows:

- What is the optimum range of technological usefulness?
- To what extent can we expect the socially most beneficial technologies to be developed and applied in any society?
- What controls (degree of free choice) do nations and individuals have over the application of technology?
- Are the best interests of nations and societies, especially less developed countries, kept in mind in developing and actually applying the range of technologies available, and
- if not, why?
- How is the nature of the family, family life, and work likely to be affected by the introduction of new technologies both within the home and at the workplace? For example, how will they be affected by the increased availability of information-intensive products and machines, systems and telecommunication facilities?
- Can we predict the likely characteristics of future technologies— what they are likely to be, and what social consequences can be expected from them?
- Do developing countries face particular obstacles to economic development because of their late start and their reliance on imported technology?
- How can developing countries acquire, adopt and diffuse imported technology that mostly comes from unfamiliar socio-cultural and industrial systems?
- Is it possible to eliminate, or even decrease, the negative ergonomic effects of imported technology in order to improve people's efficiency and national productivity?
- What environmental problems and social adjustment problems may be encountered as a result of the emergence of new tech-nologies? Do these technologies increase man's control over or effect on nature? Do they lead to the relative rise and fall of dif-ferent industries?

Doeleman (1988, p. 291) highlights a conflict involving the domain of techno-economic development:

A consensus prevails that human history has, so to speak, been caught up in the fast lane. It is widely accepted also that the cause of this acceleration in the pace of our times lies, directly and indirectly, in expansion of the body of human technological knowledge. In the event, our natural and man-made physical environment as well as our social environment and psychological, cultural and spiritual values are all subject to an unprecedented multitude of pressures. These pressures have not necessarily been intended.

This points to the need for us to consider *both* sides of technological change before coming to any judgement about development, especially where developing countries are concerned.

While technology is accorded the credit for generating innumerable improvements in human living conditions, we must also consider its negative side. The pessimism regarding technological developments offers a sharp contrast to the optimism with which they are generally viewed. Thus, while the huge benefits of technology for developing countries are acknowledged, it is also held responsible for the destruction of ecological and environmental equilibria, for causing pollution, noise, dirt, hazards, ugliness, monotonous jobs, anti-social housing, cultural disruption and other psychological distress (M. Sharif 1988). This paradox of benefits and disbenefits is caused by the introduction of a new technology or a new application of existing technology. However, while the threat of hackers, for instance, is seen as a negative aspect of Internet technology, this cannot justify ignoring the enormous benefits the technology brings to all aspects of economic and social life. Negative cultural, social and ethical impacts along with institutional imbalances may be interpreted as some common symptoms of transition from underdeveloped to developed status brought about through technological change.

Techno-economic development is in reality a complex process of structural change, heavily influenced by new generic technologies themselves closely linked with science and technology capabilities (N. Clark 1990). Science and technology have thus acquired social power in the present age of wealth production (Salam & Kidwai 1991). Generally, the more sophisticated the technology and the more technical facilities that are available, the more time is saved in going on to the next stage. This is a specific potential: that of 'technological dynamism'. This potential of technology development, particularly its capacity for self-acceleration, has meant that high technology—especially in recent years—has in turn accelerated economic and social development. Indeed, the facts show that there can be no socio-economic growth without technology. And without economic growth there is inadequate capital to support environmental protection and sustainable development (N. Sharif 1992), especially in the energy sector of developing countries.

CRITICAL CONCEPTUAL CHANGES

After the Second World War (and particularly during the 1970s and 1980s), there came a time of dramatic modification in the structure of economic and technological change at all levels. Growing international competition introduced and extended a new era characterised by a powerful role for technology. Technology came to be recognised as a key factor in the promotion of efficiency of production and continuous improvement of productivity in techno-economic systems. This technology-oriented policy has now been supplemented by new manufacturing/production environments, along with a vast increase in trade in recent years (this has now become a prominent factor in national techno-economic development). These circumstances have increased the trade and technological imbalance between industrialised and less industrialised countries; thus, despite the acceleration of endeavours towards technology acquisition by the latter, the gap still exists. The gap between rich and poor countries, and between the more and less industrialised or advanced countries, is *technology-specific* and *infrastructure related*.

Indeed, technology has become crucial not only for the potential it has for inducing development, but also for survival itself. This is true of advanced countries as well as of developing countries, which suffer from the lack of sufficient technologies. While increasing competition has been the major driving force among developed countries to reach higher stages of technical knowledge in order to guarantee continuous productivity improvement, the challenge for developing countries has been one of attaining a reasonable degree of self-reliance in order to satisfy their basic or medium-term needs. Consequently, the acquisition and adaptation of foreign technology and the progress towards technological sustainability have been much more urgent and complex in the case of developing countries.

It was not until the 1980s that the full impact of the changes that affected theoretical and practical attempts at technology creation and acquisition related to the growth of nations and their socio-economic development was felt. A series of unanticipated events seemed to unfold at the same time, affecting both advanced post-industrial economies and developing countries simultaneously, if in distinct ways. For Western countries (see Malecki 1990), it was

the ascent of Japan to economic forerunner, the stagnation of Europe in jobless growth during the 1980s, and the meteoric rise of newly industrialising countries (NICs); all of these set existing theories and policies on their heads. What had worked in the 1950s, when the economy was growing, did not appear to work in the 1970s and 1980s when the economy was constant or even shrinking .... The plight of under-developed countries, with a few exceptions, also worsened. Growth became more difficult, and imports rose dramatically while production and living standards fell (Malecki 1991, p. 2).

Thus, the post–Second World War era witnessed significant transitions in many developing countries towards modern socio-economic growth. But even now, the situation of large numbers of people at very low levels of political institutionalisation remains poor, characterised by high rates of mortality, low life expectancy, chronic malnutrition, poor health, illiteracy, and the shortage of both communication and telecommunication networks.

Given that the dynamism of the development process is intimately connected with the structure and operation of international relations, we cannot separate developing and developed countries' technological changes from the development process itself. Exploring the main elements of the technical development process, Poznanski (1984) argues that the debate on South–West technological relations begins with the magnitude and scope of the technology gap that divides these two parts of the world. In the age of dangerous competition, industrialised countries, in order to protect and maintain their own advantages in the technical, social and economic world systems, continue to transfer and reflect their numerous problems across to the techno-economic systems of developing countries. The result is that this gap continues to exist, and in some cases becomes more severe. Thus, 'economic relations among industrial countries have fallen into critical imbalance, while stagnation has become the lot of many developing countries. The drift that typifies current policies, if not corrected, could lead to a disaster which none would escape' (Galbraith et al. 1988).

Indeed, much of the southern hemisphere, comprising the developing nations, 'has been left far behind in the march forward because science and technology, which form the leading edge of development, are very weak in those countries' (Salam & Kidwai 1991). Apart from other substantial factors (such as human resources, institutionalised infrastructures, orga-managerial[3] styles and political systems), the acquisition or creation, development and diffusion of technology are crucial intervening processes in socio-economic development. Technology challenges faced by developing countries include knowledge availability and scientific capability as well as the potential for imitation and knowledge absorption in the country. Science thus becomes a *dynamic contributor* to the process of technological change (Liyanage 1993). Further, the globalisation of markets for manufacturing products has meant that factors such as standards, distribution and service are often more important than price (Malecki 1991). This has serious consequences for the process of acquisition of new technical knowledge and know-how by developing countries.

Thus, international transfers of new technology, while constituting a primary means of technological development, often perpetuate patterns of dependence (Ernst 1980). On the one hand, it is evident that stark disparities in human welfare are present at a global scale as a consequence of technological imbalance (Tata & Schultz 1988). On the other hand, policy-makers and planning systems in many developing countries are not easily able to alter the process of international transfer of technology. Technology management guidelines and related polices and standards have been laid down as requirements for the effective institutionalisation of technology in a new context. In the absence of basic prerequisites, however, developing countries are barely able to meet the relevant standards and guidelines required for importing new technologies. The theoretical bases for the study of economic and technological growth through the 1960s and 1970s tended to foster the assumption that growth and development would occur inevitably when a specific set of requirements were met. Three major factors were identified as being crucial in this regard: the choice of correct policies (Malecki 1991), a proper economic environment, and public acceptance of consequential social and political changes (Lands 1989; Reynolds 1983).

---

[3]Managerial and organisational aspects, which will be described in the next chapter.

A CONSISTENT TERMINOLOGY FOR TECHNOLOGY TRANSFER

Focusing on the crucial role of technology in the development processes of developing countries leads us to an understanding of the pathways, procedures, processes and approaches by which technology might be imported and employed in a country's techno-economic system. But we must be careful in the use of the notion of 'technology transfer'; the term 'technology transfer' must be employed in a consistent manner. In most studies on the subject, technological change and innovation in industrialised countries form the basis for understanding the process of technology transfer. Accordingly, writers refer to 'technology transfer' as the process of transferring knowledge or inventions from laboratories to the manufacturing side of production. This process differs starkly from that of exporting technology to less developed countries. Although some similarity in procedures may exist between the two situations, such analyses are very far from describing the totality of the process of technology transfer to developing countries, or even indicating the most convenient path for such transfers.

According to these studies (see, for example, Fleury 1999; *Fortune International* 1992; Sankar 1991), the most important strategic consideration for both developed and underdeveloped nations, in the light of international industrial competition, is the management of technological innovation. It is clear that industrialised countries lay a strong emphasis on technological innovation. They also emphasise specialisation in industrial restructuring for boosting international trade (N. Sharif 1994a). These trends indicate that, increasingly, the value of a product is determined by the technology that goes into it, and not by the raw materials that constitute it (Bolwijn & Kumpe 1990; C. Hill 1992; Kleindorfer & Partovi 1990; N. Sharif 1994a, 1994b, 1999). In other words, *knowledge-based* technology has become more important than *material-based* technology in the production process. But since developing countries lack the prerequisites to generate the former, they are generally limited to the latter type of technology.

This fundamental shift in emphasis from material-based to knowledge-based technology has meant that developing countries find it much more difficult to enter the competitive international market. The export of raw materials and primary goods, which is the main means by which developing countries have been able to pay for transferred technology or imported machinery and process know-how, has become a losing business (see the example of Indonesia, as reported by N. Sharif [1994a]). This is because the purchasing power of these commodities has fallen steadily, while that of technologies and machinery has been rising continuously over the last two decades.

In our framework, the concept of technology transfer is relevant insofar as it is concerned with the transfer of overseas technologies (that is, from industrialised nations, especially Western countries) to developing countries, in order for the latter to acquire, adapt, diffuse and promote technology(ies) for socio-economic development. The transfer of technology that takes place *within* industrialised countries or *among* them, apart from the existence of some similarities (such as the effects of new knowledge being introduced in the environment, requirements of specific skills, the side-effects of new technology), is outside the scope of our definition. It is necessary to make this distinction because of the different context of technology and the different position it occupies in the two systems. For example, in the modern Western economies, technology innovation is the key factor in technological change, necessary to meet the standards of international competitiveness or to maintain a competitive edge. Thus, particularly since the Second World War, the technological challenge for these areas and the notion of technology transfer has indeed mostly meant 'technological innovation' (Williams & Gibson 1990). Technological innovation includes the entire process from R&D in the laboratory to successful commercialisation in the marketplace.

INNOVATION, TECHNOLOGICAL CHANGE AND DEVELOPMENT

It is thus necessary to distinguish the concept of innovation in industrialised nations from that of technology transfer in developing countries. In most sectors of industrialised countries, attempts at or decisions about innovation arise from the imperative of technological progress, and are carried out by private enterprises seeking to maximise their profits by responding to ultimate consumer wants and desires. Many national corporations, however, try to keep their markets intact; they still thrive in these countries, and effectively continue to enhance the basis for their own maintenance and survival. This is possible because their distinctive local familiarity rests on a traditionally established competitive advantage (Pearce & Singh 1992). Since national corporations in developed countries have successfully maintained their markets, the scope for market expansion is increased by adopting a global approach, encouraging the formation and expansion of multinational enterprises.[4]

At the same time, in developing countries, the majority of people continue to try to satisfy their basic needs; accordingly, industrial organisations, more governmental than private, look for the most relevant production systems and the most suitable industrial plans for production. Starting from these requirements, their attempts concentrate upon the import and provision of technology(ies) that can meet the substantial needs of production and the crucial objectives of socio-economic development.[5] This process involves a kind of innovation within the technological system of a developing country that has its own intrinsic characteristics. Here, innovation generally occurs after the process of technology transfer. Aside from this kind of innovation, these countries also produce outputs of types of 'R&D activities' or even pure academic research (as one of the essential requirements for personal promotion and job improvement). A crucial point to note here is that these activities are closer to the conditions in advanced countries than to their local circumstances. Therefore, the results of these activities can be used in industrialised countries merely as a part of their innovation process.

DEVELOPING COUNTRIES AND THE CRUCIAL ROLE OF IN-HOUSE R&D

Empirical studies of in-house R&D in industry in developed as well as developing countries have identified two important determinants: market structure, and the mode of technology imports. Technological

---

[4]Bartlett & Ghoshal (1990) distinguish four types of innovation processes in multinational enterprises. The first two are characterised as the 'classical' or 'traditional' processes, while the second pair, the 'transnational' or 'globally linked' innovation processes, are emerging as more subtle alternatives to the traditional types of innovation.

[5]This may be distinguished from the approach adopted by developed countries, which, first of all, emphasises modernity, or the ability to sustain the competitiveness of the country's production systems outside the local market.

opportunities in the sector and product market characteristics constitute important structural factors determining the nature of in-house R&D (Chamarik & Goonatilake 1994). In addition, a firm's decision to 'make' (or to develop existing) technology locally, or 'buy' (that is, import) it from abroad, would naturally be based upon the relative costs of these two options.

Innovation is seen as a process based on the cumulation of firm-specific technological skills, leading to localised technological changes. It is, therefore, pre-eminently a differentiating process, in which firms attempt to dominate the field and to establish market controls by developing new products and new processes through internal research and development (in-house R&D). In Schumpeter's view (1934, 1939, 1947), innovation cycles drive the economy. The economic system in turn provides the incentives for new innovations and influences the rate of innovations and the characteristics that new innovations will have. Schumpeter remarks on the propensity of the capitalist system to destroy old regimes and create new ones, producing what he terms the state of *dynamic disequilibrium*. Obsolete technologies (that is, products and processes) are inevitably replaced by more up-to-date and efficient ones.

In-house R&D is thus placed at the heart of the process of innovation in industrialised countries. In-house R&D activity may be related, first, to market structures in the framework of the Schumpeterian theory of creative destruction (Kamien & Schwartz 1982). In the context of developing countries, therefore, this would suggest that technology policy ought to take note of appropriate market structures. An empirical study of Indian manufacturing, for instance, reveals that larger enterprises undertake proportionately less R&D than smaller ones (Katrak 1985), a situation that seems to obtain in a number of Indian industries. The reason for this is the greater ability of larger firms to respond to changes in demand and maintain a broad market in the presence of little or even no competition or diversification, in contrast to the situation of firms in industrialised countries where in-house R&D is increasingly becoming essential if firms are to maintain their markets. Thus, the market structure should be appropriate for spurring technological change; it must be remembered, however, that different industries have different tendencies in this regard, depending on factors such as economies of scale in production and technology development.

Second, the relationship between technology imports and local in-house R&D in the Indian context depends upon the mode of import (that is, whether technology is imported by a licensing agreement or through foreign direct investment). A number of empirical studies, at both industry level (Kumar 1987; Subrahmanian 1987) and firm level (Pillai 1979; UNCTAD 1983), confirm that firms importing technology through foreign direct investment are much less concerned with absorption, adaptation and in-house R&D than their counterparts who import technology under licensing agreements. Therefore, from the point of view of promoting indigenous technological capability through faster absorption, development and innovation, technological policy ought to restrict technology imports through foreign direct investment.

Notwithstanding some important earlier efforts by scholars such as Gilfillan (1935) and Schumpeter (1934, 1939, 1947), it was only during the last few decades that a coherent image of the structure and dynamics of technology began to emerge. Stankiewicz (1990) argues that today's technology is characterised by two fundamental trends. The first is towards increasing 'scientification', and the other towards growing 'heterogeneity and complexity'. The former manifests itself in the rapid development and diffusion of new 'basic' technologies that revolutionise the foundations on which systems technologies are based. The latter trend can be seen in the rapid broadening of the technological base on which these systems depend. These trends give rise to contradictory procedures in R&D systems on the firm level as well as on the national and international levels.

In developing countries, attention has been paid so far only to technological capability advancement through local research and development efforts. Attempts to integrate business and technology strategies in developing countries are not yet common. Capability accumulation is a process of institutional learning, which results in both increased productivity and increased economic efficiency of the enterprise.

From the point of view of industrialised countries, technological innovation, which might take the form of technology transfer and/or interchange, can be characterised as responding to both *technology-push* and *demand-pull* influences in order to meet local or international conditions (R.N. Nelson 1959). Technology-push occurs when changes in scientific and engineering knowledge make new products or processes feasible or reduce their costs. On the other hand, demand-pull occurs when the market for an innovation expands, causing the benefits realisable through product or process innovation to exceed costs (Scherer 1986). While these notions can also provide a conceptual basis for understanding technology innovation in developing countries, it is clear that, in general, studies of the commercialisation of science and technology and their transfer are based on the concept of technology and on its role in effecting changes in the industrial and economic conditions of advanced countries. Thus, for instance,

> Today, the concept of 'technology exchange' is taking on a larger role. Those words now describe the process by which an entire nation harnesses its creativity and innovation in one realm— technology research—and translates that into leadership in a different realm: the competitive world of international business (D. Rogers 1988).

The notion of technical change that is currently under discussion, particularly the characteristics of technical change as a domain of innovation in market economies, is of great concern and is the focus of a major theoretical debate. Bell & Pavitt (1993a) argue that these characteristics have led some analysts to adopt a two-step evolutionary approach to technical change. Such an approach (see, for example, Dosi 1988; Dosi et al. 1992; C. Freeman 1982; Nelson & Winter 1982) emphasises the central importance of dynamic competition through continuous innovation and imitation. This is accompanied by disequilibria, uncertainty and learning, together with interfirm and intercountry differences in competency and behaviour. All of this is substantially different from the situation in developing countries.

American experts (such as Williams & Gibson 1990) interpret technological change and innovation as processes by which the USA can go about harnessing its national research and development activities in science and technology and then transforming them into increased productivities for techno-economic growth. They believe that not only would the resulting economic growth help alleviate trade and budgetary deficits and the economic problems facing their country, but that it would also provide individual Americans with a higher real standard of living.

The rapid and unpredictable development of innovations has generated discussion on the new concept of 'key technologies'. Key technologies are mainly the result of continued technical change. When effectively controlled, these technologies offer the key to economic success and to significant social change on both sides of the world (Revermann & Sonntag 1989). Additionally, access to and control of these key technologies is a decisive factor in successful competition in the age of the modern international market, and opens the way to new fields of growth. The transfer of such sophisticated and complex systems to developing countries also addresses the problem of deficiencies in certain prerequisites for development in these nations. The key role played by these emerging technologies in any technological change and development demands that they be incorporated in models of technology transfer.

INNOVATION THEORY AND THE TECHNICAL SITUATION OF DEVELOPING COUNTRIES

Schumpeter's theory considers innovation or technological change as it occurs in the economies of the West rather than in those of the underdeveloped world. In this theory, innovation is seen in its widest context, but focusing as it does only on an industrialised country interpretation, such a theory does not appreciate the situation of developing countries and their economic structure. While Schumpeter (1934, 1939, 1947) argues that successful innovation brings about techno-economic growth, he believes that innovation is necessarily linked to the entrepreneur, who derives new economic combinations by means of introducing five parallel types of changes:

1. introducing new products;
2. introducing new production functions that decrease the input needed to produce a given output;
3. providing new consumers by opening new markets;
4. exploiting new sources of materials; and
5. reorganising an industry.

Schumpeter provides a number of distinguishing characteristics to help identify his 'entrepreneur-innovator' (see Schumpeter 1934, pp. 66, 75, 78, 92, 93). In his view, the entrepreneur-innovator is characterised by 'initiative', 'authority' and 'foresight', and is a 'captain of industry' type. Usher (1981) offers his own formulation of the terms 'invention' and 'innovation'. He argues that economic development is caused by 'acts of insight', which is more than simply the exercise of normal technical skill. Such insight calls for additional capabilities, such as the perception of problems, setting the stage, and critical revision of structures, processes, organisational systems and so on.

Technology has been viewed as central to the growth of productive agricultural and industrial sectors by a large number of scholars over the last 50 years (see, for example, Abramovitz 1956; Denison 1962; Schumpeter 1934; Veblen 1966; Weaver & Jameson 1978). Therefore, technology transfer and/or the transfer of technical know-how from industrialised countries has been considered extremely crucial for developing countries. Further, the entrepreneur has been viewed as the catalyst in the process of economic development. Rogers (1962) and Schramm (1964) describe the entrepreneur as an innovator who *destroys* the old way and *initiates* a process that will replace the old way with an innovation that is organisationally more successful.

Schumpeter's concept of the entrepreneur in industrialised countries is clearly not appropriate for the entrepreneur in developing countries. The Schumpeterian concept of entrepreneur is limited in these environments, where it is clear that innovation does not mean the expansion of already existing firms. In the light of technology transfer from advanced economies, entrepreneurial activity in developing regions needs to be interpreted differently. As Nafziger (1990) points out,

> the development of entirely new combinations should not unduly limit what is and is not considered entrepreneurial activity. People with technical, executive, and organisational skills may be too scarce in less developed countries to use in developing new combinations in the Schumpeterian sense; and in any case, fewer high-level people are needed to adapt combinations from economically advanced countries.

A comparison of these two environments is thus necessary to understand the context of the innovation process and technological change in advanced countries as opposed to the process of technology transfer and technological change in developing countries. It is useful here to refer to some general frameworks of innovation based upon theoretical evidence (see Bienayme 1986; Brinkerhoff 2000; Fransman 1986; Gilpin 1975; Maclaurin 1953; Rosenberg 1976, 1982; Usher 1981). Innovation, in the light of these frameworks, may be viewed as a dynamic process that proceeds through certain stages. To avoid using confusing terminology, both 'technical' advance and 'technological' progress are regarded as being induced by innovation, and involving five stages as follows:

1. advance in pure science
2. invention
3. innovation
4. financing the innovation
5. acceptance of the innovation

Innovation, in our view, is therefore a term covering everything from invention (the conception of a new device, approach, product, process or system) to its first commercial use, and includes improvements in existing technology. From this point of view, an understanding of the different mechanisms of the innovation and technology transfer processes in the two worlds becomes feasible. Accordingly, innovations may be divided into 'major' and 'minor' innovations. The former refer to radically new technologies that may be developed on the basis of pure research to satisfy techno-economic or market needs in developed countries. The latter, which modify or improve existing technology, are more narrowly focused on applied research and development as well as on trial and error experimentation. Major and minor innovations mostly proceed concurrently within the techno-economic systems of developed countries; both types of innovation occur at macro as well as micro levels in these systems. But, due to the various shortages and the inadequate conditions prevailing within the techno-economic systems of developing countries, major innovations cannot be addressed at the macro level, and simply cannot take place. Consequently, most innovative activity in developing countries is of the minor and limited variety, and even this activity generally depends upon foreign-imported technology.

In the technology transfer process, the *diffusion* of a new technology may play the main role. The process of diffusion may be resolved into the vertical and horizontal diffusion of the transferred technology within the techno-economic systems of developing countries. Since minor innovations have a cumulative impact on the techno-economic system, they can lead to greater productivity increases than those initially possible from major innovations, particularly in developing countries. In the long term, such a trend generates specific technological capabilities (that is, innovation capabilities). However, the capability for small innovations can only stem from organised efforts by firms to develop these capabilities. A systematic effort can lead eventually to an increasing productivity trend, which may support major innovation activities in the long run. Of course, major innovations stemming from research and development are less common in developing countries. Apart from fundamental weaknesses in capability and the paucity of available resources, the lack of major innovations in these countries is mainly the result of a variety of technologies being available for purchase; this obviates the need to develop technology locally at great expense.

Innovation in industrialised countries is a source of private profit, and then of economic growth. As Maclaurin (1953), Fransman (1986) and Nafziger (1990) argue, the links to production from technology and science are often absent in developing countries. If we see innovation as a dynamic process that proceeds through the five stages described earlier (advance in pure science, invention, innovation, financing the innovation and acceptance of the innovation), then, because of their lack of specific potential (in other words, the inadequacy of science and technology infrastructures), these countries frequently can—or have to—skip the first and second stages, and sometimes even the third stage. Further, significant linkages operate in developed countries between the social environment of organisations, satisfaction with the organisation and with individual quality of life, and the climate for innovation and creativity (Turnipseed 1994). Due to the lack of the prerequisite conditions for such relationships to emerge within the production systems of developing countries, and the nature of technological acquisition through the import of technology, developing nations cannot normally reproduce the same kinds of mechanisms for the innovation process as are operational in advanced countries. Most developing (and particularly the poor) countries do not possess a thoroughgoing innovative capacity (K. Hoffman 1990). In fact, many of them do not even have the critical minimum levels of skill necessary to operate successfully the production facilities already in place.

The shortage or absence of technical alliance relationships between companies in a developing country deprive these enterprises of the benefits of sharing knowledge and efficient and appropriate learning/innovating in order to promote technological knowledge. This is far from being the case with the mechanisms prevailing in the industrialised world, especially in Japanese companies which are operating new kinds of borderless learning networks within industrial branches (Kahen 1995b, 1999; Teramoto et al. 1993). Cooperation in strategic inter-alliances learning and technical knowledge sharing has emerged as an essential precondition for technological development in companies in the developing world. Indeed, it is clear that the entire chain of values within a nation with high levels of living standards and industrialisation must necessarily be different from that prevailing in a developing nation struggling to meet its basic needs (Kahen & Sayers 1995c). This means that innovation theories and related approaches suited to industrialised nations are not appropriate for the conditions of developing countries. While it is essential, consequently, to concentrate on the idea of 'technology transfer' as a term that conveniently represents the dynamic process of technical/technological change in less developed countries, the use of this term should be embedded within a specific conceptual framework in order to establish a relevant approach to technology management and development in underdeveloped countries.

DIFFERENT CONTEXTS FOR THE TECHNOLOGICAL GAP

Our understanding of the different contexts of technological change in developed and developing countries may be furthered by invoking the concept of 'technology gap'. The notion of the technology gap as this term is understood within developing nations is fundamentally different from that in industrialised countries. The technology gap approach underlines the existence of dependency in technological ability and economic development. Following Schumpeter and other scholars, the technology gap approach analyses economic growth as the combined result of two conflicting forces:

- innovation, which tends to increase technological gaps; and
- imitation or diffusion, which tends to reduce them.

According to Cornwall (1976, 1977), Fagerberg (1987), Lindbeck (1983), Marris (1982), Parvin (1975), Pavitt & Soete (1982), Posner (1961) and others, the following main issues are relevant to the technology gap approach:

- A close relationship exists between a country's economic and technological levels of development.
- The rate of economic growth of a country is positively influenced by the rate of growth in its technological level.
- It is possible for a country facing a technological gap (that is, a country on a lower technological level than countries on the

'world innovation frontier') to increase its rate of economic growth through imitation (for instance, by 'catching up').

- The rate at which a country exploits the possibilities offered by the technological gap depends on its ability to mobilise resources for transforming social, institutional and economic structures.

The characteristics of technical/technological change in developed countries have led many scholars (Cant 1989; Dosi 1988; Dosi et al. 1992; Dowrick & Gemmell 1991; Fagerberg 1988; C. Freeman 1991; Schumpeter 1947) to develop similar theories to account for such change in developing countries. These studies emphasise the central importance of dynamic competition through continuous innovation and disequilibrium (familiar conditions within the context of industrialised countries). We argue that, given the conditions prevailing in developed countries, the dependency of economic and technological levels on innovation activities is very high. In contrast, for developing countries, *imitation* is the most important factor maintaining this dependency. This means that while technological creation and basic innovation can be the major factors bringing about technological change, the key for developing countries is appropriate technology transfer in order to reduce the technology gap.

Through a quantitative study of a group of 25 countries, Fagerberg (1987) confirms that a close correlation exists between the level of economic development and the level of technological development. Indeed, technology policy should be seen as part of economic policy. Technology policy is ultimately concerned with wealth creation, and not with the pursuit of technological achievement for its own sake (Barber & White 1987). The success of a given technology means that it can play a vital role in the process of wealth creation. Innovation, then, can be thought of as the successful exploitation of technical change. The economic benefits of innovation are only realised when a new product is successfully brought to the market, or a new process is successfully brought into use.

The level of economic development can be measured as GDP per capita, and the level of technological development may be measured by the level of R&D or by patent statistics. Traditional neoclassical theorists believe that the level of technological development of a country depends primarily on the relation between capital and labour (see, for example, Galbraith 1967). Technology gap theorists, however, relate the technological level of a country to the level of development of its technological capabilities and its innovative activity.

Fagerberg (1987) endorses the categorisation of technological progress proposed by Soete (1981). Here, measures of technological level may be divided into 'technology input' measures and 'technology output' measures. The former are linked to expenditures on education, research and development, and employment of scientists and engineers. The latter may be assessed by, say, patenting activity. Technology inputs, however, may include the innovative capacity of a (mostly industrialised) country as well as the capacity for imitation (mostly in regard to a developing country). The historical trend of development in Far Eastern countries shows that imitation plays an important role in the initial stages of the process of growth. The role of R&D as a necessary precondition for imitation is emphasised by many scholars (Fagerberg 1987; Freeman 1982; Kahen 1995b; Mansfield et al. 1982). But in developing countries, the main problem with R&D as an indicator of technological development has been that data, and information networks generally, are of poor quality.

The long-range trend of technological change has clearly been towards ever-increasing complexity, sophistication and greater technical performance, supported mainly by the dynamic techno-economic systems of developed countries. Differences are evident in the technological strategies and attitudes to production within the production systems of developed and developing countries. As a result, technological accumulation in developed countries, which is geared towards technical change and technological generation or development, and which has been rising significantly through the use of knowledge-intensive operations, has increased the so-called technological gap between the two worlds.

In industrialised countries, with their significant and institution-alised 'national systems of innovation' (R. Nelson 1993), expenditures on R&D by leading companies are often larger than their investment in fixed capital (Bell & Pavitt 1993a, 1993b). These expenditures generally involve the creation of new knowledge, or its assimilation from elsewhere. Japan may be cited as an instance of a country that has been quite successful in designing products and production systems based on imported basic technologies (for the case of the evolution of software technology in Japan, see Kahen [1999]). However, Japan is still often regarded as an adapter as much as an innovator (Kodama 1990) within a specific system of participative technology creation (Kahen 1995b). Innovation essentially involves the use of human, technical and financial resources for the purpose of finding a new way of doing things. The capitalist system's historical success arises from its superiority at each of these levels: generating the resources required for innovation, allowing the freedom to experiment with alternative approaches, and providing the incentives to do so. Though relying primarily on market forces, the system has interacted with government at two essential levels.

The first of these levels relates to the harnessing of technological power for public purposes. Nation-states have long been major consumers of new products, particularly for military uses; the need to compete against other nation-states provided an important early rationale for strengthening national technological capabilities. Whether this rationale persists as the primary motive for government action is a major factor shaping each country's technological policies (Malecki 1991). The second level of interaction between the capitalist system and government arises from the former's dependence on its social context. The development and diffusion of advanced technologies require a viable system of education and training as a basis for supplying technology and skill, and a legal framework for defining and enforcing property rights and processes such as standardisation which reduce transactions costs and increase the transparency and efficiency of markets. These are, at least in part, public goods: the benefits of investment in education (see Liu & Jiang 2001) are appropriated by a multitude of economic actors; those of the system of property rights are even more widely spread. The way these public goods are provided, and the role industry plays in this respect, also differ greatly from country to country. This is a key component of the classic 'market failure' argument for public support for R&D (see Freeman 1974; Kamien & Schwartz 1982; Mowery 1983a, 1983b; Rothwell & Zegveld 1981).

The globalisation (W. Anderson 1999) of markets is a result of the internationalisation of customer desires, advances in communications, particularly in information technology, decreases in transportation costs, the lowering of trade barriers (for instance, through deregulation), and the growing prominence of multinational companies. In this scenario, international competitiveness in technology-based industries is the new metric of national economic achievement. In fact, a nation's competitiveness depends on the capacity of its industry to innovate (M. Porter 1990). Countries use various means to build the capacity to create and market new technology, including the adaptation of technology developed in other countries. Scholars and analysts have tried to understand these means and their effectiveness (see A. Segal [1986] for an examination of the importance of informal mechanisms in the adoption of new technology).

Non-technical Changes and Industrial Progress

Apart from technical and technological criteria, the difference between developed and developing countries in terms of their respective needs for industrial change and progress originates from differences in 'conceptual' trends: the continuous processes of inter-pretation or understanding of various phenomena, such as changes in cultural values, organisational philosophies, and changing ecological strategies. These trends are often socio-culturally determined, and are different in the two worlds. At least nine types of social influence on technological change can be identified: geographical, environmental and resource factors; scientific advance; pre-existing technology; market processes; industrial relations; other aspects of organisational structures; state institutions and the international system of states; gender divisions; and cultural factors (Edge 1995; Fransman 1985a, 1985b; MacKenzie & Wajcman 1985).

Generally speaking, the move towards a given level of technological development and industrial progress requires specific socio-cultural changes. The changes associated with the movement towards an industrial society are far removed from those characterising a post-industrial nation. Accordingly, the concepts of emerging technology and innovation in two such different contexts may be basically differenti-ated. As Emery & Trist (1973) note, a new set of values, congruent with post-industrialism, will replace the Protestant Ethic values of industrialism in industrialised countries (Table 1.1). These changes (namely, in cultural values, organisational philosophies and ecological strategies) are specific to industrialised nations, and cannot be compared with the situation of underdeveloped countries, whose efforts are geared towards achieving a suitable level of industrialisation through the transfer of technology.

We have argued that, due to the existing conditions in developed countries, their economic and technological levels are closely interde-pendent with innovation activities. In contrast, in developing countries, imitation is the most important factor maintaining this interdepen-dence. This means that while technological creation and innovation may play a major role in technological change and in reducing the gap between industrialised and developing countries, appropriate technology transfer must be seen as the key for developing countries.

The interesting point to note here is that, even when technology is imported into industrialised countries—a process that has been seen as comparable to the process of technology transfer to developing

Table 1.1
Changes associated with the move from industrial society towards post-industrial society

---

1. **Cultural Value Changes**
   (a) From achievement to self-actualisation
   (b) From self-control to self-expression
   (c) From independence to interdependence
   (d) From endurance of distress to capacity for joy

2. **Changing Organisational Philosophies**
   (a) From mechanistic to organic forms
   (b) From competitive to collaborative relations
   (c) From separate to linked objectives
   (d) From a view of one's resources as owned absolutely to a view of one's resources as shared with society

3. **Changing Ecological Strategies**
   (a) From responsive-to-crisis to crisis-anticipation strategies
   (b) From specific to comprehensive measures
   (c) From requiring consent to requiring participation
   (d) From damping conflict to confronting conflict
   (e) From short to long planning horizons
   (f) From detailed central control to generalised control
   (g) From small local government to large area government
   (h) From standardised to innovative administration
   (i) From separate to coordinated services

Source: Adapted from Emery & Trist (1973).

countries—the main objectives of this kind of transfer coincide with those motivating the innovation process within their systems. Accordingly, the transfer of new technology among industrialised countries may be expected to be linked closely to the production and international marketing strategies supporting the innovation objectives of the transferee (motivations that are far removed from the objectives of technology transfer to developing countries). The principal objectives behind the transfer of foreign technology into the UK machine tool industry serve to highlight our argument. The international competitiveness of machine tool manufacturing companies in the UK has long been in relative decline. Most policy prescriptions for restoring competitiveness in the 1980s emphasised the international dimension and the potential contribution of new technology in overall strategy development. Accordingly, priority was placed on supplementing indigenous technological capability by increasing the inward transfer of foreign technology.

According to an analytical study by Millman (1990), 'achieving and sustaining a future level of technological capability comparable with that of international best practice' are the main objectives of the type of technology transfer that we have been describing (that is, transfer inside or among developed countries). This requires establishing a tidy set of priorities:

- Executives must pay greater attention to competitor analysis and to monitoring technological developments worldwide.
- Many companies should use foreign technology to reposition themselves in existing industry segments and redirect their strategies towards growth segments.
- There is an urgent need for orga-managerial development in machine tool companies to create a balanced internal environment that is more receptive to the potential total benefits embodied in both internally generated and foreign technology.

These considerations illustrate one of the major differences between the transfer of a technology to a developed country and transfers to developing countries: namely, the objective of 'achieving and sustaining international competence in a given technology in order to maintain competitiveness'. This is clearly a competitive challenge met through innovation-oriented technological demand/change, rather than by fulfilling socio-economic needs, the main concern in technology transfer to developing countries.

The focus on enhancing technological mastery is another important point (Dahlman & Westphal 1981). Many studies (S. Cohen et al. 1984; Scott & Lodge 1985) look for the role of relative advantage in this respect. Such factors can be brought together in a dynamic socio-technical context as a 'technology delivery system' (Wenk & Kuehn 1977). This perspective on the development of technology emphasises the need for an effective enterprise to combine the necessary inputs (viz., technical know-how, raw materials, capital and managerial abilities) to deliver marketable products.

Four main factors appear critical to the performance of nations in the international market for technology-intensive products:

1. *National orientation:* A nation's use of directed action to enhance technology-oriented production.
2. *Socio-economic infrastructure:* The social and economic institutions that support and maintain the physical, human,

organisational and/financial resources essential to the functioning of a modern, technology-based industrial nation.

3. *Technological infrastructure:* The institutions and resources (physical and information-based) needed to apply technology-intensive manufacturing processes and to develop, manufacture and market technology-intensive products.

4. *Productive capacity:* The physical and human resources committed to manufacturing and the efficiency with which these are used.

THE NEED FOR A THEORY OF TECHNOLOGICAL CHANGE

No theory exists for technological change management in developing countries, nor for the process of technology transfer. Conversely, in developed countries, the trend is towards an increasing acceptance of the theory of technological innovation. Technology and/or technological change are construed in these economies as means of saving raw material. As mentioned earlier, here the drive is towards assuming that the value of a product is determined by the technology that goes into it, and not by the raw materials that constitute it (Bolwijn & Kumpe 1990; C. Hill 1992; Kleindorfer & Partovi 1990; N. Sharif 1994a, 1994b). The lack of a clear understanding of options in developing regions, on the other hand, and the lack of opportunities to apply indigenous capabilities or employ external technology, highlight the differences in perceptions of technological change within these two worlds.

In spite of these limitations, as the process of industrialisation in some Southeast Asian countries over the last 15 years has proved, sophisticated strategies and reasonable policies can help developing countries apply their potential to use their own strengths for development so as to achieve higher levels of social, technological and economic advancement. Stewart (1990, p. 310) goes further to say:

In some respects developing countries today have fantastic opportunities that were not open to the now-developed countries: there is a vast and growing array of technological knowledge, to which developing countries have potential access, that, with proper use, may transform them from a preindustrial state to a high-income, fast-growing sophisticated economy, in just a few decades.

While these opportunities exist, developing countries face many problems in using them to achieve an appropriate level of development. This is perhaps what leads Stewart (1990, pp. 311–12) to observe, following her optimistic remarks:

> Yet this opportunity is also a threat. The highly advanced state of knowledge possessed by a few economies can lead to domination over less developed countries, with a high price levied for the technology they acquire, ... the characteristics of the technology transferred leading to imbalance in forms of development and environmental degradation ... and attempts to avoid this situation by developing their own technology are thwarted by competition from the highly efficient technology of the more advanced countries.

Most developing (particularly the poor) countries do not possess a thoroughgoing innovative capacity (Hoffman 1990). Apart from the factors already discussed, many other characteristics of developing countries contribute to this situation: in particular, the proprietary or organisation-specific characteristics of developing countries, marked by lower levels of research, less competition, unsophisticated marketing, the failure to reap economies of scale, less product diversification, etc. These characteristics further distinguish the modes of innovation and means of sustaining competitiveness in these economies from corresponding mechanisms in developed regions.

A POSSIBLE THEORETICAL BASIS FOR TECHNOLOGY TRANSFER

A basic means of enhancing the technological and technical abilities of developing countries, which has almost always been ignored, is technical and technological transfer from within (for example, information technology, communication technology energy technology; see Kahen 1996a; Kahen & Sayers 1994, 1995a). Vast resources of knowledge, skills and innovation already exist within small enterprises in these countries. Actually, expatriate technical assistance specialists overlook the fact that appropriate assistance in many cases involves improving the distribution of information about existing products, processes, techniques and materials. This may be called 'people's technology transfer', which can be carried out through formal as well as informal sectors/channels.

Developing countries differ from industrialised nations in aspects such as market size, degree of tariff protection, availability of skills, managerial styles, and information distribution channels. The particular technological needs of developing countries, along with their limitations and strengths with regard to development, lead us to seek a better understanding of the technology transfer process along with its mechanisms, its main elements and significant variables. To this end, it is essential to identify development concepts, technology frameworks, definitions and characteristics of technological change, environmental factors, cultural values, the capacity for adaptation and technology development, and socio-economic planning, as these variables pertain specifically to developing countries. Subsequently, the complex process of technology transfer can be studied with a view to establishing a basis for a general theory from which a relevant model of this qualitative process may be built. Putting aside innovation theories and related approaches that are more suitable to industrialised nations and not sufficiently matched to the conditions of developing countries, we concentrate on the realm of technology transfer itself, in order to build a comprehensive approach.

Any proposed framework should, however, involve both factors already discussed in the literature and new variables. A realistic context for technology transfer to developing countries would consist of a two-sided continuum. Since any technology transfer process to a developing nation is driven by *mutual* forces both inside and outside the country, this continuum involves both external and internal elements (see Figure 1.1). In industrialised countries, on the other hand, the innovation process is free from outside forces. The inherent dynamism of innovation and its self-originated potential in developed countries differentiates it from the technology transfer process, in that innovation cannot be limited by external factors. Additionally, R&D and pure research activities are at the heart of any innovation, whereas in developing countries pure research is irrelevant to the process of technology transfer, and R&D may occur after the physical transfer of technology.

AN APPROPRIATE CONTEXT FOR TECHNOLOGY TRANSFER

The production systems of developed countries are not affected by those of developing countries. Indeed, the dominant technological

Figure 1.1: Technology transfer context: Internal and external elements

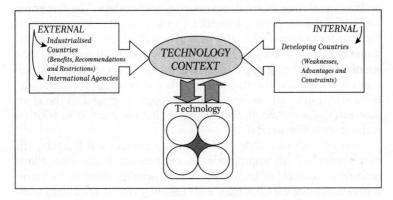

abilities of industrialised-world enterprises enables them to integrate the production systems of developing countries into a worldwide production strategy. Such a situation allows these enterprises to exercise a certain degree of control over the transfer process, which can disfranchise the developing world from appropriate choices. In fact, decisions to employ a technology to induce technological change in any given developing country are never based purely on its own internal interests (which would be normal in respect of innovation in the industrialised world).

Based on this analysis, it is evident that the process of techno-economic development in developing countries depends heavily on the availability of technology. The purposes served by technology are different in the North and the South: technology facilitates *competitiveness* in the North, and *development* in the South. This means that the processes of technology utilisation and development and technological change in the two systems are also essentially different, characterised by innovation in developed countries, and technology transfer in developing countries. The dimensions of technology, which are our main concern, need to be understood in order to highlight the differences between these two contexts. A multidimensional perspective on technology will help us address the need for a theory of technological change and technology development in the context of developing countries.

A conceptual approach to technological change in developing countries would therefore rely on a number of principles, linked to internal as well as external factors.[6] Three groups of actors are involved in these interlinked internal and external relationships. The first group consists of the developing countries (constituting the demand side of the transfer process), while the second and third groups comprise the industrialised countries and international agencies respectively (the supply side). Existing weaknesses, advantages and constraints within a given developing country, along with the benefits, recommendations and restrictions arising from the supply side, as also the characteristics of a candidate technology, define the context in which a technology is transferred.

Such an understanding of the transfer process will facilitate the development of an appropriate conceptual apparatus that allows realistic evaluation of technologies and permits them to be transferred to developing countries with minimal risk. A candidate technology is transferred together with its specific requirements and dimensions. The dimensions of technology (which will be discussed in the next chapter) are fundamental to understanding the transfer process within the technological context of a given country, ensuring that the transferred technology is compatible with the country's technical/technological capabilities and is transferable with minimal risk (see Figure 1.1). Examining this context enables us to identify the most powerful, dominant factors or constraints (internal and external) influencing the transferability of a technology and its utilisation. This constitutes the basis for an effective evaluation.

---

[6]It is, of course, possible that the technological capability existing within a country might be able to dominate the effects of external elements, providing a smooth context for technology transfer. This could accelerate technological adaptation and improvement so as to facilitate the emergence of appropriate conditions for technology generation, similar to those of innovation in the developed country context.

2

TECHNOLOGY AS A PROCESS

CONCEPTS, PERSPECTIVES AND DIMENSIONS

This book aims, first of all, to understand the reasons for the difficulties that are likely to arise in the process of transferring various technologies (such as energy, information systems, electronics, telecommunications and health care) to developing countries. Next, it proposes to develop a methodology by which to choose the best candidate technologies to be transferred, and, by identifying the important factors and understanding how they operate, to ensure that implementation is effective and sustained. As we have already stated, our approach is to conduct a detailed examination of all the important elements involved in the process of technology transfer. Thus, in this chapter, we will review the various meanings of the term 'technology'. Through the consideration and analysis of different views, we shall devise an appropriate framework by which to arrive at a comprehensive understanding of the concept of technology. Such a framework will then enable us to understand the process of technology transfer in depth.

'Technology transfer' is a process that basically involves transferring a knowledge base from one place to another. Technology itself is thus the main element in the process of technology transfer. Indeed, technology has emerged as the primary driving force of economic growth—the most important industrial and economic resource that contributes directly to socio-economic development. As a result, many attempts have been made to highlight the major factors responsible for the success and effectiveness of technology transfer. Aspects such as conditions prevailing in the transferee country, including its economic system and the modes of transaction, and the financial or even political objectives of the transferor, have been addressed frequently in the literature, but very little attention has been paid so far to the concept of technology itself as the key factor within the transfer process. Opening up the so-called 'technology black box' should therefore greatly benefit our understanding of technological choice and development, and hence the management of technology transfer. This means that the concept of technology and its essential characteristics must be subjected to analysis.

Since the majority of decision-makers at both organisational and national levels do not have—or do not utilise—any deep understanding of the *perspective* of technology, they tend to make poor decisions in the process of technology assessment and eventually in the stages of technology selection and implementation. While many scholars (Liu & Jiang 2001; Marcotte & Niosi 2000; Noori 1995; Panerai & Pena Mohr 1989; Rogers et al. 2001; N. Sharif 1999) argue that technology assessment contributes intrinsically to the national planning and policy-making systems (that is, to the formulation of a country's socio-economic policies), technology has so far only been conceived of in narrow and abstract ways. This failure to conceptualise the nature of technology rigorously is one of the fundamental reasons for the ineffective management of technology assessment and transfer and, as we argue, for misguided technological development, especially in developing countries. Given the absence of any global agreement on the definition of technology, the issue requires examination.

In general, the nature and the level of these misunderstandings depend on the nature of the technology that is chosen and transferred. For instance, a common misperception is that industrial projects transfer more easily than agricultural projects. At first glance, it might appear that the technologies involved in industrial projects would be relatively easy to transfer from one culture to another, while those involving agriculture are more obviously site-specific. It has now been argued (see, for example, Hirschman 1967; Ouma-onyango 1999; Szyliowicz 1981) that industrial projects are more likely to fail than agricultural ones, because in reality they are equally subject to environmental or local conditions and constraints. However, many policy-makers continue to regard technology in a narrow, deterministic way as consisting merely of tools or machines that can be transferred easily. Even when efforts are made to take local and environmental conditions into consideration, industrial projects often fail because of the failure to understand the dynamism[1] of technology. This is the result of underrating the significance of the environment vis-à-vis technology, as well as the complexities inherent in any technology transfer.

TECHNOLOGY: MEANINGS AND PERSPECTIVES

To reiterate, technology is the principal means adopted by nations seeking developmental progress and higher standards of human life. In our view, technology involves many elements, including engineering, organisational know-how, and economic, societal and managerial factors. All these elements may be categorised into internal (viz., cultural) and external (viz., technical) factors. These groups of factors determine the particular direction in which a technology is utilised (for example, agricultural technology, aerospace technology, information technology, military technology, telecommunications technology). While it is important to note these variations, certain aspects may be identified as characterising all technology in general. With this in mind, we shall now review various perceptions, insights and beliefs about the meaning and significance of technology.

George Kozmetsky (1990) lists five important features of technology related to its nature and its commercialisation in a modern economy:

1. Technology is a constantly replenishable national resource.
2. Technology generates wealth, which in turn is the key to power (economic, social and political).
3. Technology is a prime factor in domestic productivity and international competitiveness.
4. Technology is the driver of new alliances among academia, business and government.
5. Technology requires new managerial philosophy and practice.

It may be inferred from this list that the environment and the system of social values within which technologies are to be used demand

---

[1]'Technological dynamism' refers to the inherent potential of technology for inducing development, promotion and evolution.

specific kinds of organisation, management and communication. Thus, it is important that the managerial aspects of technology, including organisational philosophy and practice, be developed in concert with the process of technology transfer. However, it may be noted that while he tries to fit every kind of technology into a general scheme, Kozmetsky does not explicitly and adequately take into consideration a fundamental element of the dynamic system of technology, namely, personnel or the workforce.

Technology may be described as a set of specialised knowledge applied to achieving a practical purpose. In our perspective, then, the term 'know-how' contains the concept of knowledge proper to technology. *Webster's* (9th edition) defines know-how as the knowledge of how to do something smoothly and efficiently. That 'something', in our case, is the practical purpose that we identify with technology. In many studies, whether they deal with the process of technological innovation, diffusion or transfer, or are carried out by technologists, sociologists or economists, technology is perceived as a 'black box' (Layton 1977). On the other hand, technology is also frequently represented as a phenomenon whose contents and behaviour are assumed to be common knowledge. We therefore need to understand technology from the 'inside', both as a body of knowledge and as a social system.

It is also necessary to point out here that technologies encompass both 'hard technology', in the form of plant, machinery and equipment, and 'soft technology', in the form of training, know-how and more efficient means of organising the existing factors of production (services and goods). Hard technologies can only be successfully absorbed and developed if the complementary soft technologies are in place. One of the main constraints to successful technological development in developing countries has been the tendency of hard technologies to run ahead of the training, institutional capacity and infrastructural support necessary to sustain them.

As already stated, no global agreement exists on the definition of technology. It is generally left to scholars and researchers to define technology in their own terms, based on their own particular knowledge and experience. In the next section, we discuss some working definitions that seem logical and have a measure of acceptability as definitions that provide a reasonable and systematic understanding of technology and the process of technology transfer. However, as we shall show, these definitions are nevertheless incomplete and obscure significant elements.

SEMANTIC AND APPLICATION PERSPECTIVES

Technology is a special type of resource; it varies in its content and in the meanings attached to it. The term is applied widely to objects as diverse as manufacturing hardware (Woodward 1965), search procedures (Perrow 1967), or anything found 'inside one's head' (Ulrich & Weiland 1980), or skills possessed by people (Rousseau & Cooke 1984). Not surprisingly, then, technology has been defined in many different ways. For instance, it is defined as 'the ensemble of forces by which one uses available resources in order to achieve certain valued ends' (Ellul 1964), and as 'any tool or technique, any product or process, any physical equipment or method of doing or making, by which human capacity is extended' (Schon 1967). It is also defined as 'the systematic modification of the physical environment for human ends' (W. Lynn, quoted in Forbes 1971), as 'the body of knowledge that is applicable to the production of goods' (Root 1968), as 'specialised knowledge' (Richard et al. 1967), and as 'the sum of the ways in which a social group provides itself with the material objects of its civilisation' (*Random House Dictionary*, 2nd edition).

As may be observed from these examples, each definition suggests one or more aspects inherent in the concept of technology (here, these include available resources, production methods and knowledge, a body of knowledge whose final goal is the production of a commodity or an artefact). Putting all these elements together, technology may be construed as *capability*. It is physical structure or knowledge embodied in an artefact (software, hardware or methodology) that can aid in accomplishing some task. Apart from very broad definitions, the literature tends to highlight one or more special bases or elements of technology, such as its subject, method and type, whether it takes a material or non-material form, or its legal or systemic characteristics.

Existing theoretical frameworks are insufficient to encompass the concept of technology in its entirety. We need a new and wider perspective on these matters. A better understanding of the complexity of the issues involved may be derived by engaging the *semantic* and *application* perceptions of technology.

A technology actually encompasses more than just hardware (that is, machines) and software. It also includes certain skills and knowledge that, though often not mentioned, are essential to ensure the effective and efficient use of the technology. A further point to note is that while technology is embodied in tangible products such as machinery or industrial complexes, or in legal documents such as patents, licences or know-how contracts, it may also be expressed in the form of a skill, a practice, or even a 'technology culture', which finally becomes so diffuse that it is no longer noticed. The existence of such cultural aspects of technology has led some scholars to define it as 'the use of scientific knowledge by a given society at a given moment to resolve concrete problems facing its development, drawing mainly on the means at its disposal, *in accordance with its culture and scale of values*' (OECD 1978, emphasis mine). The crucial point here is that we cannot separate the parts from the whole system that technology encompasses. Empirical evidence suggests, moreover, that technical change comprises advances in both hard and soft technologies.

A definition that appears suitably to capture the notion of technology and its areas of applicability is proposed by UNCTAD (1979): 'technology means a process or the rendering of a service, including any integrally associated managerial and marketing techniques.' Thus, technology is practical knowledge of how to do and make things (Litter 1988). It may be embodied not only in products and processes (hardware), but in the form of techniques (software). In our view, technology may be viewed from two perspectives. The first concerns the essence of technology in a general sense, a perspective that we call the 'semantic side' of technology. The second perspective is oriented towards the different types of technology and the various fields in which it may be utilised. We describe this as the 'application side' of technology. The semantic perspective on technology is fundamental to a proper understanding of the process of technology transfer and development (including such elements as alternative technologies, assessment and choice of technology, adaptation and appropriateness), aspects that are incorporated in the term 'technology' in different interpretations. But before considering the semantic side of technology, it may be helpful to provide an up-to-date classification of technology on the application side.

CLASSIFICATION OF TECHNOLOGIES

Technologies can be categorised and classified in a number of ways, depending on the application, the knowledge base, organisation, and other factors. For instance, technologies may be classified as high technologies and low technologies; as modern and traditional technologies; or as labour-intensive and capital-intensive technologies (Engelsman & Raan 1994; Grupp 1992; Hannay & McGinn 1980; Mansfield 1977; Ramanathan 1988; Stewart 1978). Although knowledge about these categories is useful, they have to be carefully understood because of subtle differences among them in meaning and objectives.

Technology comprises a complicated and heterogeneous conglomeration of different fields of activities, and is characterised by many interrelated aspects. Engelsman & Raan (1994) construct a series of technological activity indicators, represented as a table of technology fields using the codes and delineation provided by International Patent Classification (IPC) symbols. The classification contains 28 fields covering the entire domain of technology, and is differentiated to emphasise recent high-technology developments. Table 2.1 lists these 28 fields (excluding the IPC codes) with code (abbreviations) and description (for details, see Engelsman & Raan, ibid.; Grupp 1992).

While this kind of typology has its uses, we need to concentrate more on the essential characteristics of technologies. One of the more misleading assumptions in current thinking about technology is that technology is the mere application of prior scientific knowledge. Rosenberg (1982, p. 143) criticises this view:

> This perspective obscures a very elemental point: technology is itself a body of knowledge about certain classes of events and activities. It is not merely the application of knowledge brought from another sphere. It is knowledge of techniques, methods, and designs that work, and that work in certain ways and with certain consequences, even when one cannot explain exactly why. It is, therefore, if one prefers to put it that way, not a fundamental kind of knowledge, but rather a form of knowledge that has generated a certain rate of economic progress for thousands of years.

Here, however, technology is still interpreted as a knowledge-oriented field; no attempt is made to categorise the functional or organisational origins of the concept of technology. Indeed, we may define a technology as a cluster of similar 'functions' based on a cluster of similar scientific and engineering 'principles'. Then, as both functions and principles can be complex and multi-levelled, technologies can be defined in a variety of ways as well as from a variety of perspectives.

Table 2.1
The standard categories for technology fields

Code	Technology Fields
BA	Mining, civil engineering, airconditioning, building materials, waste disposal
PP	Paper, printing
TE	Textiles, apparel, leisure, textile machinery
ME	Biomedical engineering (biomedicine)
NA	Agriculture, nutrition, beverages, tobacco
GP	Bio- and genetic engineering (genetics), pharmacy
OC	Organic chemistry, petrochemistry
PC	Polymer materials (polymer chemicals)
SY	Manufacturing & application of polymers (synthetic resins, paints, etc.)
IC	Inorganic chemistry, glass, explosives
CO	Coating, crystal growing
SM	Process engineering, separation, mixing
MA	Mechanical engineering, machinery, armament
MM	Material processing, machine tools
HA	Handling, conveyor equipment, robots
TR	Transport, traffic
ET	Engines, turbines, pumps
EN	Electric power, nuclear technology
EM	Electrical machinery
LA	Lasers
OP	Optical equipment
IN	Instruments, controls
MS	Metrology, sensors
DA	Data processing
IS	Information storage
TC	Telecommunication (not image transmission)
IM	Image transmission
EL	Electronics, electronic components

Source: Engelsman & Raan (1994).

Using this approach, Green & Morphet (1977) define technology as the *systematic* knowledge of technique. This technique, as the interaction of person/tool/machine/object, defines a *way of doing* a particular task. Here technology is understood as both a dynamic system as well as a knowledge system. Green & Morphet interpret technology in economic terms. The 'production function' of a technique is described as the boundary of technically efficient production possibilities. A set of techniques gives rise to a 'range' of production functions. We can now go beyond the system of technology to understand technical or technological changes or transfers. Technical change may be regarded as the effect produced by a manufacturer moving from one production function (technique) to another within the known range. If we accept this simple definition of technical change, this movement may also be construed as involving a move along any particular production function. The installation of a technology or the development of a new technology then becomes a move to a new production function.

It is, however, possible and also useful to interpret technology as a complex system in terms of technical development. Burgelman & Maidique (1988) argue that technological development refers to the activities involved in putting inventions/discoveries to practical use. For example, the three major inventions in the semiconductor industry—the transistor (invented in 1947), the integrated circuit (1959) and the microprocessor (1971)—were hugely successful and propelled new generations of technologies (such as data processing and memory devices). But all inventions and discoveries may not be translatable into 'application processes' in the same way. Experience shows that only particular types of inventions or discoveries can be put to practical use, eventually becoming technologies themselves. There is also a time lag between making an invention or a discovery and its production as a distinct technology, although rapid changes in knowledge and technology have made this time lag shorter and shorter. In any case, when an invention/discovery turns into technology, it consists of the practical knowledge, know-how, skills and special dexterity that are used to develop a new product or new service and/or new production system. This is a simple example of how technology may be defined in terms of the engineering perspective.

TECHNOLOGY IN THE ENGINEERING AND ECONOMIC APPROACHES

Returning to the semantic side of the discourse, technology may be interpreted or defined from two different perspectives: the engineering, and the economic. To the engineer, a technology means a process of transformation, a way of combining *inputs* to obtain an *output* with given characteristics. Technology here comprises the tools used for changing the material; thus, it is defined primarily in terms of the operations and equipment required. To the economist, technology interconnects inputs and outputs within a process. Input, in the economists' view, includes capital; technology is defined in terms of the type and quantity of each input required to produce a given quantity of output. In order to define technology, economists introduce the idea of *technique*. A technique is a particular method of combining inputs to make an output. In accordance with this formulation, the economists interpret technology in the following way: '*Technology* is the list of all known techniques, and the *production function* is the list of all techniques that are technically efficient' (Begg et al. 1991, emphases mine). By technical progress, economists mean an invention or improvement in a system that allows a specific output to be produced with fewer inputs than before. Accordingly, technical progress will result in changes in the production function as a consequence of changes in the set of technically efficient techniques.

To understand technology within the economic framework, we need to understand the notion of the 'production function'. Since aggregate growth refers to increases in total production in every organisation, sector or country, we can identify the growth factors by examining the factors contributing to production. We may do this by means of a production function stating the relationship between capacity output and the volume of the various inputs. Equation (1) is a generalised and summarised formula depicting this relationship:

$$Y = f(L, K, N, E, T) \qquad (1)$$

Here, Y, the output (or national product) during a given time period depends on the input flows of:

- Labour (L), representing a list of skills, together with the number of individuals possessing each skill
- Capital (K)
- Natural resources (N)
- Entrepreneurship or management (E)
- Technology (T)

Technology (T) can refer to technical knowledge; it also connotes the practical arts, ranging from hunting, fishing, administrating and agriculture through to manufacturing and medicine. T can be a direct production input as in equation (1), or a variable affecting the relationship between the inputs L, K, N and E and output Y.

TECHNOLOGY AS A BLACK BOX

From the engineering point of view, technologies are skills, knowledge, procedures and activities for transforming inputs into outputs; an increased T reduces inputs per output (Fransman 1986). It is essential to mention here that output per worker in developing countries is low in comparison to developed countries because of the low levels of capital per worker in the former. Possible causes of the low proportions of capital per worker in developing countries include insufficient training and education, inappropriate technology, mal-adaptation, lack of adequate understanding of or attention to human–machine interactions, and various socio-cultural problems, as also the lack of equipment, machinery, know-how, supportive infrastructure (such as telecommunication networks), appropriate management and organisation. All of these shortcomings hinder production and delay technological change and development. Any technological advancement would lead in turn to a lower level of both capital and labour corresponding to the same level of output, or a higher level of output corresponding to the same level of capital and labour.

It is interesting to note in this regard that what engineers call a technology becomes a 'black box' to economists. The 'black box' is a fictitious box, defined by what goes into it and what comes out. Taking only one perspective into account (either that of the engineer or that of the economist), therefore, will lead us to very different results regarding the nature of technology. Since these two perspectives on technology are not exactly equivalent, they can be used simultaneously to understand the nature of the production systems in every sector or country. This highlights the need to integrate both engineering and economics in order to make good choices and to better employ technology for developing countries.

TECHNOLOGY AS A PROCESS

Technology is not a simple or an abstract entity, nor is it a one-dimensional phenomenon. Rather, technology is a complex, multi-dimensional phenomenon that may be viewed as a process. Burgelman & Maidique (1988) define technology as a combination of people, materials, cognitive and physical processes, plant, equipment and

Figure 2.1: The process of innovation (technology creation) and its key concepts

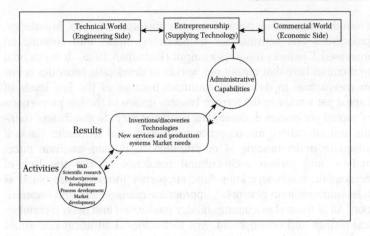

tools. They argue that the criteria for success in respect of each technology are technical rather than commercial. Technical criteria (that is, the engineering aspects) are concerned with the 'ability' of the technology (can it do the job?), while commercial criteria refer to its economic and financial aspects (can it do the job profitably?). Production processes for two kinds of product might utilise only one main type of technology. In that case, engineers would consider the two production processes as essentially the same technology, or at most as different techniques of production, given that the principles and methods used are basically the same. This is in spite of the fact that the inputs used by the two processes might be different. Economists, however, would consider this difference in processes under different criteria. For them, the difference in input requirements would turn the two production processes into two distinct technologies.

Combining the economic and engineering approaches, together with the knowledge that technology is a dynamic process, enables a better understanding of the nature of technology that will also help us influence the progress and development of technical/technological systems. Processes of invention/discovery (for instance, through scientific research, applied research or R&D) can lead to innovation and to technology creation. Figure 2.1 depicts a general approach (combining the economic and engineering perspectives) to the process of technology development. Here, *organisation* is highlighted as a key part of the process. The figure draws attention to the two aspects of the various key concepts: *activities* and *results*. It provides a simplified picture of the connections between the key concepts used to describe the process by which knowledge is transformed into new technologies.

Although it depicts the interaction between technology and the main elements of the technical process, the figure does not display the content, or the internal elements, of technology. Any given process involves special technology(ies). Technology is defined as a consistent set of processes involving related technical factors. It may be useful to provide here an outline of these practical processes. Generally speaking, following Leontief (1947), Morishima (1976) and Gomulka (1990), the entire system of processes for each enterprise and in every industrial sector may be represented in the form of a tree and of clusters. Assuming that the system contains, for instance, four processes ([i]–[iv]), we can show how different techniques can produce different goods (see Figure 2.2). In our hypothetical enterprise, the process (i) combines inputs 1, 2 and 3 to produce item 8:

(i):   (1, 2, 3) ——————▶ (8)

To produce good 9, two alternative methods may be used:

(ii):   (4, 5) ——————▶ (9), or

(iii):   (5, 6, 7) ——————▶ (9)

The next stage in this production system is process (iv). This is the final process, and represents the way of obtaining the system output. Items 8 and 9 are used now as inputs to produce 10, the final output of the production unit. Two alternative methods of producing item 10 exist in this firm: since product 9 can be produced by employing either process (ii) or process (iii), one alternative for producing 10 involves processes (i), (ii) and (iv), and the other involves (i), (iii) and (iv). This practical scheme allows us now to introduce the key concepts of technique and technology.

The different methods of producing the final product or goods in terms of the schema provided in Figure 2.2 are called *techniques*, whereas the set of all techniques available to a firm is its *technology*, in the narrow sense of the word. However, since human resources

Figure 2.2: Genealogy of production

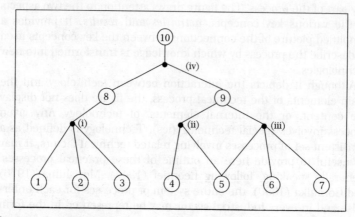

Source: Gomulka (1990).

are required for management, and since decision making is crucial in the system, we must include the broader sense of the term in our definition of technology. This leads us to a consideration of technology as a dynamic state. Now, technology includes not only purely technological processes reflecting different ways of combining inputs, but also organisational processes reflecting different ways of combining the processes themselves. The orga-managerial aspects of each system cannot be omitted, even when considering detailed technical features or very sophisticated technologies.

Finally, for convenience, we may relate each technique to a specific 'organisation' of the process. Thus, to each technique of production (or technology), there would correspond one particular organisational process that includes the necessary services of the firm's management and related staff and other resources as its inputs but has zero outputs. In fact, the final product or output of the technological process includes the outputs of such organisational processes, outputs that sometimes may not be sharply defined.

THE SPECTRUM OF TECHNOLOGY

It is vital to understand fully the complexity of the term 'technology', although this requires more information than is available at present.

This understanding is key to finding the best definitions of the economic and engineering processes (that is, transfer, change, development, design) that apply to technologies. While there is no precise and universally accepted definition of technology, practically every expert in this field (see Freeman 1974; Gendron 1977; Jequier & Walker 1983; Szyliowicz 1981) accepts a broad definition that alludes to technology as 'any kind of practical know-how', or as 'any set of standardised operations that yields predetermined results'. Technology would then include, in addition to machines and tools, all kinds of methods, routines and procedures as well as patterns of organisation and administration. It is worth quoting again the brief and precise definition of technology offered by Storper & Walker (1989), along with their classification of the elements involved: 'technology refers to the general capabilities of human society to transform nature into useful products for human consumption'. Technology involves four main elements:

1. General theoretical and practical understanding of how to do things (social knowledge)
2. Objects (goods)
3. Installed techniques of production (processes)
4. The personal know-how and abilities of workers (skills)

Technology must be perceived within the framework provided by such a conceptual apparatus; then, technological change due to the transfer of technology may be perceived as occurring along all these dimensions.

An appropriate framework for technology that facilitates the analysis of technology transfer would require us to introduce certain other perspectives into the picture. Management science provides a very important perspective, known as the 'orga-managerial'[2] approach (Kahen 1994, 1995a, 1995b; Kahen & Griffiths 1995; Kahen & Sayers 1995a, 1995b, 1995c). In the orga-managerial approach, technology is considered together with organisational and managerial capabilities (see Batstone et al. 1987; Buchanan & Boddy 1983; Buchanan & Huczynski 1985; Child 1985; Clark & Staunton 1989; Kanter 1989; Lash & Urry 1989; Pettigrew 1973; Winner 1986; Woodward 1965). The relationship between technology and organisation is defined as

---

[2]We use the term 'orga-managerial' to refer to this approach for the purposes of the present volume.

Table 2.2
Technology spectrum

Technical		Social
Apparatus	Technique	Organisation (Winner 1986)
Physical objects	Hardware related	Human activities and skills (MacKenzie & Wacjman 1985)
Physical pieces of machinery: instruments of production		Relationships of production (Batstone et al. 1987)

Source: Batstone et al. (1987).

either technology determining organisation or vice versa (despite this mutuality, however, technology still dominates organisational structure and communication). Thus, as shown in Table 2.2, technology is often presented as part of a spectrum that ranges from 'hardware' at one extreme to social and organisational structures (viz., 'software') at the other.

According to Winner (1986), 'the adoption of a given technical system … requires the creation and maintenance of a particular set of social conditions as the operating environment of that system'. Organisations, then, have little choice in this respect. It is clear that they must adapt their structures, skills and work processes to the requirements of technology. In any given context, the relationship between technology and organisation is largely determined by managerial intentions and values (Buchanan & Boddy 1983). In order to take this mutual interaction between technology and organisation into account, therefore, technology must be viewed as a process, rather than as an aggregation of machines and systems (Clark & Staunton 1989; MacDonald 1983). A process-oriented view of technology regards technology as being generated and diffused by the transfer of knowledge and artefacts between three different processes: the invention process, the exchange process, and the process of use or the production process (Scarbrough & Corbett 1992). But it should be understood that due to the characteristics of developing countries, the technology process in these regions is generally limited to a combination of the 'use process' and the 'exchange process'.

Scientific knowledge and the knowledge of social structures are the two fundamental elements within this integrated, processual

Figure 2.3: The technology process with special reference to developing countries (a transfer-based technology system)

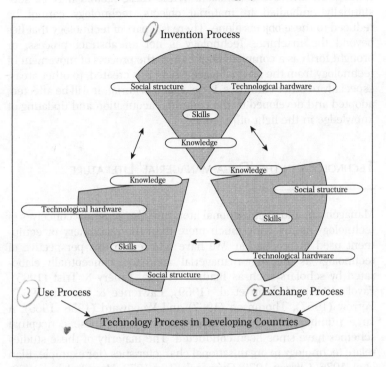

view of technology. The former comprises the forms of knowledge assembled within the technology process. The latter is the knowledge of the context in which the technology is to be used. The various social processes overlap and interpenetrate with the production process and technology in a variety of ways. This makes it all the more difficult to unfold the technology process so as to understand it better. Figure 2.3 depicts technology as just such a multi-interaction process, highlighting the specific state of the technology process in developing countries. The cyclical and reciprocal chain indicates the flows of knowledge between different social contexts.

We have established that a clear idea of technology transfer and technological change may only be had if we conceive of technology as a multidimensional phenomenon. It may be clear by now that we understand technology as the art of transforming nature to serve human ends, and as involving two main parts. Technology consists of the knowledge, equipment and practices that direct human activity towards an effective conclusion. While these factors may be substantially embodied in material objects, technology cannot be reduced to these objects alone. There is a part of technology that lies beyond the machine. Technology is not an abstract process, or brought forth as a complete entity; thus, the process of movement of technology from the original place where it is created, to other areas, especially to other countries, is not mono-criterial. It will be affected, adopted and developed by the continual acquisition and updating of knowledge in the light of practice.[3]

TECHNOLOGY IN THE 'ORGA-MANAGERIAL' LITERATURE

Management and organisational literature also generally conceives of technology as involving much more than the machinery or equipment used in production. We have referred to this perspective of technology as the 'orga-managerial' approach, conceptually elaborated by scholars such as Blauner (1964), Emery & Trist (1965), Fayol (1949), Hickson et al. (1969), Lawrence & Lorsch (1967), Perrow (1967), Thompson (1967) and Woodward (1958, 1965). A large number of empirical investigations using these conceptual schemes have since been conducted. The majority of these studies relate technology to organisational characteristics (for example, Blau et al. 1976; Glisson 1978; Grimes & Klein 1973; Hage & Aiken 1969; Harvey 1968; Hickson et al. 1969; Hrebiniak 1974; Mohr 1971; Van de Ven & Delbecq 1974; Withey et al. 1983).

Researchers in organisation theory generally agree that technology refers to the information, equipments, techniques and processes required to transform inputs into outputs in an organisation. The importance of the connection between technology and organisation does not need to be emphasised further. But within the literature, there is much debate about the nature of the connection between technology and organisational structure (see Fry 1982). For instance, Gerwin (1981) distinguishes between technology and structure, but maintains that 'there is no clear-cut distinction between tasks and technology; rather, there is a more or less gradual shift from ends to means'. Gerwin thus analyses the

---

[3]We will discuss these issues in detail when we consider technology transfer processes and models in subsequent chapters.

task–technology combination to point out that technology can determine task as well as vice versa.

Clearly, technology reflects *how* the inputs in a process are converted into outputs. The problem begins when we move from the abstract to the specific. How exactly does one measure technology, and how may adaptation, technology implementation, adoption, development and innovation be increased? To answer these questions, researchers have used a number of technology classifications. A partial list would include operations techniques (used in work flow activities), characteristics of material (used in work flow), varying complexities in the knowledge system (used in the work flow), the degree of continuous, fixed sequence operations, the extent of automation, and the degree of interdependence between work systems.

These classifications suffer from several problems that it will not be possible to examine in detail here. Instead, we shall restrict our discussion to only the landmark contributions in the technology–structure debate. Three main paradigms may be identified within the orga-managerial approach that are cited most frequently, and adopt very different perspectives of the relationship of technology to organisational structure and the resulting socio-cultural atmosphere.

PARADIGM I: WOODWARD'S THREE TYPES OF TECHNOLOGY

On the basis of an extensive research project utilising information and data from 100 firms and a series of case studies, Woodward found that several critical structural variables were directly linked to the nature of the technology in the industrial firms being studied. Woodward (1970) defines technology as 'the collection of plant, machines, tools, and recipes available at a given time for the execution of the production task and the rationale underlying their utilisation'. During 1958–70, Woodward introduced her research and developed her theory in three major publications (1958, 1965, 1970). She categorises firms in terms of their utilisation of three major types of technologies:

1. The unit or small batch production system, exemplified by ship building, manufacture of turbines for hydroelectric dams, or aircraft manufacturing
2. Large batch or mass production system (radio or automobile production firms)

3. Process or continuous production firms (chemical or petroleum manufacturers)

The scales to which these three classes of technology were applied in Woodward's first book varied slightly in the next version published in 1965. Miner (1982) explains these variations by clarifying the criteria of the original and revised systems for the classification of technologies (see Table 2.3). In the second version, the scale was characterised by increasing technical complexity, in that the production process was more controllable and yielded more predictable results.

Based on this categorisation of technologies, Woodward concluded that: (a) distinct relationships existed between these technology classifications and the subsequent structure of the firms; and (b) the effectiveness of the organisation was related to the 'fit' between technology and structure.

PARADIGM II: PERROW'S KNOWLEDGE-BASED TECHNOLOGY

Charles Perrow proposed a broader view of technology by looking at knowledge technology rather than at production technology. Perrow defines technology as 'the action that an individual performs upon an object, with or without the aid of tools or mechanical devices, in order to make some change in that object' (Perrow 1967). Thus, for Perrow, 'technology is a technique or complex of techniques employed to alter materials (human or nonhuman, mental or physical) in an anticipated manner' (Perrow 1965).

Perrow identifies two underlying dimensions of knowledge technology: *task variability* (which considers the number of exceptions encountered in one's work) and *problem analysability* (if there are exceptions, a search must be instituted to determine the appropriate response; thus, problem analysability refers to the type of search procedures followed to find successful methods for responding adequately to task exceptions). Operational definitions of technology have focused on such things as work flow, raw materials, or perceived worker tasks. Perrow (1967, 1970) describes organisational technology as the actions employed to transform inputs into outputs. His approach to technology is based on the 'raw material' that the organisation manipulates. This raw material may vary in the extent to which it is perceived as uniform and stable by members of the

Table 2.3
Original and revised systems for classifying technologies

Original System (Woodward 1958)	Revised System (Woodward 1965)
Unit and small batch production	
1. Production of simple units to customers' orders	1. Production of units to customers' requirements
2. Production of technically complex units	2. Production of prototypes
3. Fabrication of large equipment in stages	3. Fabrication of large equipment in stages
4. Production of small batches	4. Production of small batches to customers' orders
Large batch and mass production	
5. Assembly-line type production of large batches	5. Production of large batches
	6. Production of large batches on assembly lines
6. Mass production	7. Mass production
Process production	
7. Process production of chemicals in batches	8. Intermittent production of chemicals in multipurpose plant
8. Continuous flow production of liquids, gases and solid shapes	9. Continuous flow production of liquids, gases and crystalline substances
Combined systems	
9. Production of components in large batches, subsequently assembled diversely	10. Production of standardised components in large batches, subsequently assembled diversely
10. Process production combined with the preparation of a product for sale by large batch or mass production methods	11. Process production of crystalline substances, subsequently prepared for sale by standardised production methods

organisation, paralleling the 'number of exceptions' variable in technology. It may also vary in the degree to which it is well understood (analysable). This is the reason that organisations generally seek to standardise raw materials, making them as uniform and stable as possible so as to minimise the number of exceptions.

Table 2.4
Measuring technology with the help of Perrow's approach

Exceptions (task variability):

1. How many of these tasks are the same from day to day?
2. To what extent would you say your work is routine?
3. People in this unit do about the same job in the same way most of the time.
4. Basically, unit members perform repetitive activities in doing their jobs.
5. How repetitious are your duties?

Analysability (problem analysability):

1. To what extent is there a clearly known way to do the major types of work you normally encounter?
2. To what extent is there a clearly defined body of knowledge of subject matter which can guide you in your work?
3. To what extent is there an understandable sequence of steps that can be followed in doing your work?
4. To do your work, to what extent can you actually rely on established procedures and practices?
5. To what extent is there an understandable sequence of steps that can be followed in carrying out your work?

Source: Adapted from Withey et al. (1983).

Withey et al. (1983), in an empirical assessment of Perrow's approach, measure task variability (exceptions) and problem analysability in an organisational unit using a questionnaire comprising 50 technology items. Employees answered 10 questions on a one-to-seven scale that indicated their degree of agreement with each item as a description of the work done in their unit (see Table 2.4). These two dimensions of technology form the basis for four categories or classes of technology, as illustrated in Figure 2.4.

The two dimensions of technology suggested by Perrow have major implications for organisational structure.[4] Using his *cognitive* concept of technology, Perrow places organisations at various points in the two-dimensional space created by the two variables (see Table 2.5). A two-by-two matrix with four cells is constructed, creating four types of technology, as follows:

1. *Routine technologies* (with few exceptions and easy-to-analyse problems, such as mass production of steel or automobiles; see cell 1 in Figure 2.5)

[4]Perrow's schema is especially crucial for developing countries, with their different organisational structures and technology management styles.

Figure 2.4: Perrow's technology dimensions

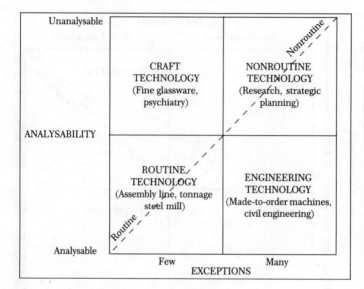

Source: Withey et al. (1983).

Table 2.5
Positions of types of firms in terms of Perrow's dimensions of technology

Number of Exceptions	Type of Search
Many	
↑ R&D firms (2)	↑ Custom craftsmanship (1)
Engineering prototypes (3)	R&D firms (2)
Nonroutine manufacturing (aerospace) (2)	Craftsmanship (1)
Engineering (heavy equipment) (3)	Nonroutine manufacturing (aerospace) (2)
Custom craftsmanship (1)	Engineering prototypes (3)
Craftsmanship (1)	Routine manufacturing (tonnage steel mills) (4)
Routine manufacturing (tonnage steel mills) (4)	Engineering (heavy equipment) (3)
↓ Continuous processing (4)	↓ Continuous processing (4)
Few	

Source: Miner (1982).
Notes: Numbers in parentheses are the quadrant designations (types of technologies):
1. *Crafts* (few exceptions—unanalysable search)
2. *Nonroutine* (many exceptions—unanalysable search)
3. *Engineering* (many exceptions—analysable search)
4. *Routine* (few exceptions—analysable search)

Figure 2.5: Perrow's technology classification

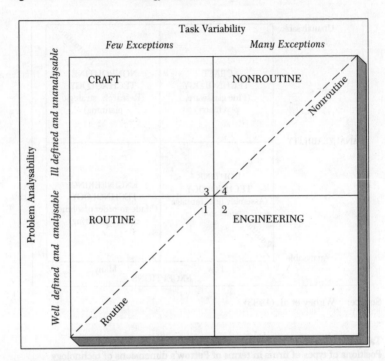

Source: Robbins (1987).

2. *Engineering technologies* (with a large number of exceptions, which, however, can be handled in a rational and systematic manner, an example being the construction of office buildings; see cell 2 in Figure 2.5)
3. *Craft technologies* (dealing with relatively difficult problems but with a limited set of exceptions, such as shoemaking or the work of performing artists; see cell 3 in Figure 2.5)
4. *Nonroutine technologies* (characterised by many exceptions and difficult-to-analyse problems, such as basic research activity and strategic planning; see cell 4 in Figure 2.5)

Accordingly, if problems can be studied systematically, cells 1 or 2 would be appropriate. Problems that can be handled only by intuition, guesswork or unanalysed experience require the type of technology described by cells 3 or 4. If new, unusual or unfamiliar problems appear regularly, they would belong in either cells 2 or 4.

existence of a positive correlation between task variability and problem analysability means that the four types of technology may be placed along a routine–nonroutine continuum, represented in Figures 2.4 and 2.5 as a diagonal line. The routine–nonroutine diagonal thus contains elements of both exceptions and analysability.

PARADIGM III: THOMPSON'S TECHNOLOGY CLASSIFICATION

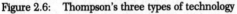

Thompson (1967) took Woodward's paradigm a stage further by developing a technology typology that encompasses all organisations. Thompson sought a classification scheme that was general enough to deal with the range of technologies found in complex organisations.

Figure 2.6:   Thompson's three types of technology

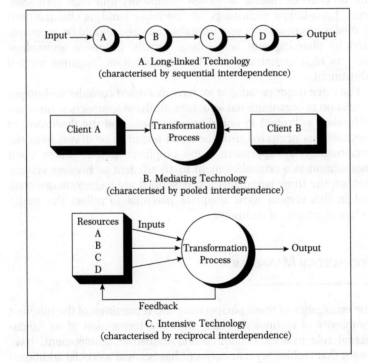

Thompson's technology classification (represented in Figure 2.6) comprises three types of technologies:

1. *Long-linked technology*, involving 'serial interdependence in the sense that act z can only be performed after successful completion of act y, which in turn rests upon act x, and so on' (Thompson 1967); for instance, mass production assembly lines.
2. *Mediating technology*, which links clients on both the input and output sides of the organisation (for example, computer dating services, telephone utilities, banks).
3. *Intensive technology*, which draws upon a variety of techniques in order to achieve a change in some specific object, but the selection, combination and order of application are determined by feedback from the object itself. This form of technology is found in work dealing with humans (for instance, technologies dominant in hospitals, research laboratories).

Mediating technology is coordinated most effectively through rules and procedures (owing to its low complexity and high formalisation). Long-linked technology, on the other hand, is characterised by moderate complexity and formalisation, and should be accompanied by planning and scheduling. Finally, intensive technology, with its high complexity and low formalisation, requires mutual adjustment.

The three major paradigms we have discussed consider technology in relation to organisational structure. In these approaches, however, technology is limited to one dimension only, and the dynamism of technology is neglected. But the main lesson to be drawn from the 'orga-managerial' approach is the emphasis that it places upon organisation as a crucial element in an efficient technology system. Further, the three paradigms just described are technique-oriented, and in this respect have adequate potential to reflect the multi-technical criteria of technology.

TECHNOLOGY MANAGEMENT

The emergence of these perspectives and recognition of the inherent complexity of technology, along with the recognition of its fundamental role in socio-economic and industrial development, have meant that technology management has become a crucial additional component in the technology discourse. Technology management comprises one level in the management hierarchy (consisting of society management, economy management and technology management). In spite of the generality of technology management, it takes different forms in different socio-economic environments (Huijiong 1993). Technology management can generally be classified into macro technology management and micro technology management. Macro technology management commonly refers to technology management at the national or sectoral level. Micro technology management concerns technology management at the firm or project level. Micro technology management forms the basis for macro technology management, while the latter provides the guidelines for the former.

Reviewing the various concepts, categories and approaches that have so far been linked with the term 'technology', we understand that it is not a mono-dimensional or an isolated concept. On the contrary, it is a multidimensional, interrelated phenomenon encompassing *hard* (physical) as well as *soft* (knowledge-based and orga-managerial) aspects. The different paradigms elaborated in the literature suffer from certain limitations in this regard: they have been largely unable to satisfy the broad conceptual spectrum represented by the idea of technology. In this context, a 'techno-economic' approach may offer a viable alternative paradigm for a more comprehensive understanding of technology.

A TECHNO-ECONOMIC APPROACH TO TECHNOLOGY

In order to overcome the limitations of earlier paradigms for understanding technology, we propose a 'techno-economic' framework that integrates technology and technical considerations in economic analysis. We may consider technology as the means for transforming natural resources (or even data and intellectual matter) into produced resources (or processed data). Then, technology may be regarded as the key actor converting certain inputs into desired outputs. As M. Sharif (1988) suggests, the efficiency of this transformation (or its productivity) is influenced by the national economic and socio-political culture, including the science and technology climate. According to the Technology Atlas Team (1987a), any transformation of natural resources into produced resources may be described in terms of the following elements (see Figure 2.7):

Figure 2.7: Technology and transformation

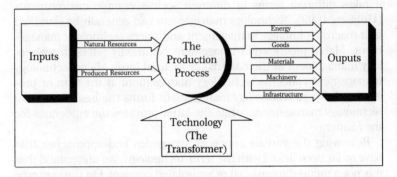

- Inputs: natural resources and produced resources (semi-finished products and goods)
- Outputs: produced resources (consumer goods, semi-finished goods, capital goods)
- Production activity: the mode of converting inputs into outputs
- Technology: the transformer and the core of the transformation facility

From this perspective, wherein technology is viewed as a complex process for the transformation of resources, four basic components of technology may be identified: (Kahen 1994, 1995a, 1995b, 1996b; Kahen & Griffiths 1995; Kahen & Sayers 1995a, 1995b, 1995c, 1996a; M. Sharif 1988):

1. Technoware: Object-embodied technology
2. Humanware: Person-embodied technology
3. Inforware: Document-embodied technology
4. Orgaware: Institution-embodied technology

We shall now explore each of these major components in depth.

'Technoware' includes any tools and facilities. It consists of equipment, machinery, vehicles, physical facilities, instruments, devices, structures and factories. Skills and experiential knowledge, qualities of perseverance and wisdom, expertise, proficiency, creativity, diligence, dexterity, ingenuity and so on are referred to as 'humanware'. 'Inforware' includes all kinds of documentation and all accumulated facts and figures pertaining to process specifications, procedures, theories, designs, observations, equations and charts. The arrangements and linkages required to facilitate the effective integration of technoware, humanware and inforware may be referred to as 'orgaware'. Orgaware comprises allocations, systematisations, organisation, network communication, groupings and all other aspects of management practice.

The effective usage of these four components as an integrated set requires that certain minimum conditions be satisfied. Thus, all types of technologies and facilities, namely, technoware, that enhance the muscle power and brain power of individual human beings, need operators with certain abilities. Adaptation and motivation are required for humanware to enhance abilities and to improve the effectiveness of the system (Kahen & Griffiths 1995). Inforware, or facts representing accumulated knowledge, needs updating, while orgaware or the managerial and organisational framework must evolve continually over time to meet changing requirements and conditions within and outside the transformation facility. In all cases, all four components of technology are required simultaneously. Thus, no technical or transformational operations can take place in the absence of any of these components.

Figure 2.8: Dynamically interacting components of technology

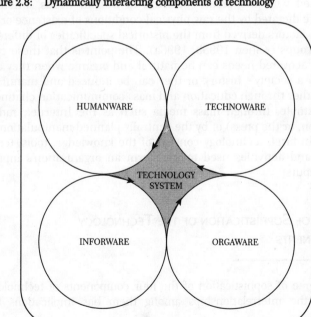

Figure 2.8 depicts these dynamically interacting components of technology, which may be summarised as follows:

- Technoware forms the core of any technology (that is, a transformation facility), which is developed, installed and operated by humanware.
- Humanware, or individual abilities, represents a key element of any transformation operation that is, in turn, guided by inforware.
- Inforware, or documented facts, stores accumulated knowledge for time compression by individuals in learning and doing. It is generated as well as utilised by humanware for the process of decision making and for operations.
- Orgaware, or the organisational framework, acquires and controls inforware, humanware and technoware in order to effect the operation. Orgaware consists of the activities of planning, organising, activating, motivating and controlling the operation.

Technology, however, is not only associated with an abstract socio-economic system. Technology and inventions are intimately associated with the broad spectrum of human needs, whether these are dictated by the raw physical conditions of existence or by cultural factors derived from the historical specificities of different social groups (Kahen 1995b, 1996a). The point is that these cultural or acquired needs can be natural and organic when they are given by a society's history, or they can be induced and manufactured either through education and mass communication channels (for example, through mass media such as the Internet, radio, television, or the press) or by the centrally planned manipulation of needs. In brief, technology consists of the knowledge, tools, techniques and activities used to transform an organisation's inputs into outputs.

LEVELS OF SOPHISTICATION OF THE TECHNOLOGY COMPONENTS

The degree of sophistication of the four components of technology and of the interrelationships among them has implications for technological advancement (The Technology Atlas Team 1987a). In general, increase in the sophistication of technoware, humanware, inforware and orgaware entails corresponding increases in operational complexity, levels of skills and experience, the value of knowledge and the complexity of interactions. For instance, a greater degree of sophistication of technoware will cause changes in the required levels of sophistication of inforware and humanware as well as orgaware. With more sophisticated inforware, better choices of technoware and humanware are possible. As the degree of sophistication of humanware increases, more sophisticated inforware will be generated, and, in parallel, the utilisation of technoware will improve. Finally, improved orgaware will generate parallel improvements in the quality of technoware, humanware and inforware. Thus, augmentation of the level of sophistication of any of the four components of technology implicitly leads to the improvement of the set. To summarise, greater sophistication entails:

- increased requirements of skills and experience in the case of individual abilities (humanware);
- increased operational complexities in the case of physical facilities (technoware);
- increased value of knowledge in the case of documented facts (inforware); and
- increased interactions in the case of organisational frameworks (orgaware).

Table 2.6 classifies these components in terms of the effects produced by increasing sophistication.

The perspective of technology elaborated here has specific reference to the context of technology transfer to developing countries (Kahen 1995c, 1996a; Kahen & Sayers 1995b). As may be clear, the interrelationships among these four components have significant implications for the choice of technology in a socio-techno-economic context. A particularly important aspect is the fact that this paradigm allows us to conceive of the possibility of substitution of the components with each other. However, the technological policies of many developing countries reveal a flawed perception of technology as a singular factor that must either be imported or created at home. As we have emphasised throughout this chapter, technology is and need to be understood as a systemic set of components, consisting of technological

Table 2.6
Levels of sophistication of the components of technology

	Level of Sophistication	Examples
Technoware		
	Manual tools	Screwdriver, hand drill
	Powered equipment	Grinder, powered drill
	General purpose facilities	Milling machine, lathe
	Special purpose facilities	Textile power looms, airjet weaving loom
	Automatic machines	Soft drink bottling plant
	Computerised facilities	Numerical Control (NC) machines
	Integrated facilities	Completely robotised assembly plants
Inforware		
	Familiarising facts	Brochure, pictures
	Describing facts	Technical booklet, process description
	Specifying facts	Performance and usage specifications
	Utilising facts	Standard operating and maintenance manuals
	Comprehending facts	Process theories, design data and calculations
	Generalising facts	Product and process development information generated through indigenous R&D
	Assessing facts	Comprehensive information on the latest developments (design, etc.) of technoware
Humanware		
	Operating abilities	Unskilled and semi-skilled operator
	Setting-up abilities	General technician, skilled operator
	Repairing abilities	Special technician, maintenance engineer
	Reproducing abilities	Scientist, production engineer

(Continued)

Table 2.6 Continued

	Level of Sophistication	Examples
	Adapting abilities	Design engineer
	Improving abilities	Improvement engineer
	Innovating abilities	Development engineer (creator)
Orgaware		
	Individual linkages	Small firm, garage shop
	Collective linkages	Cottage industry
	Departmental linkages	Small-scale industry
	Enterprise linkages	Medium-scale industry
	Industrial linkages	Large-scale industry
	National linkages	Multi-location industry
	Global linkages	Transnational corporations, international firms for transfer of technology

Source: Adapted from the Technology Atlas Team (1987a) and M. Sharif (1988).

information, technological means, and technological understanding, acting in a continuous relationship with technical humans. The question for technology acquisition or for the achievement of technological change, then, is not whether to import technology or to create it at home (Dahlman et al. 1987), but rather to determine which elements to import, which to obtain from domestic sources, and which have the potential for technological improvement. To summarise our argument, we may identify the following principal characteristics of technology:

1. Technology involves a particular set of elements for the production of a given service or commodity.
2. Technology is a dynamic phenomenon that changes over time to develop new methods of production (in industry, services) and new products.
3. Any technology set (for example, energy, manufacturing or information technology) is associated with a unique range of outputs in terms of type, quantity and quality (for the case of energy technology, see Kahen [1995a]).

4. Technology is characterised by the dynamic of continuous improvement, which means that it needs to be continually updated.
5. Just as technology is determined by the designer, the environment and the user, it also needs to be looked at in terms of 'location' (regardless of which definition of technology is used, technology tends to differ according to the place in question).

This view of technology offers a suitable basis for studying technology transfer under various classifications: for instance, in terms of the nature of its internal, specific factors, the hardness or softness of the technology being transferred, whether it is a high level or low level technology, its size and application (production or consumption), its social/cultural effects, simplicity or complexity, hazardous or non-hazardous nature (Kahen & Sayers 1995a). It also allows the consideration of methods of optimising macro and micro level benefits through the selection and acquisition of technology.

As we have shown, improvement in the degree of sophistication of any of the four components of technology gradually enhances the technology capability potential of an enterprise. Conceptual and actual trade-offs between the different components of technology may be studied in order to make the best choices in the process of technology transfer. The key point here, as we have said earlier, is that a view of technology as a set of components offers the opportunity for substitution of one component for another. Humanware and technoware are the most easily interchanged or substituted among the four components, while orgaware and inforware are less easily substituted. Thus, substituting labour for capital, for instance (or capital for labour), makes sense in the context of technology transfer to developing countries.

This chapter has analysed the complex content of the term 'technology'; we expect that this analysis can also demonstrate the complexity of the system of technology transfer in an illuminating way. It must be remembered, however, that the potential for substitution among components as stressed here may be limited given the influence of quite a large number of technical, environmental, cultural, physiological, organisational, anthropometric, global and ergonomic factors—factors that are often neglected in the literature discussing the concept of appropriateness of technology. The following chapters will explore in detail the implications of adopting such a perspective on technology for the analysis of technology transfer to developing countries.

3

TECHNOLOGY TRANSFER

THEORETICAL ISSUES AND SYSTEMATIC MODELLING

The first chapter delineated our perspective of the context and nature of technological change as it occurs in developing countries. In the second chapter, we undertook a comprehensive discussion of the concept of technology. These chapters laid the groundwork for a detailed examination of the process of technology transfer, the relevant variables, and the characteristic issues associated with this process. In the present chapter, we confront the 'black box' perspective of technology transfer prevalent mostly in the one-dimensional (economic and financial) literature on the subject, and establish the major elements within the process and the linkages existing among them. This systematic analysis of technology transfer will pave the way to the elaboration of a theoretical approach involving both engineering and economic views of transfer. The objective is to develop a rigorous methodology for the assessment and rational choice of technology.

The emergence of many newly independent countries facing problems of social and economic underdevelopment has created favourable conditions for various forms of technology transfer, especially since the Second World War. Changing world economic and development structures have entailed that technical knowledge has become an increasingly significant factor in the development process of nations. As a result, the trading of technology has emerged as an important politico-economic activity. Technology transfer is a principal means of industrialisation for underdeveloped nations, given their weak or non-existent indigenous technological and R&D capabilities. Such countries therefore depend heavily on the acquisition of proprietary know-how from foreign sources, and on the inflow of foreign technology either in the form of foreign investments or in the form of direct technology flows (Jansizewski 1981). These countries have now become better prepared to deal with the complexities of international technology transfers.

The transfer of technology from developed to developing nations has grown vastly within the last three decades (Frame 1983), and it seems as if the growth trend will continue. Post-war patterns of industrialisation in developing countries have generally been based on the promotion (via the import substitution strategy) of a modern sector using advanced technologies imported from industrialised countries (James & Bhalla 1993). Technology and science policies in underdeveloped countries are thus closely bound up with economic policy at both national and international levels. As a result, the acquisition of technology cannot be regarded as a neutral phenomenon.

Different technologies and different industrial policies are associated with particular approaches to strategic techno-economic development. The priorities of related sciences cannot be established until decisions have been taken on appropriate economic policy and technology. Technology transfer, regarded as a crucial component of socio-economic and industrial development, is thus closely linked with all the elements of the national production system. This is why many researchers emphasise that any transfer of technology divorced from the consideration of local variables is doomed to failure (see, for example, Ahmad 1986; Au 2000; Dearing 1993; Georgantzas & Madu 1990; Hague 1991; Hill & Still 1980; Huijiong 1993; J. Jones 1985; L. Kim 1980; Lee et al. 1988; Meshkati 1989a, 1989b; Murphy 1985; Ndebbio 1985; Prasad 1986; C. Rodriguez 1985; Shahnavaz 1992). The present work avoids this pitfall by looking at technology as specialised knowledge (including orga-managerial skills and systems, information, expertise and human skills, and tools) pertaining to the production of goods and services through organised activity to manage a set of interrelated, technical processes. While technology may appear in various forms or be viewed from different perspectives, we focus in this chapter on clarifying the notion of technology transfer and the process of transfer itself.

The crucial question of why developing, or even developed, nations strive to transfer certain types of technology into their socio-technical and production systems is linked to the inherent needs and situation of the country. It is useful here to examine existing definitions and concepts to be found in the literature on technology transfer. This would help clarify some of the issues associated with the sophisticated process of technology transfer, as well as inform our own comprehensive framework elaborated at a later stage.

On Terminology

The first reference to technology transfer in modern times was made in 1967 (Cairncross 1967). Indeed, it was only in the early 1960s that the subject of technology transfer began to receive serious attention from scholars and academia. This was followed by an explosive growth in the literature on technology transfer from the mid-1960s through the 1970s and into the 1980s. But several questions still remain unanswered. There exist three major issues: (*a*) the lack of a single accepted definition of technology or of what constitutes its transfer; (*b*) the absence of a rigorous formalisation of the process of technology transfer to, and its impacts on, developing countries; and (*c*) the lack of universal, comprehensive measures of volume or value by which to aggregate relevant data when examining the different mechanisms of technology transfer (for example, within a dual economic–engineering perspective). These lacunae in the literature led us to begin the present study by conceptualising the terms technological change and technology in the previous two chapters.

'Technology transfer' is sometimes substituted, in terminological debates, by the term 'technology transmission', which some believe is the more appropriate of the two. The *Oxford English Dictionary* (4th edition) defines 'transfer' as 'to move from one place to another', or 'to hand over the possession of property or right', implying that the transferee's gain is the transferor's loss. 'Diffusion' is defined as 'spreading out', implying no loss on the diffuser's part. As Dunning (1981) points out, the word 'transmit', with its emphasis on the communication or passing on of ideas, assets, etc., seems to embrace both 'transfer' and 'diffusion'. In this work, however, we use the word 'transfer', which is more commonly used in the literature than 'transmission'.

If a nation has been unable to develop its indigenous technological capability sufficiently to compete, it can obtain technology through transfers from other sources (Malecki 1991). However, this need not always comprise a real, full-scale transfer. In Malecki's view, innovation diffusion and technical education are both types of technology transfer, although more frequently transfer is a market process in which technology is bought and sold. The content of the transfer is significant. Technology transfer may take place within firms (through training sessions and experience), among firms as information diffuses, through interfirm personnel mobility, and when specific knowledge is passed on to suppliers and customers (Fusfeld 1986). In this respect, two or more firms in developing countries can transfer technology internally as they attempt to incorporate new products, processes and organisational forms.

As the term 'technology transfer' carries slightly different connotations in different contexts, it is necessary to reiterate at the outset that in this research we are concerned chiefly with technology transfer between countries, and specifically between industrialised and developing countries. The concept of 'transfer' within this context covers a range of activities that have particular reference to developing countries. 'Transfer' is a difficult concept to pin down, as has been pointed out by various authors (H. Brooks 1966; Manning 1974; OECD 1981). The term has been used to refer to the transformation of a technical concept of proven feasibility into a development state closer to its end use in the production of services or goods (including, possibly, another tool or machine). However, the concept of 'transfer' has subsequently become identified with the systematically organised exchange of information between two enterprises generally located in different countries.

In the sociological literature also, technology transfer is an unfamiliar term (Chatterji 1990), but the impact of technological change on social groupings and institutions in developing areas has been examined extensively since Lerner published his *Passing of Traditional Society*, dealing with issues of tradition and modernity, in 1958. Other authors (for example, Barnett 1953; Katz et al. 1963; E. Rogers 1962) were also publishing works on innovation, the flow of influence, and diffusion around the same period. The generally accepted notion of 'enterprises' (broadly defined as parties to technology transfer that have tended to diversify) has led to the identification of 'transfer' with the systematically organised exchange of information. Such exchange generally takes place between two enterprises (transferee and transferor).

TECHNOLOGY TRANSFER: DEFINITIONS AND APPROACHES

Traditional economic analysis can be dangerously misleading in the study of technology transfer. If the silent assumptions on which such studies are based are explicitly articulated, the lack of any fundamental analogy between technology transfers and goods/payments transfers becomes evident (Sagafi-nejad 1979). From false analogies flow false conclusions. Further, although technology transfer appears to be at the core of international political economics, most major studies and researches on this topic have tended to be plagued by a lack of conventions and a certain degree of liberty in the use of terms and concepts. This is because discussion of the technology transfer question has been severely handicapped by a lack of uniformity in definitions or the use of key words (Robbins & Milliken 1976). The term is used in various fields and associated with different concepts. Therefore, definitions of technology transfer appear unique and specific to each study (Fisher 1976). This underlines the need for establishing a relevant framework for the study of technology transfer to developing countries.

It is often argued that the term 'technology transfer' is complicated and confusing, leading to frequent misunderstandings regarding the nature of the process of transfer of technology (Odedra 1990). The problem arises because the term involves two complex and multidimensional concepts: 'technology' and 'transfer'. Thus, several definitions of technology transfer may be found in the literature. For instance, van Gigch (1978) suggests that technology transfer involves the acquisition of *inventive activity* by secondary users. This definition implicitly incorporates the transfer of hardware (that is, transfer of physical systems such as production systems) as well as software (the information and knowledge base that is essential for the smooth running of the hardware). Emanuel (1982) states, on the other hand, that technology transfer is 'a problem of transfer of knowledge and of know-how: therefore, of people's education'. In a cognitive sense, Dore (1984) defines technology transfer to developing countries as a process that aims at 'getting knowledge that is only in some foreigners' heads into the heads of one's own nationals'.

Generally, confusion still prevails as to the difference between 'technology trade' and 'real technology transfer'. The former is merely the import of equipment and the execution of development projects on a turnkey basis. The latter involves mastering the imported know-how of core technologies and the development and generation of technologies utilising indigenous scientific and technological capacities. For our purposes, the concept of technology transfer involves both the short-term and the long-term technological movement—through acquisition, adaptation and utilisation—of technical and technological knowledge in a country other than that in which this knowledge originated. It is essential to stress again that physical machinery is only a small part of the technology transfer process (Murphy 1985). As we have been saying, it is apparent that technology transfer may not always involve the transfer of machinery or physical equipment. Technology, as discussed in the previous chapter, must be viewed as comprising four major components: technoware, humanware, inforware and orgaware. The essential point here is that, on the one hand, the framework and the forces involved in the process of transfer (of whole elements) of technology are broadly the same, whether it takes place within a country or between countries. On the other hand, there are of course differences in the magnitude of forces and their relative importance in each individual case. One should then be able to apply experience acquired in one type of transfer, for instance, the process that occurs within one country, to transfer between countries (that is, from developed to developing countries).

A broad definition of technology transfer is provided by H. Brooks (1966): transfer of technology is 'the process by which science and technology are diffused throughout human activity'. This definition, Brook explains, covers any activity by which systematic rational knowledge developed by one group or institution is embodied in a way of doing things by other institutions or groups. This can take the form either of transfer from more basic scientific knowledge into technology, or of the adaptation of an existing technology to a new use. Alternatively, as Kottenstlette & Freeman (1971) argue, technology transfer is 'a global concept to encompass any transfer of a technology from the environment in which it was generated for original use to another, and usually unintended, secondary environment for subsequent application'. Gee (1981) considers technology transfer from the application perspective, arguing that technology transfer may refer to the application of technology to a new use, or to a new user for economic gain. Rubenstein (1976) goes further and describes the effect of transfer as the improvement of capability: 'technology transfer generally involves the transfer of a capability to not only use, but also to adapt and modify and, in many cases, to innovate with respect to a product, process, piece of equipment, or field of technology (broad and narrow).'

Technology transfer differs from the ordinary transfer of scientific information in that, to be really transferred, it must be embodied in an actual operation of some kind. This leads us to one of the fundamental features of technology transfer: transfer is the outcome of a *deliberate, systematically organised act*. The process may thus involve the transfer of systematic knowledge for the manufacture of a product, for the application of a process or for the rendering of a service; it does not, however, extend to transactions involving a mere sale or lease of goods (UNCTAD 1982). Hence, technology transfer is a 'two-way' process: there is always a 'sender' and a 'receiver', and, sometimes, an intermediary. Each transfer may have a range of specific effects—including positive contributions or losses—upon the national developmental process. This means that although the transfer can stimulate development, the ultimate requirement of the receiving country is to build up the capacity to generate its own technology.

While many different definitions and meanings have been attributed to the notion of technology transfer over the years, the literature on the subject remains confined by and large to the discussion of innovation approaches. The term 'technology transfer' is yet to be accorded a comprehensive and universally acceptable definition.

TECHNOLOGY TRANSFER IN DIFFERENT DISCIPLINES

Technology transfer is a complex concept, as well as a process that is difficult to operate or manage. The reason is that the circumstances surrounding the interaction between technology development sources and technology receivers differ from transfer to transfer, even within the boundaries of a single organisation. Most economists (Holloman 1966; Murphy 1967; Ruttan & Hayami 1973; Sakuma 1995; Stewart 1992) have viewed the goal of the process of technology transfer as being either increased productivity in general or the production of specific new goods and services (new techniques) at some social cost. The *economic* perspective thus focuses on the country's technological capacity (L. Hoffman 1985) as the object of the transfer process, given that the transfer of knowledge improves a country's technological capacity.

From the economists' point of view, therefore, technology

is embodied not in aggregate capital nor in particular factors, but in the whole economic process that extends from factory suppliers on the one hand to marketing outlets on the other. It involves the harmonious meshing of a number of subsystems. This makes technological transfer and diffusion a function of the *ability* to change processes that require system adaptation (Murphy 1967, p. 7, emphasis mine).

In this approach, then, new or sophisticated technology from industrialised nations can be transferred only if the economic system of a developing country parallels that of the advanced industrial state.

In the *sociological* perspective, the process of technology transfer has been perceived as basically a form of communication. Lerner (1964) suggests that transfer is a 'process by which the behaviour codes of more developed societies are communicated to less developed societies'. Here, the success of technology transfer depends on the overcoming of various barriers to communication, for instance, the barriers that arise when individuals use different vocabularies, have different motives, or represent organisations of widely differing cultures, or when transactions vary from those involving highly abstract concepts to transactions in concrete products (see Williams & Gibson 1990). Sociologists are therefore concerned less with the economic goals of technology transfer than with the effects that such a process produces on styles of living and on social institutions.

The transfer of technology, from an *anthropological* point of view, takes place only in the context of cultural evolution. In this respect, Merrill (1972), for example, points out:

a technology is adopted when people or groups find it desirable and possible to change what they are doing in ways that involve particular uses of that technology. Such people and groups are the active, initiating elements in the change in technological practices. Beyond that, it is the circumstances of the society involved, and how they work which determines the wider effects of a technology on cultural evolution.

Like the sociologists, then, anthropologists are more interested in studying and facilitating the agents and objects of change (mostly intangible) as well as the 'spin-off' effects of change. In this, both differ from the economists who are concerned primarily with the (tangible) goals of technology transfer.

Technology transfer may be interpreted as a 'chameleon' process that may be harnessed for differing applications, environments, participants and problem areas (Kleiman & Jamieson 1978). Transfer involves four major issues:

1. Transplantation of technology from within one set of well-defined conditions to another set in which at least one key variable may differ; how the recipient applies the technology may vary greatly from the donor's mode.
2. A sense of opportunism, whether justified or not, that prevails in the technology transfer phenomenon.
3. A rich variety of mechanisms and relationships between recipient and donor. These may vary from a routine, people-less, passive transfer to a turnkey contract.
4. The critical dependence of the success of the transfer upon the nature of the transferred technology and how it is transferred.

TECHNOLOGY TRANSFER AS A DYNAMIC PROCESS OF TECHNOLOGY USE

Technology transfer, as should be apparent from the preceding discussion, tends to mean different things to different people. From the *engineering* point of view, 'technology' does not refer to a 'thing'. Rather, when engineers talk about the transfer of technology they really mean the transfer of knowledge. Knowledge may be seen as the state of knowing through study or experience. It can be stored and conveyed in many ways: the written word is knowledge; the spoken word is knowledge; computerised data banks are knowledge. Further, the term 'transfer' does not mean movement or delivery. Transfer inherently contains a dynamism, and may be defined as the 'knowledgeable use of technology'. The fact that a technical book is written does not mean that its contents are or will be read. If it is read, it does not mean the author's words were understood. If they were understood, it does not follow that knowledge has been transferred until that knowledge has been *applied*, or used in a conscious manner. Therefore, our definition of technology transfer includes the ability to use knowledge. Such an ability is based on adequate understanding of that technology, and generally proceeds to create a potential for technology development.

In our view, the potential for development is, in essence, an inevitable result of the ability to use. It is sometimes argued that if technical knowledge is sent and the receiver acknowledges that it has been received, then technology has been transferred. What this really means is that something has been *delivered*. If this 'something' is never used or developed knowledgeably by local receivers (such as a firm, an organisation or a country), then, by our definition, nothing has been transferred. The achievement of a practical purpose (for example, knowledge or technical application) by someone who has not previously been able to accomplish that purpose is the hallmark of technology transfer.

Technology transfer is not restricted to transfer in a scientific or engineering sense only. As noted earlier, technology transfer may be described as the process by which science and technology are diffused through human activity (H. Brooks 1966). Accordingly, wherever systematic, rational knowledge developed by one group or institution is embodied in a way of doing and understanding things by other institutions or groups, technology transfer may be said to have taken place. To reiterate, no transfer of technology can occur until and unless the technical knowledge is put to use locally, that is, in an organisation or a country. The success of a transfer therefore depends on the mechanism of use, and not on the state of transfer. Although we defined technology in the previous chapter as a set of specialised know-how (including human skills, information, orga-managerial expertise and tools) applied to achieving a practical purpose, technology transfer is not merely the transfer of know-how from one person to another. Rather, it is a dynamic process in which not only knowledge is transferred (in the form of the four components of technology), but also its socio-cultural organisation, along with its societal use.

In light of the conceptual development of the term 'technology' undertaken in the last chapter, and the notion of technological change applicable to developing countries elaborated in chapter one, we now use the term 'technology transfer' to refer to the dynamic process of knowledgeable use of technology that fulfils the following knowledge-based (or knowledge-oriented) roles:

1. satisfaction of the system requirements needed to install and apply the new technology: that is, the four major elements comprising technology;
2. enhancement of general knowledge and information in the society;
3. improvement of industry- (or sector-) specific knowledge: that is, technical knowledge common to most firms belonging to a

particular industry or a sector (this type of knowledge is necessary for manufacturing a product or implementing a process);

4. improvement of system-specific knowledge (theoretical and technical knowledge needed to produce a specific product, or to manage a process)—for instance, how to manufacture computers designed for process control applications;

5. improvement of organisation- or firm-specific knowledge— knowledge that is technically unique and belongs to an organisation or a firm within the industry or sector (such know-how results from the institution's own capabilities, and often constitutes a competitive advantage over other firms);

6. improvement of ongoing problem-solving capability (that is, improvement of the organisation's acquired know-how as a result of gaining experience in solving production problems on a continuing basis: see Wallender [1979]).

Whatever definition of technology transfer is used, we must recognise the importance of the more qualitative aspects of the process and the difficulties involved in attempting to quantify transfers. This difficulty is magnified when it becomes necessary to distinguish between the 'ability to use' and the 'ability to master' a complete process from design and development through to production and marketing. It is this second capacity that characterises a more complete technological mastery.

THE NATURE OF TECHNOLOGY TRANSFER: MAJOR CONCERNS IN THE LITERATURE

The concept of transfer may be said to concern the enrichment of any given field through an input from the 'outside'. In fact, the notion of the 'outside' provides a useful basis for understanding technology transfer to developing countries. 'Outside' is relative to 'region', 'field' or 'sector'; transfer occurs when technology previously applied or developed in one country (that is, the 'outside'), is applied in a second country (the 'inside'). In other words, technology transfer may be regarded as the operation whereby knowledge is diffused. Such diffusion leads to the improvement of the country's technological capabilities for development of the initially imported technology. Through transfer, technology, as we defined it in the previous chapter, is moved from one physical or geographical location to another for the purpose of application and for development towards an end product. Technology transfer may involve new (the latest) or old (mature) technology (Hall & Johnson 1970; Perlmutter & Sagafi-nejad 1981). It may occur through the international transfer of documents (blueprints, formulas, plans and other communications on technique or organisation), people, or products embodying the technology.

While technology has been identified with the specialised knowledge or 'know-how' applied to achieving a practical purpose (see the discussion of technology as know-how in chapter two), technology transfer is not the mere transfer of know-how from one person to another—although the transfer of know-how is a very important step in the technology transfer process. Rather, we use the term technology transfer to mean not only knowledge transfer, but also its societal use. Transfer thus comprises a series of steps, the culmination of which is the achievement of a practical purpose. Going beyond the strictly scientific or engineering perspective of technology transfer, the use of knowledge is recognised as its application.

Technology transfer is often thought of as being product-embodied, process-embodied or person-embodied. In other words, the transfer of technology may be said to occur through the specific transfer of products, processes or people. Much of the emphasis in the research and practitioner literature has been on the latter two types of technology transfer, namely, process-embodied and person-embodied transfers. However, referring back to our description of technology as a system comprising four main components or elements (see chapter two), it may be stressed here that the transfer of technology, whether in the form of tools, processes or persons, never occurs except within an overarching information and orga-managerial framework.

To reiterate: transfer, in our view, consists of the acquisition, utilisation, assimilation (that is, knowledgeable use), and eventually the development of technological knowledge by a country other than the country in which this knowledge originated; transfer is inherently a two-way process. This process generally involves two sides (sender and receiver), sometimes mediated by an intermediary or a third party (Derakhshani 1980). Although transfer of technology can stimulate development, its ultimate purpose for the receiving country is to build up the capacity to generate its own technology. Technology transfer presents a crucial opportunity for learning for the host country. Effectively managed, it could provide suitable opportunities for the recipient country or firm to acquire new technological knowledge, technical know-how and skills otherwise unavailable to them (Hoffman & Girvan 1990).

At this juncture, it is important to note a significant bias in a large part of the literature concerning the transfer of technology. Recognition of the importance of technology in the modern world for the promotion of employment, export development, the enhancement of living standards and acceleration of national socio-economic growth, along with the general acceptance of the fact that technologies often need to be obtained from outside sources to speed up the pace of national techno-economic development, has meant a vast increase in the literature surrounding the notion of transfer of technology. The main body of this literature, however, has focused on analysing concepts or models of technology transfer, generally viewed as the outcome of innovation, in industrialised countries (see, for example, Bar-Zakay 1970; Stock & Tatikonda 2000). A predominant view is that technology transfer is merely 'business practice': Ariga (1981), for instance, describes the international transfer of technology as a business practice with substantial implications for international economic growth and the welfare of people. Indeed, 'international transfer of technology' for commercial purposes has become a catch phrase in the development literature in advanced and less industrialised countries, and in the international debate on technology transfers. In 1964, the United Nations Conference on Trade and Development (UNCTAD) was among the first international forums in which technology transfer was discussed as an autonomous topic in the general context of development.

Given that technology transfer, from the point of view of developed countries, is viewed merely as 'business practice', it is necessary, therefore, to be realistic with regard to the framing of technology transfer policy in developing countries. The majority of proposed recommendations or agreements issued by relevant United Nations organisations reveal a somewhat hasty, idealistic approach that have made them unrealisable in practice. The owner of technology is generally a company or a business enterprise that pursues its business interests not only domestically but also internationally. Therefore, technology tends to be used as leverage, either to maximise profits or to protect or strengthen competitiveness. The owner of know-how—a technology undisclosed to others—may also enjoy a degree of monopoly, or at least a better position than others (that is, from a purely business-oriented perspective).

MECHANISMS OF TECHNOLOGY TRANSFER

New technology may be acquired in either of two basic ways: by *developing* it or *importing* it (M. Sharif 1986). Developing countries import technologies for two fundamental reasons: because little or no R&D investment is needed, and because technical and financial risks are very low since the new technology is usable immediately. From the supplier's point of view, too, good reasons exist for selling technology:

- the sale of technology may imply increasing returns on R&D investments;
- the transferred technology may have no immediate use for the supplier;
- the technology may have already been utilised up to its limit.

Two kinds of transfers of technology occur: vertical and horizontal (Brooks 1968). Vertical transfer refers to transfer of technology along the continuum from the more general to the more specific. In particular, it includes the processes by which new scientific knowledge is incorporated into technology, by which 'state-of-the-art' technology becomes embodied in a system, and by which the confluence of several different and apparently unrelated technologies leads to a new technology. On the other hand, horizontal transfer occurs through the adaptation of a technology from one application to another that is possibly wholly unrelated to the first (that is, without the two necessarily being linked). An example is the adaptation of a military aircraft to civilian air transport (through the process of *spin-off*, common in industrialised countries). This type of transfer is concerned with the application of a technology in an area or a way in which it was not really intended to be used, while vertical transfer is concerned with obtaining the intended application.

The different types of technology that are transferred may be categorised into sophisticated (the latest) technology, established technology and old technology. Technology may be viewed as consisting of a series of techniques; the technology available to a given country cannot then be identified with all known techniques (Stewart 1978). In the absence of perfect communication, the methods available to any particular country will be only a part of the total methods known to the world taken as a whole.

The transfer of technology has been described as taking place through three main mechanisms: first, through the mobility of personnel; second, sourcing (which is the agreement between two producers to manufacture fully compatible products); and third, cross-licensing agreements (Rada 1982). This classification, however, does not take into account the education and training needed to use a particular equipment as a technology transfer channel. As we have been saying, technology is not a purely abstract thing (which it is from the engineer's perspective); rather, it is a knowledge set comprising the four main elements of technology discussed earlier. Further, 'transfer' does not simply mean 'movement' or 'delivery' (that is, just physical or 'static' movement). We define transfer as the dynamic application and utilisation of technology. We thus move beyond the conventional interpretation of transfer (see, for instance, Miller 1979; Mogavero & Shane 1982) as simply the use of knowledge without any adoption and development. Such a process may be described as a 'static technology transfer'. In our perspective, since technology transfer is regarded as a dynamic process, it can involve both the physical movement of a technology from one place to another as well as diffusion phenomena (including the acquisition, adoption, adaptation and development of that technology).

A combination of these mechanisms is needed for successful technology transfer to occur. The mechanisms most frequently used in developing countries include:

1. purchase or licensing of already developed technology in the form of patents, products or know-how packages;
2. direct purchase of specialised machinery embodying needed technologies;
3. use of foreign experts as technology transfer agents;
4. the bodily transfer of technology through the establishment of foreign industrial enterprises, often multinational corporations or joint ventures, in a developing country;
5. the training of personnel abroad;
6. establishment of specialised centres for technology transfer, mainly for the training of personnel (this technique has been used effectively in Taiwan and Mexico);
7. establishment of institutions of education, research and development, and agricultural extension services in the developing country; and
8. maintenance of a suitable economic and social climate for innovation and technological change (as has been achieved, for instance, in Korea and Taiwan).

This is only a partial list of the various mechanisms available to a developing country for the transfer of technology (Schechter 1982). Certain common elements may be observed among these mechanisms, in particular the series of processes that must be undertaken in each case if the transfer of a technology is to succeed. Such processes would include:

1. defining the need or the market;
2. searching for pertinent technologies;
3. screening these technologies for relevance and appropriateness;[1]
4. modifying the technology to suit local conditions, including social, political and cultural as well as economic factors;
5. demonstrating the value of the technology in social and economic terms;
6. implementing the project in physical terms; and
7. diffusing the technology to relevant sectors of society, including both producers and consumers.

Technology transfer usually occurs over a lengthy period of time. It is rare for technology to be sold (assigned) to the licensee in a once-and-for-all sale of patents and know-how. Hence, the price of a transferred technology is usually disbursed over time in the form of a series of payments by the licensee to the licenser, although the payments may not extend for the same duration as the benefits that accrue to the licensee from the transferred technology. Technology transfer is a process that takes place over time because its purpose is to create a 'technological capability'[2] in the licensee that matches, in whole or in part, the capability of the licenser (Root 1981).

MODES OF TRANSFER

Much of the discussion about the acquisition of foreign technology in the literature focuses on how the technology is transferred, rather than on what technological elements are being transferred and why they are being acquired overseas. From the transactional perspective (see, for example, Fontes 2001b; Kahen 1996a; Karani 2001; Lan 1996; Rubin

---

[1] The process of appropriate technology choice will be discussed comprehensively in chapter five.
[2] We will analyse the different concepts and types of technological capability in the next chapter.

et al. 1995), technology transfer can take place through two channels: the 'commercial' and the 'non-commercial' (these modes of transfer are described in the next section). Commercial transactions constitute the main form of technology transfer in various fields.

According to the International Code of Conduct on the Transfer of Technology (UN 1980), a number of distinct operations may be identified, as follows:

- assigning or granting of industrial rights;
- handing over technical or non-technical know-how in the form of documents, plans, diagrams and so on;
- the communication of technical or other know-how in the form of supply of services;
- providing a combination of services with a view to commissioning an industrial complex; and
- providing technical services related to the selling or leasing of machinery.

Many authors have attempted the classification of the methods by which foreign technologies can be transferred to developing countries. Adeboye (1977) bases his schema on UNCTAD (1975), wherein the transfer of technology can take place through one or more of the following means:

1. transfer of published material (such as journals, books);
2. purchase of machinery, equipment and other intermediate goods;
3. transfer of data and personnel;
4. granting of licences and trademarks;
5. collaborative agreements;
6. direct foreign investment by transnational corporations (this procedure entails a combination of mechanisms);
7. technologists' mobility (movement of technical personnel from one organisation to another);
8. technological entrepreneurship (technologists moving out of established firms to set up their own businesses); and
9. interpersonal communication (gatekeeper networks).

Baranson (1975) classifies these mechanisms into three principal modes: licensing, subcontracting, and supply of equipment and materials. Goulet (1977) adds 'consultants' to the list proposed by Baranson.

The process of technology transfer has also been described as consisting of three elements: transferor, transferee, and the linkages (or the ways and means of transferring technology) between the two partners (M. Sharif 1986). These linkages may be direct or indirect. Direct linkages include:

1. the operation of transnational corporations;
2. licensing arrangements;
3. hiring of experts and contractors; and
4. training of technical staff abroad.

Indirect linkages include:

1. purchase of machinery, equipment and components;
2. exchange of information at international meetings;
3. flow of books, journals and other publications; and
4. exhibitions and trade fairs.

A study carried out by the UNCTC (1987) distinguished between two types of technology transfer: commercial and non-commercial. Commercial technology transfers are described in this study as including foreign direct investment, joint ventures, licensing, franchising, marketing contracts, technical service contracts, turnkey contracts and international subcontracting. Non-commercial technology transfers include the review of technical publications (journals and books) and the training of foreign students.

Two further major modes of technology transfer may be identified: the conventional and non-conventional modes. Unconventional modes of transfer are now viewed as the most beneficial and cost-effective approaches, and are adopted particularly by newly industrialising countries (NICs) to establish and to promote the computer industry, which is usually labelled as 'high technology'. Unconventional modes of transfer are generally adopted in addition to the well-established conventional modes of technology transfer to developing countries, and include:

- reverse engineering
- reverse brain drain
- foreign direct investment in industrialised countries

Reverse engineering or product imitation has been the mainstay of the process of industrial development in Japan, and continues to be employed as a principal means of technology acquisition in many developing countries (for example, the computer industry in Brazil: see Erber [1985]; for Taiwan, see 'The Pirate Invasion', *Asia Week*, 6 May 1983; for Japan, see Kahen [1995b, 1999]; and for South Korea, see Sacerdoti [1986]). Attracting expatriate entrepreneurs and experts who have gained adequate experience abroad to set up or develop technological institutions in their countries of origin is another form of unconventional technology transfer that has been used by some NICs in Southeast Asia (such as Taiwan and China: see Crawford [1985, 1987]). Foreign direct investment, finally, represents an attempt to expand the dynamics of technology transfer in developing countries from the mere diffusion of technology to the globalisation of technology application. Factors such as market access, fiscal incentives, favourable rates of return to investments, political stability, access to technical knowledge, internalisation and location advantages appear to be at the heart of this unconventional mode of transfer.

In the present study, we focus primarily on non-commercial transfers of technology to developing countries. Such transfers, as opposed to purely commercial transfers, include transfers of technology under 'multilateral' or 'bilateral' cooperation agreements with developing nations. They generally relate to infrastructural projects of all kinds (government services, urban management, scientific, educational and research services), but they also cover other activities such as agriculture. Moreover, the transfer agents involved are usually national authorities, non-governmental or international organisations who operate within the framework of agreements that are usually explicitly designed to further the host country's development. However, the non-commercial transfer is often carried out in the same way as the commercial transfer. Documentary information and training courses are provided alongside various other services by expert teams.

The process of technology transfer to developing countries begins with the formation of a linkage between 'technology sources' (developed countries) and 'technology users' (developing countries). The presence of an appropriate leverage is dictated by the achievement of such a linkage (Mogavero & Shane 1982). By leverage we mean 'bridging agencies' such as UNCTAD, WHO, UNDP or MNCs. Figure 3.1 depicts technology transfer leverage as a model of non-commercial transfer.

Sources of technologies include firms, industries or countries in which original technology has been generated. Users or consumers of technologies include firms and organisations in the public or private sectors within the techno-economic systems of developing

Figure 3.1: Technology transfer leverage as an initial model

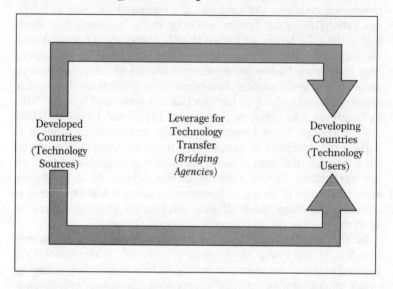

countries. Leverage for the transfer is provided by countries and agencies (in the national systems of industrialised nations or within international authorities) that act as facilitators who try to make the technology transfer happen. These agencies are supposed to make available to a country any existing pertinent technology that would satisfy a perceived or real societal need.

Whatever the mode of transfer, multinational corporations, as the main suppliers of technology, dominate the process (Buckley & Casson 1976). The mode of technology transfer is affected by the following four groups of factors, which play crucial roles (see Figure 3.2):

1. Industry-specific factors, such as product and structure factors
2. Region-specific factors, such as cultural aspects
3. Nation-specific factors, such as political aspects
4. Firm-specific factors, such as management and technical knowledge

The complexity of the transfer process may be demonstrated by a discussion of the interaction among these groups of factors. Each particular element within the process of technology transfer interacts with systems existing in the environment. Once a technology is introduced and spreads widely, it gets locked into a set of 'institutional

Figure 3.2: Major factors dominating the mode of transfer

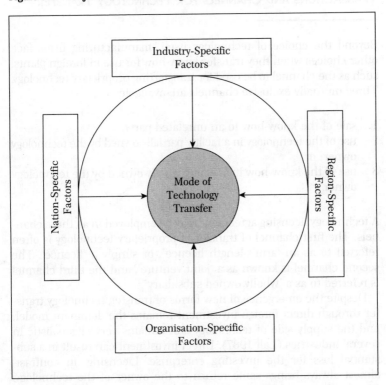

arrangements', making it difficult to dislodge. The attributes of a technological system are inexhaustible, self-reproducing and, above all, dynamic, diffusible and adaptable. Control over the dissemination and application of technology is therefore necessary to retain technological advantage in domestic and foreign markets (Marton 1986). It is also essential to manage techno-economic growth in a planned fashion (see Figures 3.5 and 3.6; the model is developed conceptually later in this chapter). Looking at technology transfer as a dynamic process, our conception of a technological system possesses an important implication: the *entire* system can never be transferred, just some of its elements. The technologies being transferred are not just inanimate objects. So for a transfer to be successful, and for the characteristics and elements of the technology to be productive and effective, the entire system must be well understood.

TRANSACTIONS AND CHANNELS FOR TECHNOLOGY TRANSFER

Beyond the choice of technology itself, manufacturing firms face other choices when they transfer know-how for use in foreign plants, such as the channel to be used for transferring proprietary technology. Three mutually exclusive channels are available:

1. sale of the know-how to an unrelated party;
2. use of the technology in a facility partially owned by the technology owner; or
3. use of the know-how in a facility wholly owned by the technology owner.

A technology licensing agreement may be employed in all three channels. The first channel of transfer of proprietary technology is often referred to as an 'arm's-length licence', or simply a 'licence'. The second channel is known as a 'joint venture', and the third channel is referred to as a 'wholly owned subsidiary'.

Despite the emergence of new forms of transfer, technology transfer through direct foreign investment remains the dominant model, and the supply side of technology still remains very oligopolistic in several industries (Lall 1987). Direct investment can result in a substantial loss for the investing enterprise. Licensing, in contrast, almost always brings some return to the owner of the technology. Clearly, there is no evidence that any one channel is ideal for all developing countries in all situations. Certain characteristics of the country to which the technology is being transferred also affect the decision about the transfer channel.

The international transfer of technology takes place through a number of formal and informal organisational modes (for a discussion of these modes see Cusumano & Elenkov [1994]). These modes can involve governments, academic institutions, companies and individuals, and may range from direct contact with foreign sources to indirect contact with such sources. Simon (1991) identifies five basic organisational modes:

1. the international technology market, which is made up of independent buyers and sellers;
2. intrafirm transfer, wherein organisations (such as multinational corporations) do not resort to the market but transfer technology

either through an internal venture or through a wholly owned subsidiary;

3. agreements or exchanges directed by the government, where the counterparts can be either public or private actors;

4. education, training and conferences, through which information is disseminated publicly for consumption by either a general or a specialised audience;

5. pirating or reverse engineering, through which organisations obtain access to technology without resorting to the market but at the expense of the property rights of the owners of the technology.

Thus, the type of transaction adopted and the procedures followed are affected by many factors. Given local market conditions, and depending on the economic situation, level of industrial development and political circumstances of the host country, the receiving enterprise may be a joint venture or may be totally independent. Indeed, there is considerable overlap between these forms. Lack of necessary levels of skills also affects the conditions surrounding the transaction. In many cases, the receiver of technology may not possess the ability to repair and maintain, modify, adapt or develop technology, or to design and produce new equipment or products.

THE MACROPROJECT AS A TYPE OF TECHNOLOGY TRANSFER TRANSACTION

Project developers as well as governments are increasingly involved in technology transfers aimed at designing, engineering, constructing and operating 'macroprojects'. Such technologies and the associated skills are no longer the purview of a few industrialised nations (Davidson & Meador 1992). A new type of multinational joint venture has emerged that deals with multiple transfers of technologies for macroprojects in developing countries (for example, Jubail in Saudi Arabia; Shoubrah el-Kheima in Egypt; the New Zealand Gas-to-Gasoline Project; see Hull [1992]). Macroprojects involve the transfer of a vast variety of technologies, including, for instance, energy, medical, transportation and information systems. In the Jubail macroproject, technology transfer provides the major basis for ensuring that local inhabitants are able to reap the benefits of an industrial society and live and work as fully productive citizens. To meet the massive objectives of the project, planners instituted a global programme for training and development through the establishment of a human resources training centre which would graduate over 1,000 students per year after training them in various skills. This programme runs in parallel with another programme training government administrators in various aspects of municipal government management and operation.

Macroprojects require greater awareness of deep technological interrelations. For example, the Jubail project involves 16 major technological projects including steel, fertiliser and petrochemicals among others, 300 support industries, and other essential services such as airport, railroad and seaport. This also illustrates why high-risk issues, vast technical domain allocations and issues concerning 'macro-ethics' within macroprojects should be given adequate attention (see Barquin 1992).

STAGES IN THE TECHNOLOGY TRANSFER PROCESS

The process of technology transfer to developing countries involves a complex series of stages. The precise nature of the process in each case depends on prevailing local conditions and on the type of technology that is to be transferred. Two major stages may be identified in general; each stage consists of related minor stages or components. While the first of these two principal stages deals with technology policy planning and decision making (that is, technological planning and technology assessment),[3] the second revolves around the implementation and operational processes of technology transfer.

According to UNCTAD (1975), the operational stage of the technology transfer process includes five different, but coordinated, parts. The steps in this sequence (depicted in Figure 3.3) may be summarised as follows:

1. Assignments, including sale and licensing agreements covering all forms of industrial property including patents, inventor's certificates, utility models, industrial designs, trademarks, service names and trade names.
2. Arrangements covering the provision of know-how and technical expertise in the form of feasibility studies, plans, diagrams, models, instructions, guides, formulations, service contracts and

---

[3]As the principal focus of this volume, these will be discussed fully in the following chapters.

Figure 3.3: Operational sequences for technology transfer

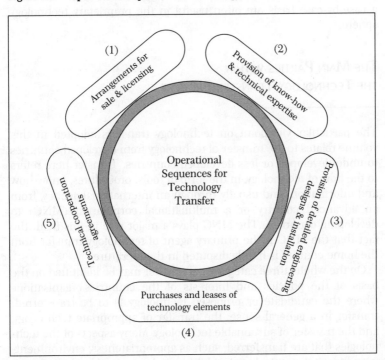

specifications, and/or involving technical, advising and managerial personnel and personnel training as well as equipment for training.

3. Arrangements covering the provision of basic or detailed engineering designs, and the installation and operation of plant and equipment.

4. Purchases, including leases and other forms of acquisition of machinery, equipment, intermediate goods and/or raw materials, insofar as they are part of transactions involving technology transfers.

5. Industrial and technical cooperation agreements of any kind, including turnkey agreements, international subcontracting as well as provision of management and marketing services.

Technology is not a homogeneous phenomenon. There are different types of technology, each posing fundamentally different problems and demanding different solutions in the international transfer process. It is now accepted (Kolds 1981) that ad hoc negotiations on a case-by-case basis are often useful in the proprietary technology sphere.

The Main Parties within the Technology Transfer Process

The particular viewpoint on technology transfers adopted in this volume relates to the transfer of technology from developed countries to underdeveloped or less developed countries. Transfer here refers to the flow of technology, in the form of tools, procedures, know-how and information, and usually through an international agency, from an advanced country or a multinational corporation (MNC) to developing countries. The MNC plays a major role in this field: the fact that the MNC is the primary agent of technology transfer from the home country is hardly disputed in the literature.

On the whole, three categories of transfer may be identified on the basis of the policies and interests of the countries/organisations where the candidate or proposed technology is to be transferred: transfer in a general sense, the transfer of appropriate technology, and the transfer of sustainable technology. Many aspects of the technologies that are transferred, such as appropriateness, environment-friendliness or political acceptability, are determined by the interests and objectives of the main parties to the transfer. The rigorous definition of criteria for appropriateness or sustainability by the major parties involved (home and host nations, MNCs and local firms) obliges them to fulfil these requirements during the transfer process. On the other hand, if these requirements, specific constraints or objectives are not spelled out clearly in the initial stages, the category of 'general transfer' is put into force. Thus, successful transfer requires the mutual understanding of interests and cooperation among the principal participants in the process.

A model of the process of transfer of technology would therefore take account of two points of view: (a) MNCs'/foreign firms' objectives; and (b) local firms' objectives. Furthermore, in modelling international technology transfer we also need to consider: (a) the recipient country's goals; and (b) the donor country's goals. The donor country's motives in transferring technology might be wholly business-oriented, or may involve political objectives as well; the recipient country, on the other hand, might be seeking developmental benefits from the technology transfer, and may even be motivated by non-economic goals. This points to the possibility of a divergence of interests in the process of technology transfer. It must not be forgotten that political and non-developmental issues may also influence decision making in the recipient country.

In view of these facts, it is not surprising that there is a greater coordination between MNCs' strategies for technology transfer and the interests of firms in the recipient country than between MNCs, or the donor country, and the development strategy of a developing country. Thus, any attempt to establish an approach for evaluating or planning technology transfer must carefully consider a series of elements concerning the two primary parties to the transfer process: the home country and the host country (the home country being the country where the technology originates; host country denoting the recipient).

The present work develops a model of the complex process of technology transfer that will help better understand the process, and provides guidelines to enable transfers to be as effective as possible. Such a model requires a new theoretical approach based on an understanding of the fundamental elements, both theoretical and practical, that are responsible for effective technology transfer to developing countries. The existing literature on the subject mostly discusses the commercial and economic aspects of transfers, which are not the whole story even if they are partly responsible for the effectiveness and success of the system. These aspects of transfer may be seen as a set of specific, necessary factors generally applicable to micro level, firm level and/or project level analyses of the process of technology transfer. However, they are not sufficient to an understanding of the process as a whole, since they do not account for the many failures of technology transfer that have been reported.

CONCEPTUALISING A MODEL OF TECHNOLOGY TRANSFER

Prior efforts to establish a framework for the study of technology transfer have emphasised three distinct aspects:

- the international political dimensions of the transfer process
- commercial transactions
- issues of operational relevance and those pertaining conditions

Frameworks focusing on the international political dimensions of transfer concentrate attention at the level of the nation-state, and evaluate issues related to cooperation and confrontation between the transfer countries. The commercial framework, on the other hand, by emphasising firm level activity, seeks to determine the outcome of individual projects as the interplay of corporate motives and negotiating strategies. A predominant focus on the host country characterises the operational framework.

International technology transfer has both a *horizontal* and a *vertical* dimension, each with its own constituent elements. Seen horizontally, the three basic elements in international technology transfer are the home country, the host country and the transaction. The vertical aspect of transfer refers to issues specific to the nation-state, or to industries or firms within the home and host countries. We may categorise these various elements as follows:

1. Home country (supply side):

   Impact of technology transfer on the home country
   Government policy
   MNCs and technology transfer

2. Host country (demand side):

   Impact of technology transfer on the host country
   Government policy
   Technological capability and appropriate technology
   Technology acquisition and adaptation
   The type of industry or service the candidate technology is to be transferred into

3. Transaction:

   The role and nature of technology transfer
   Technology transfer costs and payments and funding
   Pricing of technology
   Conflicts and code of conduct in technology transfer
   Mode and control of technology transfer
   Effective transfer of technology

As we have been saying, the lack of a consistent theoretical framework relating to the process of technology transfer to developing countries is a major weakness of much of the current literature dealing with this subject. Problems associated with technology transfer are discussed mostly in terms of limited descriptive considerations: indeed, most studies dealing with technology transfer to developing countries concentrate exclusively on its financial or economic aspects. Transfer of technology, however, is a complex process that involves the engineering, management, economic, politico-social, environmental and anthropometrical sciences. Ample scope therefore exists to develop an interdisciplinary theoretical approach to the subject. Such an approach would integrate the concepts and methodologies of these various sciences into a multidimensional understanding of technology transfer.

Technology transfer has emerged as an important part of the new international economic order, wherein multinational corporations are the main suppliers of technology to developing countries. However, it is clear that the interests of MNCs are mostly far removed from the national goals and interests of developing countries. Fayerweather & Kapoor (1976) suggest that the goals of the nations within which MNCs operate are best considered first. This is because they appear constantly as reference points against which to measure the strategic capabilities of the country. The following forms of participation of MNCs in the process of industrial development of developing countries have been examined:

1. direct foreign investments, and
2. joint ventures (which have emerged as the result of intervention by the governments of developing countries and demands for local ownership).

Technology Transfer as a Simple Triple-System

In recent years, for both political and economic reasons, the governments of many developing countries have played a larger role in the process of transfer of technology. However, these host governments are still more or less passive participants in the process of technology transfer. Multinational corporations, as the major suppliers and financiers of technology to developing countries, have dominated the environment of international technology transfer, particularly until the 1980s. Figure 3.4 shows the relationships between the major participants in the transfer process at the organisational or firm level (that is, at the micro level).

Figure 3.4: A conceptual model of technology transfer at the micro level

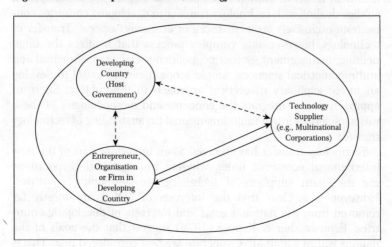

During the second half of the 1970s, the international debate on the issue of fair distribution of the world's resources led to several UN policy declarations, as a result of which three sets of financing bodies appeared on the scene as the major facilitators of technology transfer in the 1980s: development banks, bilateral aid agencies and multilateral aid agencies. Agencies that assist developing countries achieve techno-economic and social development are basically of two kinds: multilateral and bilateral. Technological aid provided by one government to another is considered bilateral assistance, while multilateral assistance is provided by agencies that give aid on behalf of several governments (for instance, the World Bank). International development assistance agencies have been under increasing political pressure to adopt policies and programmes that take into account in a comprehensive manner the prevailing local conditions in developing countries (for example, by helping to protect limited natural resources in these countries).

From the viewpoint of the parties involved in the process of technology transfer, two issues emerge. First, the transfer process should be considered as a *system* involving three major, interrelated parties. Second, the role of the UN and related institutions should be recognised alongside that of MNCs and developing countries within each transfer project. These relationships, as depicted in Figure 3.5, affect the supply of foreign technology to underdeveloped countries. Therefore, the process of policy making for technology transfer in

Figure 3.5: A conceptual model of technology transfer at the supranational level and the major parties involved

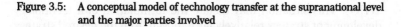
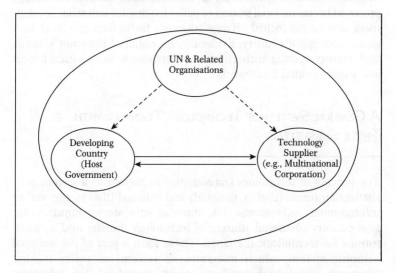

developing countries is dependent in each case (of country and/or technology) on existing relationships and on the atmosphere of international relations. This means that the national strategy of techno-economic development (a dominant political issue in developing countries) not only depends on national macroeconomic and internal socio-political factors, but is also significantly affected by the UN (and its relevant departments and declarations) and by international suppliers of technology (such as the MNCs).

Technology transfer to developing countries involves a host of technical, socio-cultural, political, economic and environmental problems. For each of these factors, an appropriate function should be defined which affects, in turn, the techno-socio-economic system of the country. From the point of view of economics, the problem here is to link two economic systems with different production functions through the transfer of knowledge (Chatterji 1990). For the purpose of deriving this linkage, a new system of interrelated production functions may be developed.

The point to be noted is that while the relationship between a developing (that is, host) country and a supplier of technology is facilitated by a two-way and direct mechanism, the process is also crucially affected in an indirect and one-way manner by the UN and its related organisations (for example, the UNDP, UNCTAD and

WHO). This situation may dictate the formulation of a technology development strategy relatively far removed from the desired strategy proposed by the national system of policy making for industrial development and technological change (through technology transfer) in a given developing country. Evidently, the national planning systems and strategy-making authority systems require to work within logical and expert-guided frameworks.

A GENERAL SYSTEM OF TECHNOLOGY TRANSFER WITH THREE SUBSYSTEMS

The process of technology transfer may be viewed as a system consisting of internal (that is, national) and external (that is, regional or international) subsystems. The internal subsystem comprises the host country's national strategy of technology transfer and its institutions for technological change. These form a part of the national planning system, which integrates all systems of policy making (economic, social, educational, etc.) at the macro level. This subsystem is also interrelated with and coordinated by the overall strategy for industrial development prescribed by the national planning system, a strategy generally framed by the political authority system (PAS) that is in place in the host country. The external subsystem of the technology transfer process includes, first, the international financing and support structures (UN institutions, aid agencies), and, second, the international system of technology suppliers.

The transfer process presented pictorially in Figure 3.5 may now be perceived as a comprehensive system involving both national and international domains, and containing three subsystems, S_1, S_2 and S_3, where:

S_1 is the developing country's internal system for technology transfer based on national interests (the national protocol for technology transfer);

S_2 is the international financing and support system for the transfer of technology to developing countries; and

S_3 is the international system of technology suppliers.

Each of these subsystems, obviously, involves its own set of elements. For instance, S_1 contains the national economic system, political and socio-cultural institutions, the educational system, technological

Figure 3.6: Technology transfer as an interrelated and comprehensive system

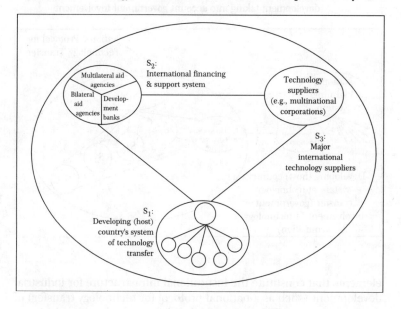

capabilities and the industrial situation, etc., of the host country. It is also interrelated with the policy-making and planning systems for national development, the strategy for technological change and industrialisation, and so on. Figure 3.6 depicts the transfer process as a system consisting of three interrelated subsystems. The elements within each of these subsystems change according to the targets defined by any given country at a specific time (in this study, the focus is exclusively on S_1). Further, each system may be defined for a particular level of analysis (micro or macro) and the relevant factors may be assessed accordingly.

TECHNOLOGY TRANSFER AND POLITICAL DOMINATION

With industrialisation being perceived as the unique vehicle of socio-economic development, and thereby as a fundamental goal in any developing country, there is an accelerating tendency to institutionalise local systems for technology acquisition and absorption in these countries. Such a system may form the whole or the heart of S_1, with

Figure 3.7: Institutional infrastructure for technology transfer and industrial development taking into account government involvement

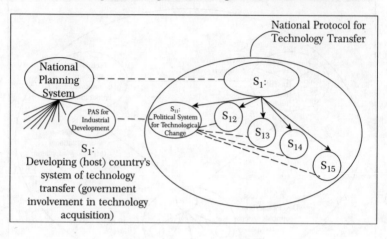

elements that constitute the institutional infrastructure for industrial development (such as a national protocol for technology transfer) of the host country. The responsible authorities within the decision-making and planning system for technology transfer may focus on the prerequisites for and implications of direct government involvement in the selection of technologies and industrial projects, enter into negotiations with foreign technology suppliers, and participate in project implementation. Where such local systems exist, the evaluation of S_1 should be carried out using a new set of elements (namely, those that make up the institutional infrastructures for technological and industrial development), as follows:

S_{11}: Political system for technological change and development (this subsystem, per se, is also a component of the political authority system, or PAS, for industrial development within the national planning system: see Figure 3.7)

S_{12}: System for consulting services in the development of technological or industrial projects

S_{13}: System for negotiation of foreign technology acquisition

S_{14}: System for financing of technology transfer (industrial) projects

S_{15}: System for implementation and absorption of foreign technology, followed by the operational stage of transfer

The first party (that is, the transferee) within the process of technology transfer (S_1) may thus be divided into functional subsystems for the acquisition and development of foreign technology. As Figure 3.7 shows, S_{11}, S_{12}, S_{13}, S_{14} and S_{15} (that is, the internal subsystems of S_1) are interrelated, but the latter four are dominated by the first subsystem (viz., the political system for technological change and industrial development, or S_{11}). This is due to the fact that technology transfer and industrialisation in developing countries have become increasingly politicised domains. Further, while S_1 is a subsystem of the national planning system, S_{11} may be seen as a subsystem within the political authority system (PAS) that governs technological change and industrial development in a given country. Experience shows that this domination by the political sphere plays mostly a negative role and causes the transfer of inappropriate technology. Political domination is generally considered a major bottleneck in effecting technological change and industrial development in these countries.

In terms of the conceptual and schematic model we have proposed, the achievement of a viable transfer requires that these institutional infrastructures be developed in such a way as to improve technological capacity in the host country. The framework just outlined addresses the transfer process in terms of the functional elements (that is, the subsystems) involved within the national process of technological change and industrialisation. Each subsystem, at any stage (or activity phase) of the transfer process, plays its own role in facilitating the transfer of technology within the national economic and production system. For instance, at the stage of selection of a technology transfer project, the chief participants within the system (in other words, the responsible subsystems) will mainly be S_{11} and S_{12} (see Table 3.1).

Table 3.1
Stages within the process of technology transfer

Stage of the Transfer Process (Activity Phase)	Subsystem Involved
1. Plans for (industrial development via) technology transfer/priorities setting	S_{11}
2. Selection of technology transfer project	$S_{11} + S_{12}$
3. Feasibility studies	S_{12}
4. Negotiations and contracting of technology acquisition	S_{13}
5. Technology transfer financing	S_{14}
6. Implementation of technology transfer projects	S_{15}
7. Operation (of the transferred technology)	S_{15}

EXTERNAL AND INTERNAL FORCES AFFECTING TECHNOLOGY TRANSFER PROTOCOLS

The effectiveness or success of any transferred technology in a developing country depends on five kinds of forces:

- changes in indigenous technological capabilities
- changes in society and individual lifestyles (that is, socio-cultural changes)
- changes in the economy, human resources system and working conditions
- changes in the political system
- changes in international relations

Together, these five kinds of forces affect the supply of and demand for technology, and influence government policies on technology transfer, or, in other words, the national protocols on technology transfer (see Figure 3.8). Technological changes or breakthroughs occur continuously, and have implications for all areas of the host country's techno-economic system (from facilitating research and development and improvement of the services and manufacturing

Figure 3.8: External and internal forces affecting changes in protocol

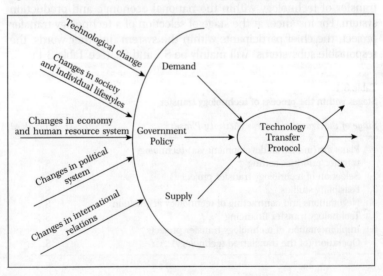

sectors, to encouraging the expulsion of foreign technology). With the appropriate strategies and policy-making authorities in place, changes in indigenous technological capabilities can rapidly enhance a country's ability to absorb and manage transferred technologies. Rapid increases in technological capability, however, also raise certain concerns. The introduction of foreign technologies in these situations should involve careful management and evaluation. Further, technological changes wrought by transferred technology require a re-examination of all arrangements for the initial and ongoing training of professional staff, and have a profound effect on hitherto accepted working practices.

Any major change in a society's lifestyle is mutually interrelated with changes in the economy; as a consequence, human resources and working conditions may determine some aspects of the technology transfer protocol. In the absence of responsiveness to socio-economic changes and to emerging new individual lifestyles, institutional mechanisms that intended to facilitate the acquisition of technology may instead act as constraints and barriers. Further, for any technology transfer project to be successful, instabilities in the existing political and policy-making systems, internal economic conflicts and institutional constraints will have to be dealt with. The stability of a country's political system affects both the process of transfer and the dynamics of the protocol, which are also influenced by other forces such as foreign government policies, international relations and even by private corporations. The building of capacity on the basis of a relevant national protocol for technology transfer requires identifying these various interrelated internal and external forces and determining the intensity of their respective impacts.

A Systematic Approach to the Process of Technology Transfer

At this point, it is useful to recapitulate briefly the approach to technology transfer that we have outlined until now, in order to lay the groundwork for the next stage in our analysis. A review of the literature concerning the difficulties faced in the transfer of technology to developing countries led us to conclude that the methods previously proposed to resolve these difficulties have all focused on one or the other aspect of the process, without taking a panoptic view. We contend that in order to arrive at the optimum practices, a thorough review of all the aspects involved in the technology transfer process is required, and this forms the basis of the approach developed here.

In the light of the disparate viewpoints and definitions appearing in the literature, it seemed important to us to consider afresh what is meant by 'technology' and by 'technology transfer'. We then assembled a conceptual model of 'technology transfer' treated as a process, and identified the principal elements and stages involved in this process.

The major elements in this conceptual system include: (a) the home country (supply side); (b) the host country (demand side); and (c) a transaction that involves each side along with its relevant variables. The transfer process itself has been analysed into two main stages, each further divided into minor stages or components. The first of these major stages involves 'technology policy planning and assessment'; the second concerns the 'implementation and operational process' of technology transfer. With this background, it is possible now to consider how the transfer process essentially works, how it is affected by the various factors involved, and which groups of variables play key roles in the assessment of candidate technologies.

It is evident that political decisions play a major, even dominant, role; it is pertinent to ask how this factor can be taken into account systematically in terms of its effect on the technology transfer process. A number of other questions have to be answered before choosing a technology and implementing the transfer process. For instance, the choice of appropriate technology for transfer is a crucial issue: how can the assessment of technology for transfer be carried out in as objective a manner as possible? Evolving a rigorous approach to technology assessment requires us to explore the internal characteristics of the process of transfer. We shall now undertake an in-depth analysis of this nature. In chapter four we analyse the major steps involved in the implementation of technology transfers, with a view to addressing the crucial issue of improving technological capability, the main objective of any technology transfer.

4

TECHNOLOGY DIFFUSION

ASSIMILATION AND CAPABILITY IMPROVEMENT

The ability of different countries to benefit from technical knowledge (as embodied in the four principal elements of technology, namely, humanware, orgaware, technoware and inforware) varies with levels of indigenous technological capability. The efficient use of imported technology requires the existence of considerable technological capability in the recipient country, for installation, adaptation to local conditions (technically, anthropologically, socially, politically, environmentally, and so forth), and for operation and maintenance. This is one of the main concerns underlying technology assessment within the process of technology transfer.

An extensive review of the literature reveals the lack of comprehensive treatment of indigenous technological capability as the major determinant of the effectiveness of foreign technology transfer. Most works (mainly case studies at the micro level) take into account the relative importance of indigenous technological efforts in technology improvement, but these studies lack any clear, systematic framework to relate indigenous technological capability factors to the management of foreign technology utilisation and development. In this volume, the acquisition of foreign technology by an organisation or a firm in a developing country is seen as serving two strategic purposes, based on the engineering and economic perspectives respectively: (a) improvement of direct economic returns; and (b) strengthening technological capability and competence.

Technology transfer is a dynamic, continuous process aimed at achieving and improving sustainable technological capability. This involves the improvement of elements within the operational process of technology transfer, from acquisition to the development of imported technology (stages that constitute what we describe as the technology transfer 'pyramid', discussed in the next section). In this chapter, we examine the major stages within this process through a systematic analysis. A rigorous understanding of what constitutes the essence of national technological capability and the requirements for its improvement will allow us to address the factors responsible for successful transfers of technology.

As we shall argue, the achievement of sustainable technological development and productivity improvement involves upgrading technology through a sequence of minor changes to the original plant, equipment and related orga-managerial elements, rather than bringing about radical changes through the employment of new sets of technologies (see Vongpanitlerd [1992] regarding the development of Thailand's technological capabilities; see also Dahlman et al. [1987] for the case of Brazil). Stewart (1990) draws attention to the dangers of dualism associated with the excessive and unselective use of advanced country technology, and argues that technology development involves a chain-like process. The changes that follow from small improvements, when added together, often amount to as great an overall effect upon resource use and productivity as the changes induced by radical techno-logical changes. The manner of technological development evi-dently has considerable implications for the process of technology transfer.

THE TECHNOLOGY TRANSFER PYRAMID

Technology development is not an autonomous process, but is inti-mately associated with the needs and pressures created by environ-ment and society. Technology transfer, in our view, is about *continuous* technological improvement of technical know-how and information viability, organisational and managerial ability, techno-logical capability, and human skills and knowledge capacity, brought about through the utilisation of imported technology for the achievement of sustainable industrial capability. Achieving technological sustainability involves passing through a series of stages, including:

1. technology assessment and selection
2. technology acquisition
3. technology adaptation
4. technology absorption and assimilation
5. technology diffusion
6. technology development

It may be noted here that the first of these stages represents the main objective of this book, which is to develop a comprehensive approach to technology assessment and selection. The second and third stages may be seen as sub-steps within the process of 'adoption'. Each of these six stages may drive the process of improvement of transferred technology. In order to evolve a method for achieving a sustainable transfer, in this chapter we translate each stage into a set of practices involving core activities or procedures. These activities or procedures describe how to achieve that particular stage of technology improvement. They may be seen as a set of sub-stages that define the path of the operational process of the transfer. These practices comprise the key-role factors within the process of continuous technology improvement.

Each stage involves a specific capability; taken together, they form what we may describe as a technology transfer 'pyramid'. Figure 4.1 provides a representation of the technology transfer pyramid.

The receiving firm or organisation needs to be guided through the various stages in the technology transfer pyramid on the basis of the principles provided by the technology management and control system (that is, the micro level guidelines established by the national protocol for technology transfer). Thus, the transfer of technology cannot be viewed as a 'quick fix', a solution towards achieving a short-term goal that will be met simply with the physical import of technology. Indeed, technology transfer is the management of a *techno-social* process that recognises the importance of utilising, adapting and improving an imported technology in order to eventually develop technological capacity. The entire process of transfer may thus be seen as a system for the continuous improvement of a new technology within the techno-economic system of a country.

Figure 4.1: Technology transfer pyramid and the system of continuous improvement of technology

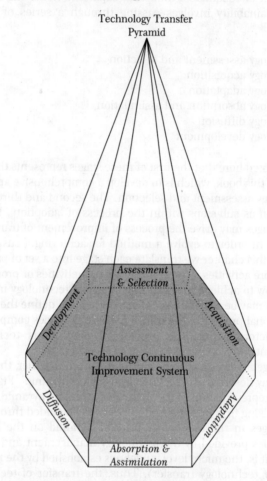

Technology Transfer
Pyramid

Assessment
& Selection

Development

Acquisition

Technology Continuous
Improvement System

Diffusion

Adaptation

Absorption &
Assimilation

ADOPTION: ACQUISITION AND ADAPTATION OF THE TRANSFERRED TECHNOLOGY

In many developing countries, much effort has been devoted to seeking technological progress through technology transfer in order to realise development in a much shorter period of time than that originally taken by industrialised countries to reach their present levels of development. However, the process of technology transfer is not a simple matter of taking a technology developed in one place and installing it elsewhere, where operations and productivity will be duplicated. When technology transfer projects are being considered, it should be recognised that considerable adaptation of the initial technology is almost invariably needed, often requiring research, investment and training to make the transferred technology work in its new context.

The weak technological basis of less developed countries means that both the technological process and the process of technology development in these countries differ from those of industrialised countries (see the discussion in chapter two of this volume; see also Kahen & Sayers 1995c; N. Sharif 1999). The problems originate from differences in the socio-economic and technological levels of the country of origin, which is almost always a developed country, and the recipient country. It is a proven fact that any technology embodies features corresponding to the comparative advantages of the country where it was developed.

Since technology is conceived of as organisation-specific information concerning the characteristics and performance properties of the production process (of services and goods), and to the extent that it is tacit and cumulative in nature (Rosenberg & Frischtak 1985), the transfer of technology is not as easy as the purchase of a capital good or a blueprint. It involves positive and sufficient costs, reflecting the difficult task of replicating knowledge across the boundaries of organisations and nations. Recipients would normally be obliged to devote substantial resources towards adapting, assimilating and improving upon the original technology.

An imported technology can often be re-engineered or modified significantly to match the socio-economic and technological situation of the importer. This constitutes the stage of technology adaptation within the process of technology transfer. We have described transfer as involving the knowledgeable application of already existent technology to new uses or, for that matter, to nations, areas or users where that particular technology had not previously been known or utilised. Generally, new technologies from more advanced countries tend to dictate the requirements for adaptation to existing technologies in their new circumstances (that is, the circumstances prevailing in the developing countries that import these technologies).

No technology is made available by industrialised nations that is already perfectly suited to developing country conditions. Technology does not come ready to work at a 100 per cent efficiency rate. Further, despite the call for more technical cooperation between developing countries and the efforts in this direction spearheaded by the United Nations Development Programme (UNDP), the literature contains few examples of actual cases of such cooperation. Any transferred technology, in any case, needs to be developed in accordance with local user characteristics and environmental variables in order to achieve both adequate productivity and human satisfaction. This is because, in general, technologies are created to meet the objectives of their countries of origin. For these reasons, many efforts in developing countries are geared towards adopting imported technologies into their production and process systems and adjusting them to local conditions. It is therefore essential that, not only in the evaluation and selection stages, but also before importing the technology and during installation and utilisation, developing countries try to identify relevant local weaknesses and advantages in order to minimise the adaptation and adjustment period. A serious attempt in this direction would aid viable technology transfer and technological change in non-industrialised countries.

Several efforts to assist developing countries to boost agricultural production, for instance, have focused on the transfer of agricultural technology from countries with successful 'green revolutions' to those still aspiring towards a green revolution. To cite an example, Kaatawee Farm was developed during 1978–89 by the People's Republic of China as a state-owned rice seed plantation in rural Liberia (Braautigam 1993). This was an instance of the transfer of Asian technology to Africa, involving the provision of technical assistance by one developing country to another. The project sought to establish the feasibility of plantation-scale rice production in Liberia. The Kaatawee Farm experience revealed that successful technology transfer depends partly on similarities between the source environment and the destination, and partly on successful adaptation. In some ways, the rice growing environment in Liberia is not unlike that in China. On the other hand, there are some significant differences between the two environments. While China is a densely populated country with low labour costs, labour in Liberia is limited in relation to land, and labour costs are consequently high. Furthermore, China's technology transfer was part of a package that included both the technology and the systems necessary for its sustainability, which depended upon the high maintenance and management demands of Chinese practices, information and training. The presence of these elements, together with easy access to commercial inputs, would be critical for successful transfer and continued usefulness. Some of the technical difficulties experienced in the transfer process in this case were a function both of lack of experience and unorganised government support. It is clear that with greater skill development and more efficient agricultural services, these difficulties can largely be overcome.

Adaptation of a new technology also involves matching it with the anthropometrical characteristics of the technology utilisers (or human resources, including workers/operators of the technology; in the case of process technology, this would include the end users of the technology). This is an 'ergonomic' consideration in the process of technology transfer, and plays an important supporting role in the success of any transfer (see Gurr et al. 1998; Kahen & Griffiths 1995; Meshkati 1989a, 1989b; Meshkati & Robertson 1986; O'Neill 2000).[1] Thus, technology transfer must be viewed as a complex process, comprising distinct components and involving a multitude of attributes; furthermore, transfer involves relationships not only between various elements (men, machines, rules), but also between the donor and the recipient.

Adaptation in the operational stage of the process of transfer is not costless—it requires the allocation of resources towards purposive technological efforts. The changes are typically implemented through trial-and-error testing of modifications, somewhat like applied research, even though the process often does not involve inputs from specialised agents of R&D. Adaptation is a continuous process spread over the entire life cycle of the project operation, as depicted in Table 4.1. It also often involves elements of 'investment capability' (Westphal et al. 1985), because adaptations are frequently embodied in minor changes or additions to physical capital. In some cases, such adaptations involve all aspects of investment capability, even though the amount invested may be small.

Much of the effort of recipient countries is thus geared towards the continuous adaptation of imported technology to local conditions and to the receiving firm's operational characteristics and particular productive constraints. Adaptations have been observed to take place through modifications and changes that stretch the capacity of existing plants, overcome bottlenecks in particular processes, improve the use of by-products, facilitate adjustment to new input sources, alter the product mix and introduce a wide variety of incremental improvements in process and product designs.

---

[1] We will discuss this issue in greater detail in chapter five.

Table 4.1
Elements of investment capability

Manpower training: to improve skills and abilities of all kinds

Pre-investment feasibility studies: to identify possible projects and to ascertain prospects for viability under alternative design concepts

Project execution: to establish or expand facilities, including:

> **Project management** (to organise and oversee the activities involved in project execution);
>
> **Project engineering** (to provide the information needed to make technology operational in a particular setting, including:
>
>> **Detailed studies** (to make tentative choices among design alternatives);
>>
>> **Basic engineering** (to supply the core technology in terms of process flows, material and energy balances, specifications of principal equipment, plant layout);
>>
>> **Detailed engineering** (to supply the peripheral technology in terms of complete specifications for all physical capital, architectural and engineering plans, construction and equipment installation specifications).
>
> **Procurement** (to choose, coordinate and supervise hardware suppliers and construction contractors);
>
> **Embodiment in physical capital** (to accomplish site preparation, construction, plant erection, manufacture of machinery and equipment);
>
> **Start-up of operations** (to attain predetermined norms).

Source: Westphal et al. (1984).

ADAPTATION AND THE TRANSFER OF MANAGERIAL KNOWLEDGE AND KNOW-HOW

Adjustments are also required in the orga-managerial aspects of any transferred technology. It is often necessary not only to change the specifications and technical dimensions of equipment, but to adapt the managerial structure as well (see Kahen 1997b). For instance, during the start-up of a certain project in Brazil, the transferor encountered problems in transplanting the administrative structure from a large (original) plant at home to a smaller one in a setting characterised by fewer experienced technical personnel and less-skilled workers (Dahlman et al. 1987).

For a technology supplier to transfer its know-how is regarded as a difficult task within the operational process of technology transfer, a task that often proves more difficult than anticipated. Acquiring the requisite expertise, however, is one of the most important benefits a country expects from foreign investment. In this respect, high expectations are generally hard to achieve and the transfer of know-how easily becomes a problem area. In general, and particularly in the case of the orga-managerial aspects of technology, it has been observed that skills which succeed in one culture may fail in another; control systems are differently interpreted; and marketing techniques prove ineffective. Sometimes local preferences will obstruct all efforts to promote methods that have succeeded elsewhere (M. Brooks 1986).

No doubt many of the problems of transferring know-how are inescapable. To minimise difficulties, however, it is important for technology suppliers to recognise that the orga-managerial element is culture-bound, and that some techniques reflect values of the home country that are not necessarily those of the host. It should be understood that technology is not neutral in its political and social effects, and that an appropriate technology needs to be adapted to the local environment (for example, the economic system, market characteristics, traditional channels of communication). Industrialised countries and international suppliers of technology are often reluctant to recognise that these are circumstances in which the elements of the package are inseparable. For instance, with a simple technology, the sale of patents may be adequate, but more advanced technologies are likely to have been developed with built-in training schemes, re-engineering and organisation redesign, research and development frameworks, marketing programmes and other orga-managerial activities.

R&D, Adaptation and Technological Capability Improvement

Technology adaptation today differs fundamentally from the experience of countries that industrialised early. Indeed, it has been argued (Nakaoka 1987) that it is far more difficult for developing nations today to absorb fast-moving technologies. This is due to the greater dependence of these technologies on specialised activities (such as corporate R&D, design, and production engineering) than on line-production experience. The introduction of existing technology into a new environment therefore requires specific adaptation capabilities.

Most R&D units established abroad by transferors of technology take the form of technical service laboratories that help to transfer the technology efficiently before the product or process technology has stabilised. These laboratories, or 'technology transfer units', also provide related technical services to their foreign customers. A study of 55 R&D units (Ronstadt 1984) established in other countries by seven American multinationals revealed that they fell into four distinct categories:

1. Transfer technology units: R&D units established to help certain foreign subsidiaries transfer manufacturing technology from the parent while also providing related technical services for foreign customers.
2. Indigenous technology units: R&D units established to develop new and improved products expressly for foreign markets. These products were not the direct result of new technology supplied by the parent organisations.
3. Global technology units: R&D units established to develop new products and processes for simultaneous—or nearly simultaneous—application in major world markets of the multinational organisations (this particular sample also included non-MNC American companies).
4. Corporate technology units: R&D units established to generate new technology of a long-term or exploratory nature expressly for the corporate parent.

When we analyse the objectives and missions of these units, it becomes clear that none of them takes into account the *long-term* adaptation and development of the transferred technology within the host countries. This is because the transferor of technology generally does not appreciate the possibility of mutually benefiting from the outcome of R&D units with the transferee. Had this been the case, a technologically dynamic atmosphere could develop within the receiving country or the firm, and even encourage the local generation of a significant part of the technology (Bell & Pavitt 1993a). This could be achieved by incorporating local technical staff in the designs of the capital goods to be transferred, and encouraging their interaction with suppliers in developing designs and specifications, as well as local *control* of a part of the installation and development processes of the technology. We believe, therefore, that the effectiveness of a transferred technology and its potential for capability improvement depend most heavily on the mode of transfer (whether it takes the form of wholly owned ventures, joint ventures, etc.).

Many studies (for instance, Dahlman & Valadares 1987; Katz 1987) examine the domestic technological research and development efforts that developing countries undertake for the purpose of adapting foreign-designed technologies to local market conditions. Various studies also confirm the crucial importance of minor technological changes as a source of productivity growth in developing countries. After achieving the initial stages within the technology transfer pyramid, however, the capacity to develop technology or to innovate is the highest stage in the accumulation of knowledge of technology by a country. The Indian science and technology infrastructure (including in-house R&D units and national laboratories), for instance, as well as adapting and localising foreign technologies, has begun the process of innovating. In some areas, these efforts have yielded tangible outcomes. For instance, of the 34 models of tractors sold in the country, as many as 16 are products of in-house R&D, and one was developed by a national laboratory (Mani 1987). Other significant product developments include battery-operated electric locomotives, low-cost digital switching technology for telecommunications, and the technology for electronic-grade silicon. In the last two instances, the locally developed technology involved a much smaller capital outlay than the available imported alternatives, resulting in lower product costs. A crucial point revealed by these case studies is that 'cost reduction' has not necessarily been a priority of the technological research efforts undertaken by developing countries (particularly in Latin America). Quite to the contrary, product mix diversification (Vitelli 1978), quality (Fidel et al. 1978), and the more effective use of imported and installed technology and of its normal capacity (Katz et al. 1988) appear as the important objectives of such technological research and development efforts.

SYSTEMATIC ADOPTION, ACCEPTANCE AND APPLICABILITY OF TECHNOLOGY

The adoptability and applicability of new technology within the context of organisations in developing countries determine the degree to which the transfer of a particular technology is successful. It is clear that merely the purchase of new technologies does not ensure their successful application. In many cases (see, for example, Davis et al. 1989; Preece 1990; Voss 1984), promises of productivity

Figure 4.2: The main frameworks of stages in new technology adoption

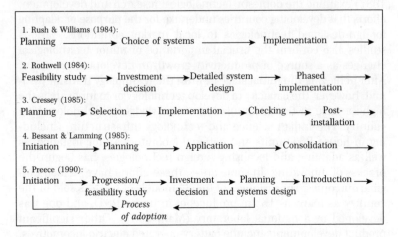

gains are only partly realised, often because the social organisation cannot adapt to the use of these new technologies. At the micro level, or in other words at the level of the organisation or the firm, various stages may be discerned within the adoption process of a new technology, comprising the initial stages within the operational process of the technology transfer. To summarise the findings of various case studies (Bessant & Lamming 1985; Caloghirou et al. 2000; Cressey 1985; Preece 1990; Rothwell 1984; Rush & Williams 1984), the stages in the adoption process may be classified into five different frameworks (see Figure 4.2).

Each of the frameworks represented in Figure 4.2 emphasises a certain part of the adoption process. Rush & Williams (1984), in their study of a sample of companies in the electronics sector, focus on the stage at which 'consultation' with the human resources sector occurs in connection with the adoption of new technology— that is, at the relatively late stage of implementation. On the basis of case studies of 23 organisations, Rothwell (1984) finds that the feasibility study is an initial requirement for adoption, paying less emphasis to application design and implementation. In a study on the introduction of new technology in 21 organisations in various sectors in Denmark, England, Ireland, Italy and Germany, Cressey (1985) proposes a framework for adoption comprising five stages: planning, selection, implementation, checking and post-installation.

Bessant & Lamming (1985), on the other hand, argue that initiation (that is, providing reasons for going ahead with change) is the first step in the adoption of a new technology, followed by planning (preparation for technological change), application (actual introduction of the technology in production), and consolidation (bedding-down and evaluation). Of all these frameworks, that provided by Preece (1990) may be viewed as a dynamic framework. Preece defines the process of adoption as consisting of initiation, the progression/feasibility study, the investment decision, and planning and systems design.

Effective utilisation and the successful transfer of technology entail the achievement of the full potential of a new technology, described as its 'integrative potential'. For this potential to be tapped, the process of adoption must address all aspects of micro level analysis. In other words, adoption must occur at the organisational, technological and human resources levels. It may be noted that for certain technologies (like nuclear technology), the adoption process should also take into account other factors, for instance, macro level factors such as national consciousness.

A broad review of experiences with successful transfer and technological change in developing countries would seem to suggest that the adoption of new technology in a new environment generally involves an element of faith. Be that as it may, successful transfer demands a careful consideration of the internal, external and contextual elements pertaining to the process of introduction and transfer of new technology. Internal elements are related to the field, type and characteristics of the candidate technology that is to be transferred and to the type of transaction and the mode of transfer. External elements include such factors as government regulations, international relations, some policy-based constraints, strategic advantages and even facilities provided by international institutions (such as the World Bank, UNCTAD and WHO). Contextual elements pertain to the country's technological context and existing technical/technological capabilities, and the degree of risk involved in this respect. An adequate understanding of the context in which a new technology is to be introduced and utilised would, further, include a consideration of the following factors.[2] These factors affect both the acceptance and the applicability of new technology within a new environment:

---

[2] Land (1987) refers to these factors as a typical set of *contingency* factors.

1. The extent to which those who work in the organisation share its goals and values: this depends on the external and internal industrial relations climate, management style/distance, personal relations, management goals, cultural and political factors.
2. The approach chosen for the introduction of new technology
3. The philosophy that underlies the way in which systems are expected to operate
4. The extent to which the organisation is used to technological and organisational change
5. Economic factors
6. Government regulations and legislation
7. The extent of trade union knowledge of and influence on technological change

In general, the influence of these factors should be studied empirically on a case-by-case basis. Such a practice would ensure that a technological system is recognised as being confronted with a reality that is influenced and determined by factors partly out of the organisation's range of control, sometimes not even predictable. If models are images of reality, then the 'facts' that make up reality (that is, local characteristics) must be interpreted into a structure of words, which must then have something in common with the structure of the facts. Such a structure is therefore deeply affected by cultural environment: symbols and meanings within the model will be differently interpreted in another cultural context where technology users are embedded in different social, environmental, technical, cultural and economic networks. Information, hence, is not culturally neutral; 'current information is a reflection of a certain way of thinking and of a certain economic and social organisation: it is the product of a rationalist and Western culture' (Kalman 1981). Ignoring this can and must lead to hazardous results—the case of Bhopal in India is representative—or to complex and completely unpredictable situations (see Kahen 1996a, 1999, 2001b, 2001c; Kahen & Griffiths 1995; Meshkati 1989a, 1989b).

ABSORPTION AND ASSIMILATION

Developing countries differ greatly in their capacities for technological absorption, in their technological needs and in their goals in seeking technology transfer (Prasad 1986). A large component of technology is tacit, residing in the skills of technicians who implement the projects and operationalise them (Chamarik & Goonatilake 1994). The indigenisation of technicians, therefore, is an indicator of the absorption of 'know-how', if not of 'know-why'. Further, transfer arrangements must recognise that absorption is a dynamic process. As a general rule, when a developing country can at least use a product efficiently and support its use, we can say that this technology has been absorbed in that country. 'Full' absorption may include the capacity to process a service or manufacture a product and ultimately to develop it further. Briefly, the absorption of a technology requires:

- the acceptance of the technology (mentally by local people and physically within the environment);
- the motivation to make it succeed (for example, where there exists a perceived need or benefit within the developing country, supported by appropriate government policy measures such as regulation and pricing to create a positive climate);
- the ability to support the technology (either a finished product and/or a production process) locally. Ultimately, this includes the availability of indigenous skills to adapt technologies to the local environment and to further develop them.

Further, the absorption of a technology is significantly affected by the process of adaptation, potentially an important source of knowledge acquisition, understanding and absorption of 'know-why'. For instance, there is evidence (Chamarik & Goonatilake 1994) that Indian firms have undertaken considerable adaptation of imported technologies for various reasons: to facilitate the substitution of imported raw materials by local ones; to adapt the product to the local climate, environment or tastes; to scale down plant size to suit the size of the market; to upgrade the technology, etc. These adaptations have resulted in the indigenisation of the imported technologies, or, in other words, in technology absorption.

Another indicator of the indigenisation or absorption of technologies in the Indian case is the evidence of technology exports from India to other developing countries through joint ventures and licensing agreements (see Desai 1980). A survey of 52 Indian firms that undertook joint ventures abroad revealed that, although 42 of them had obtained their initial technology from foreign sources, 47 had indigenised these technologies before exporting them. The fact that 'Indian machinery' was the source of know-how in most of the Indian investments abroad makes it apparent that these firms exported locally adapted technology to their affiliates. The adaptations rendered these technologies 'most appropriate' for conditions in developing countries (Thomas 1982). An empirical study of 12 Thai industries also confirmed that Indian firms often used absolutely efficient technologies; they operated at costs below the theoretical minimum cost (Lecraw 1977).

Although absorption and acceptance of an imported technology mutually reinforce each other, acceptance is often a prerequisite for viable absorption. Technology acceptance is based on motivation and on the scope for its enhancement. Motivation may take a number of forms:

1. Economic incentive: If a technology is commercially viable in its own right, there is an immediate incentive for its introduction.
2. Political incentive: The political agenda may include a desire for self-sufficiency, to generate employment, to maintain subsidised supplies (technology or its production), and so on. These will all have a direct bearing on technology preferences.
3. Social pressure: Born of custom, of demand for increased welfare, or of conscience, social pressures exert an influence on the acceptability of a technology.
4. Awareness: The complexity of technological debate makes it very difficult for people to be aware of the exact nature of the technological problem and of the most appropriate solution for their particular circumstances. This has consequences for acceptance of the technology.

The process of transfer must address the question of 'absorption' of the technology on the part of the people of the recipient country. International transfer of technology has not taken place until the technology under consideration has been assimilated to some degree by the recipients in the host country (Kanz 1980). Assimilation may be described as the recipients' capacity to utilise the technology on their own. National diffusion within the recipient nation occurs when nationals leave the original transfer channel (such as the MNC) for other jobs within the national techno-economic system where they utilise the acquired technology, or when still other nationals acquire the technology by whatever means.

Many researchers address the important issue of the indigenous capability of developing countries to assimilate imported technology (see, for example, Dahlman & Sercovich 1984; Fontes 2001a; Katz 1984; Kwon et al. 1987; Lall 1982; Lee et al. 1988; Pang & Hill 1991;

Quinn 1969; Stewart 1981; Tolentino 1993). Assimilation is a crucial stage of technology transfer, and may define the effectiveness and success of any transfer. Assimilation results in technological change (set in motion by technology transfer) through adaptation and accumulation of technical expertise. The assimilation of an imported technology within the recipient country's techno-economic and production systems leads to an accelerated development and localisation of the imported technology. One of the main consequences of this process is a continuous increase in the potential of indigenous dexterity and technical knowledge. This means that a new and dynamic system of learning is being provided to support and facilitate the process of technological change and progress.

According to Bell (1984), learning mechanisms may be divided into two broad categories:

1. Mechanisms where learning is a costless by-product of doing (that is, learning by operating, learning by changing)
2. Mechanisms where learning depends on the allocation of resources (that is, system learning, and learning by training, by hiring personnel for this purpose, and searching for solutions through the investigation of published sources or the Internet)

Thus, technology assimilation results in specific learning, which leads in turn to technology development and generation. A cumulative process of learning is thus initiated within the process of technology transfer, enhancing the national system of technological change and innovation (ibid.; see also Andersen & Lundvall 1988). Such a cumulative process of learning results from producing, using and changing, as well as from training, searching for solutions, and the interaction of producers and users. The result of this learning is a 'synergistic' combination of skilled manpower and expertise (Wilmot 1977), achieved through a combination of *newly* acquired skills and *existing* levels of indigenous knowledge and skills.

SUPPORTABILITY

Supportability is basically a function of soft technologies. As infrastructure and local know-how develop, transfer progresses through a number of stages:

- Initially, equipment or products may be made available as imports for local use.
- Later, skills for the local provision of the service or for the local manufacture of products may be transferred.
- Eventually, circumstances may be created for the full absorption of the technology, with the emergence of indigenous capacities for adaptation and innovation (examples include the electronic load controllers project for micro-hydro schemes in Peru, and the phosphate rock beneficiation plant in Egypt: see Touche Ross [1991]).

The supportability of technologies depends on: (a) the ease of use of the service or product (consumer or industrial) and its maintenance requirements; and (b) the ease of process or manufacture, including investment (for instance, capital versus labour intensity, economic scale of production), operating, management and maintenance needs. Raw material availability is also a factor.

One of the main constraints to successful technology transfer and development has been the tendency of technoware to run ahead of the rest of the technology system, namely, inforware, humanware and orgaware. This focus on hard technologies has meant little or no consideration of such issues as the availability of the institutional capacity, training and infrastructural support necessary to sustain the technology. Therefore, a new technology lands in a recipient country before the requisite institutional and infrastructural capacity is in place, in the absence of appropriate organising, training and management programmes as well as know-how and technical information, and with maintenance practices and the accountability and transparency of operations in a poor state and in need of improvement.

TECHNOLOGICAL DIFFUSION

Diffusion of technology is one of the main elements in the process of technological change in any country. 'Technological diffusion' may be viewed as a complex phenomenon involving two simple elements: the extent of *use* and the extent of *time*. Any technological change takes time to spread to its potential users. But while many technologies take decades to achieve widespread use, others become familiarised within production systems relatively quickly. A variety of terms have been used to describe the spread of technology within a given area, country or society, such as 'rate of adoption', 'rate of imitation', 'rate of diffusion' and 'rate of substitution'. Although they are often used interchangeably, these terms belong to different conceptual frames; in this study, geared to the situation of developing countries, we use the term technological diffusion to mean the rate of adoption or imitation of a given technology within both the production and consumption systems of a country.

The extent of diffusion of a technology at any given time is defined by the degree to which it is being applied at that time. Freeman (1986) suggests that any new technology that diffuses through half of a potential adopter population, or affects more than two-thirds of the relevant output of a good or service in less than 10 years, has enjoyed a rapid rate of diffusion. Diffusion may thus be seen as the continuous or 'gradual' process of growth of the application of a technology as time passes. Although this looks like a simple definition, technological diffusion in developing countries contains a number of complexities that are specific to each case and should be dealt with as such. The particular characteristics of each country influence the nature of the diffusion process. The rate at which technologies diffuse also varies widely according to the technology and the processes involved. Further, it must be remembered that diffusion of a technology is always preceded by the diffusion of *information* about that technology. Diffusion, in addition, includes the diffusion of industrial process innovations, diffusion in business, government and among people, etc. In fact, technological diffusion may be defined as a set of quite heterogeneous phenomena in which the particular nature of a technology, its characteristics, and the circumstances in which it exists, is applied, and grows, are the basic determinants of the causes, mechanisms and rates of its diffusion within the industrial or social system of a country.

The phenomenon of diffusion has been addressed by scholars in various disciplines: anthropology (Y. Cohen 1972; Kroeber 1934), sociology (Brown 1979; Katz et al. 1963; Williams & Gibson 1990), economics (Mansfield 1973; Nabseth & Ray 1974) and geography (Blaut 1977; Yapa 1977). The economic perspective suggests a relatively simple picture in which technology diffusion is driven primarily by economic incentives and constrained by economic obstacles (Grubb et al. 1992). Mansfield (1968), for instance, discusses two factors as particularly important in governing the pace of diffusion: the profitability of the new technology or its product for both producers and adopters, and the scale of investment required, which is inversely related to the rate of diffusion (bigger outlays induce greater hesitance in moving to new processes). However, in reality, economic factors, while important, do not always dominate the process of diffusion (Ausubel 1991); many other factors—economic, social and cultural—also affect diffusion.

A distinction may be made between the transfer of technology across national boundaries and its 'developmental impact' (Sagafi-nejad 1979). Here, the developmental impact of a transferred technology is its eventual effect upon processes of industrialisation and technological change in the host country. These effects are most pronounced if transferred technology is diffused and eventually institutionalised within the technological system of the host country. The dual processes of diffusion and institutionalisation are realised to the extent that the transferred technology induces technological linkage/multiplier effects. These effects, in turn, are co-determined by four sets of variables: societal, organisational, technological and transfer variables.

Technology may be diffused by the action of the organisation or body undertaking the transfer, or by the action of other parties through the parallel development of technology, competitive imitation and other modalities. Different types of technology transfer result in different scales of technology diffusion in the recipient economy. Only management skills seem capable of being rapidly transferred and diffused (Artemiev 1981). Some resources, such as land, climate and undeveloped natural resources, cannot be transferred at all due to their immobility. The pattern of application and scale of diffusion of technology in the host country's techno-economic system are likely to depend, to a certain extent, upon the channel of transfer chosen by the counterparts to the transfer. In this respect, the scale of diffusion may be understood as a function of many factors, of which two sets of factors are crucial:

1. The efforts of the transferor to provide his counterpart with all the elements needed to apply the technology successfully (the completeness of the technology transfer, reasonable pricing of technology, refraining from restrictive business practices).
2. The absorptive capabilities of the transferee (the stage of technological development of the transferee, availability of complementary resources, infrastructure).

The process of technology transfer between firms in different countries is necessarily costly, not only because of the need for adaptation to local levels of technological capability, but also due to differences in market structures, policies on the role of foreign technology in host countries, resistance to foreign technology, large differences in infrastructure, and the geographical distance which entails travel and communication costs (Caloghirou et al. 2000; Contractor 1979; Findlay 1978; Teece 1977). The fit between the existing and the required socio-institutional frameworks for a particular technology influences the rate of diffusion and the growth potential of new technologies (Freeman & Perez 1988; Johnson 1988; Perez 1988). The achievement of this fit constitutes an important priority of the national system of industrialisation (Andersen & Lundvall 1988), which supports industrial 'learning by doing' and 'learning by interacting in the key sectors of the techno-economic system'.

Following the analysis presented in chapter one, we now draw a clear distinction between innovation and the diffusion of technology. Technology transfer to developing countries deals with the diffusion of technology rather than with the innovation of technology. Clearly, developing countries can benefit from the diffusion of technologies without spending the time for and incurring the costs of technological innovation.

Technological Capability: Concept, Categories and Stages

Attempts to implement the pattern suggested by the technology transfer pyramid are geared towards improvement of the country's or firm's 'technological capabilities': capabilities of knowledge acquisition and technology digestion that enable mastery of the transferred technology in terms of both know-how and know-why. For convenience, we use the term 'technological capabilities' to refer to all types of capabilities and capacities in this regard.

A small part of the technology transfer literature appreciates the notion of 'technological capabilities'. When countries or firms choose a technology, they choose more than just a tool or method for making something with expected costs, benefits and engineering norms: they also choose the *capabilities* they can acquire from experience with that technology. Technological capabilities reflect not only ability in using resources, but also capacities in the sense of resource endowment (that is, training, R&D, maintenance). Acquisition of capabilities through such selection would enable countries or firms to move on to new productive activities, or to use these capabilities elsewhere in the techno-economic system. Different technologies afford different possibilities for subsequent adaptation and improvement in order to increase productivity and to enhance technical/technological abilities (see Kahen [1996a] and Jimba [2000] for the case of information technology transfer).

Application of technology in a new environment requires a set of specific capabilities. These capabilities are different in nature from those involved in innovation in industrialised countries, as commonly defined. The application of technology requires the ability to make effective (and knowledgeable) use of technological knowledge. The crucial point here is that 'technological knowledge' and 'technology' must be viewed as two separate concepts. Technological capability does not reside permanently in the knowledge that is possessed, but rather exists in the understanding and use of that knowledge and in the proficiency of its use in four broad areas: production (of both services and goods), development and design, investment, and, finally, technological change and innovation. In fact, technological capability is the primary attribute of *human* and *institutional capital* (Westphal et al. 1985). Institutional capital refers to the know-how and expertise used to combine human skills and physical capital into systems for delivering appropriate services, products or processes (see Hall & Johnson 1970). In our conceptual framework, therefore, institutional capital includes elements that are society-specific, system-specific and organisation- or firm-specific, as well as the four general elements of technology: humanware, technoware, inforware and orgaware.

Capabilities may be categorised into various levels or dimensions. On the basis of a case study of technology transfer conducted in Brazil, Dahlman et al. (1987) infer that technological capabilities include the abilities to acquire, use, assimilate, adapt, change and create technology. We may categorise the different types of technological capability into a set of five aggregate capabilities: production capabilities (including the capabilities of operating current or new technology effectively); capabilities for making major and minor changes (the ability to execute major and minor product or process changes); investment or acquisitive capabilities (the capabilities of seeking new technology, finding the required technology and completing a successful transfer); technological resources (characterised by: the capacity to train manpower, the quality of investments in training programmes both in-house and externally, and the capacity to carry out true R&D); and integrative capabilities (the capability of effectively integrating the other kinds of capabilities just described). Accordingly, successful technological development depends on a long-term effort to build systematically on foreign technological inputs and on accumulated experience.

In a study conducted jointly by technologists and economists in Thailand (Westphal et al. 1990), technological capabilities were defined through the use of a scoring process that reflected the researchers' attempt to consolidate both objective and subjective information into coherent indices of firms' or organisations' abilities for utilising new technology. These indices ranged across a number of dimensions concerned with transfer, assimilation and adaptation of industrial technology. Technological capabilities of four different kinds were identified: acquisitive, operative, adaptive and innovative. While operative capabilities pertain to production know-how, adaptive and innovative capabilities relate to technological efforts that are central to the effective assimilation of technology and to simultaneous as well as subsequent adaptation to fit local circumstances better.

TECHNOLOGY CHOICE AND THE IMPROVEMENT OF TECHNOLOGICAL CAPABILITIES

We may distinguish three main stages in the process of improvement of technological capabilities. Each stage forms a link in a chain, and together they constitute the basis for overall technological capability improvement. *Adaptations* may be understood as activities associated with technological development. This technological development takes place through the *transfer of technology*, complemented by indigenous efforts at adaptation, assimilation and extension. Finally, *acquisitive capabilities* relate, in turn, to the ability to search for, assess and acquire (transfer) technology.

Although most capabilities may be classified into one or another of these three broad categories, every technology requires specific capabilities, or certain 'aggregate' capabilities. Each category, further, may be seen as a set of capabilities, with subsidiary capabilities such as those involving information, orga-managerial abilities, means, skills and understanding as well as appropriate resource allocation geared towards a systematic effort to achieve comprehensive technological development. An important point to note here is that the majority of developing countries set themselves the unrealistic goal of gaining 'global' capabilities. A country is generally capable in one technical aspect, which could be different from the capabilities of other countries. It does not need to possess everything itself in order to utilise, expand and modernise its industrial production.

If a technology is to be successfully chosen and adopted, it should be evaluated against existing technological capabilities in the host nation, as well as in terms of prevailing supply and demand conditions. Just as the recipient country formalises its demand function for a given technology based on its own requirements, any supplier of that candidate technology also requires to satisfy certain policies and interests in both the short and the long terms. Here, technology policy becomes a major strategic concern for both sides. Further, the ability of the recipient firm or country to select, adapt, absorb, combine and develop the transferred technology is dictated by its indigenous technological capabilities. The size of a developing country, the extent of labour surplus, and other demand-side typological characteristics such as the nature of the industrial structure, the levels of overall competitiveness and the nature of policies crucially affect the demand for transfer of technology as well as the intensity of the search for indigenous technological activity (Ranis 1984). Equally important determinants are factors such as a suitable cultural and socio-economic environment, an adequate infrastructure which includes scientific institutions, research and development facilities, vocational, technical and management training institutes, and skilled personnel of different specialisations within the recipient country who support technological negotiation, modification and capacity development (Dore 1984; Freeman & Perez 1988; King 1984; Mansour 1981).

Different levels of capability exist among the various nations. Intercountry comparisons of technological capability are fraught with difficulties because of the lack of a precise indicator, although one broad classification (Bhalla 1987) divides countries into three basic categories:

- Technology leaders: the United States, Japan
- Technology followers: other OECD countries
- Technology borrowers: developing countries

The transfer of technology between countries at different levels of development involves certain costs. Rosenberg (1976) suggests in this regard that the total costs of the process of technology transfer between firms or countries at different stages of development are greater than those of transfer between countries/firms at relatively closer stages of development. This is because of the distinctive characteristics—economic, technical, social, cultural, organisational and political—of technology in developing countries. In particular, these countries are marked by smaller markets, higher rates of tariff protection, weaker competitive atmosphere, stronger distortions in technical information and market imperfections, more acute shortages of skills and more dramatic levels of uncertainty than developed countries (Katz 1984). State controlled mass media and difficulties in communication and training are other factors that cause the process of technology transfer between developed and developing countries to be costlier. Developing countries are further characterised by lower levels of entrepreneurship, education or absorptive capacity, and by the need for more specialised and updated technology (Lall 1984; Slaybaugh 1981). The distortions produced by these factors in developing countries make it highly uneconomical to attempt the straightforward replication of 'off-the-shelf' technology (technology used previously in developed countries) in these regions.

Most technological learning takes place at the micro level: in organisations or firms where the imported technology has been launched. The process of learning is not generally organised within a specific department. Both historical studies and contemporary researches on developing countries show that departments under-taking R&D, design and production engineering within firms are often involved in other activities such as quality control and pro-duction organisation (Bell & Pavitt 1993b; Kim 1980; Mowery & Rosenberg 1989). Successful implementation and capability improvement at the project level (or the micro level in the process of technology transfer) depend on related internal and external factors:

- the effective integration of specialised disciplines, functions and divisions within the organisation or firm; and
- outside links with sources of expertise and with the needs of the local community.

The failure to recognise the organisation or firm as the central player in the accumulation of technology has been a major shortcoming of technology policy in developing countries. The most conspicuous examples of this (see, for instance, Bell & Pavitt 1993a, 1993b;

Hanson & Pavitt 1987) were the former USSR and other centrally planned economies. In these countries, the design, research and development functions were separated (geographically and organisationally) from the production units. Similar policies may be observed in the majority of developing countries today who have adopted more or less the same type of techno-economic system; these policies are sometimes buttressed by empirically inaccurate theory.

All types of capabilities in a country may be seen within a sequence: from production to investment capability, and then to innovation capability. Since any given country will have its own specific capabilities, it is reasonable to start with the capability most likely to be available in that country (mostly production capability), and then try to build on such a basis in order to develop other capabilities. It is clear that a systematic effort in this regard needs sophisticated technological planning and management systems as well as a time period of several decades to succeed (for example, through the establishment of a national protocol for technology transfer).

NATIONAL OR SOCIAL CAPABILITY AND NATIONAL CONSCIOUSNESS

In order to avoid any potential conflicts that might occur in the face of technological change in a developing country, it is crucial to achieve a measure of public acceptance before implementation. This acceptance would be based on public awareness created and supported by public communications through official (that is, the educational system, mass media) or unofficial (including common and traditional) channels. The achievements of developed countries, in the form of high levels of social security, sophisticated health systems, socio-economic progress, modernism, social success and self-gratification, encourage developing nations to focus on technological development. However, to be successful, this process requires public support, backed up by an appropriate social pathway for the transfer of specific technologies, as well as a cultural facilitator for the process of technological development.

In this respect, it is essential to recognise the importance of 'social' or 'national' capabilities, factors that have by and large been overlooked in the literature. The expansion of capabilities in a broad sense and within a reasonable time period, given the specific situations and characteristics of developing countries, requires an element of emotional support from the public. Such support represents a non-technical/non-technology-oriented capability among the population. We may call this capability 'national will', which is based on the nature of national consciousness in a given developing country. The effect of national will has been demonstrated by the experience of Japan (see Kahen 1995b, 1999). It is certainly possible to create and facilitate national will or volition and to extend its capacity through sophisticated processes: for instance, by means of expanding public education, through mass communication channels, and through political challenge (for example, by encouraging nationalism). We should recognise, also, that 'social' or 'national' capability is unique for every nation.

Social or national capabilities depend, in essence, upon local anthropocentric factors, including the dominant beliefs, human behavioural systems and the socio-cultural characteristics of a nation. They are also linked to other characteristics, such as those concerned with the mental capacities, physical abilities and behaviour styles of the population of the nation that employs the transferred technology. National capabilities affect productivity within any production process irrespective of level of technology and type of operations. The relatively quick utilisation, adoption and development of Western technologies by Japan and other Far Eastern countries may partly be related to such nation-based capabilities. Although these capabilities depend largely on the historical background of people and on specific local elements (such as geographical conditions and institutionalised beliefs), it is also evident that national capability may be expanded and improved by increasing social consensus.

TACIT KNOWLEDGE AND ORGANISED IMPROVEMENT OF TECHNOLOGICAL CAPABILITY

Apart from operating know-how, which concerns any transferred technology, the most important knowledge required for successful and sustainable transfer is 'tacit knowledge'. This crucial knowledge involves uncodifiable, person-embodied and institution-embodied knowledge. It may refer to the 'rules of thumb' that exist in both the content and the context of any technical knowledge, or to the technological know-how that can be acquired only with experience in coping with complexity.

Tacit knowledge includes the 'intellectual properties' that are crucial for a country's industrial development.[3] Experience shows that these kinds of knowledge may not be acquired either free of cost or quickly; indeed, the transfer of tacit knowledge is slower and more expensive than the transfer of operating know-how (Scott-Kemmis & Bell 1988; Yang 2001). It is evident that tacit knowledge will increase in response to increasing technical/technological complexity. Therefore, the use of experts and the expansion of different kinds of expertise may be interpreted as the expansion and improvement of technological investment and technical support. 'Brain drain' has been viewed as a crucial factor in the continuing underdevelopment of underdeveloped nations in much of the industrial development literature. The movement of experts and experienced people has also been seen as a key mechanism in the international transfer of technology during the industrialisation of a number of countries: for example, of Britain (see Herrick & Kindleberger 1983; Kindleberger 1978; Todaro 1983, 1994), France and Germany (Henderson 1965; Landes 1969), Norway (Bruland 1989) and North America (Jeremy 1981).

Experience also shows that while foreigners may dominate the processes of engineering and project management to establish the plant and implement the operational process of transferring technology, if local personnel work closely with them from the beginning, it will be much easier for the developing country to acquire and promote technological capabilities (see Hsiao 1997). Such a procedure was carried out by a steel manufacturing firm in Brazil (Dahlman et al. 1987), an example which showed that this is an excellent way of learning many aspects of the design, equipment, selection, installation, construction, start-up and operation of the plant.

Evidence from developing countries that have been most successful in this regard shows us how technological capabilities may be locally accumulated. Across a wide range of sectors in Korea and Taiwan, for instance, firms have accumulated substantial capabilities for generating continuous change in acquired technologies, for synthesising diverse elements of technology into new processes and products so as to replicate imported technologies, and for developing innovations that improve performance (Enos & Park 1988; Westphal et al. 1985). And this has paralleled the growing importance of training and informal international networks in providing theoretical or

---

[3] We will analyse the system of intellectual properties as a key factor within the process of technology transfer in chapter five.

scientific support to these endeavours. The accumulation of these kinds of technological capability in Latin America, India and China, however, has been much more limited, or narrowly focused, and, as Bell & Pavitt (1993a, 1993b) point out, it has been virtually absent in Africa. In total, effective technological development depends on two crucial issues: first, a long-term effort to build systematically on foreign technological inputs, and, second, the effort to accumulate experience. This serves to reinforce our contention, made in the third chapter, that technology is not simply a product to be bought and sold.

The experiences of Japan, East Asia, Taiwan, Korea and recently China (Yin 1992) clearly underline the crucial role of technological development in support of socio-economic development (Vongpanitlerd 1992). South Korea, which seriously started to develop its industries in the early 1960s, decisively achieved the status of newly industrialised economy in just two decades. Several studies (for instance, Dahlman et al. 1987) suggest that the success of Korea's industrialisation was due, in large part, to clear and consistent 'science and technology' policies and strategies, which helped in firmly establishing a sound science and technology infrastructure as part of Korea's overall industrial strategy.[4] These strategies were devised to assimilate foreign technologies by developing the necessary technological capability to efficiently use and adapt imported technologies, especially in targeted industries.

It may be inferred from the preceding discussion that not only the modality of transfer, but its rate as well as the nature of benefits accruing from such transfers depend upon the existence of potential technological capabilities within the techno-economic system of the host country. Whenever such inherent capabilities have been present in organisations, firms or countries, technology transfer has fulfilled an advantageous role in their developmental processes (Tolentino 1993). The comparatively higher levels of indigenous technological

---

[4] Examples include the establishment of the Korean Institute of Science and Technology in 1966, 10 industrial research institutes during the 1970s, and the Korea Advanced Institute for Science and Technology in 1970; also, the development of technical human resources, the promotion of overseas study and training, visits to foreign factories and product fairs and attending overseas conferences were encouraged as an important means of acquiring foreign technology. An emphasis was placed on technological innovation from the mid-1970s, and on the provision of facilities to support basic science and technology research in the 1980s.

development and innovation in the newly industrialised developing countries of Asia (Singapore, Hong Kong, Taiwan, South Korea) and Latin America (Argentina, Brazil, Mexico, Chile) have enabled them to attract and utilise foreign investment effectively.

On the other hand, several examples may also be cited of developing countries where the weakness or lack of inherent technological capabilities has caused foreign technology to be ineffective (Desai 1985, 1987). The relatively lower levels of production experience and capacity for localised technological development in African countries (with the exception of Kenya and Zimbabwe) illustrate this point. The existence of such limitations in these countries, combined with their inward-looking industrialisation strategies sustained by measures that discriminate against the private sector and especially against foreign firms, has resulted in less significant inflows of foreign investment and low levels of technical catching-up compared to other developing countries (Lall 1987). In this respect, the theory of technological competence as an important determinant of international competitiveness (Blomstrom 1986) can be used to highlight the effectiveness and benefits of international diffusion of foreign technology into the socio-economic and technical systems of developing countries.

The concept of technological development or capacity adopted in the present study is consistent with that provided by Stewart (1984) and Ranis (1984), which includes not only the capacity to create new technologies, but also the ability to choose, obtain and then locally develop, assimilate, adapt, improve or modify technology already known elsewhere, and to diffuse the best practice with appropriate modifications across the techno-economic system of a country. Technological capacity is therefore acquired only through *human capital* formation. Indigenous technological capacity pertains to the technological capability of the nation defined as an economic unit (Bienefeld 1984). The extent of 'catching up' and 'leapfrogging' is greater where there are initial capabilities in closely related types of activity (Cant 1989). This, in turn, is determined by the national system of technological change or innovation, including such elements as the supply of entrepreneurial skills and scientific and technical knowledge involved in the transfer of technology (related to know-why and to know-how capabilities), a reasonable level of knowledge necessary for the assimilation and eventual development of the imported technology, and favourable locational advantages related to the general infrastructure and other engineering, economic and institutional conditions exogenous to the organisation or firm. It is also affected by social and political changes in the international community, for instance, by increased protectionism in developed countries (Freeman 1988; Hsiao 1997; Perez 1988; Perez & Soete 1988; Unger 1988).

CAPABILITY IMPROVEMENT THROUGH THE SYSTEMATIC TRANSFER OF TECHNOLOGY

analysis undertaken in this chapter leads us to conclude that, to 'fective, the process of technology transfer should harness the ')pment of indigenous capabilities. Such development would s a broad range of capabilities, including capabilities for tech- search, assessment and selection as well as for negotiation a 'uisition, adaptation and assimilation, replication, develop- m 'l, ultimately, innovation. Foreign technologies represent an im ' means of achieving rapid technological progress in dev ' countries, through the improvement of the productivity or ei y of existing industries (UNCTC 1987), as well as through open new areas of industrial production.

Mu 'nological learning can in fact take place over a period of time w outside technical assistance (Fontes 2001a; Slaybaugh 1981); sic purpose of procuring technology from outside, therefor 'ually to save the time and expense that would be required 'elop it indigenously. Foreign-imported technology employed 'echno-economic and social systems of a host coun- try is com considered a dominating factor. A strategic policy framework 'nagement strategy for utilising foreign technology should redu straints, while simultaneously exploring ways of increasing th ry's potential to improve its national capabilities in general, o ional capability in particular (capability in a specific techn ect or in an industry), in order to achieve an effective techn insfer.

A characteris any developing countries is the dualism that exists between a n export sector and the traditional sector. While the export d sector (for example, mining and agricul- tural plantations) extends the most productive technology available into the e the traditional sector (smallholder agri- culture and small b , conversely, is frequently characterised by traditional techn vhich are typically less productive. This has an important be n our discussion of the technological capabilities of countries or firms. One problem with using modern and sophisticated technology is that it is easy to lose touch with the reality of the situation. To bridge effectively the gap between the modern and traditional sectors, it is not enough to undertake a simple transfer of technology. Rather, it requires the transformation of new scientific knowledge and capabilities into services and products. Furthermore, all the parties involved in the process—individuals and organisations—need to facilitate effective mutual interactions and act as translators between institutions and groups with diverse capabilities, objectives and languages (see, for example, Fontes [2001b] for the case of biotechnology transfer; see also Putranto et al. [2003a] for the case of the transfer of transportation technology). In technology transfer planning or in the strategic modelling of technological development, the 'thinking part' (that is, correctly and adequately assessing the local situation in terms of dualism and related issues) may be misunderstood or even omitted from the process. This happens particularly when non-quantifiable elements are neglected in the choice of inputs and the interpretation of the output. These omissions and miscalculations are inevitably reflected in the final decision-making process, leading to errors in judgement regarding the validity and feasibility of a candidate technology in terms of the technical and technological capabilities of both modern and traditional sectors.

As pointed out earlier, technology is not just a simple tool; therefore, along with human and information issues, the orga-managerial aspects of any transferred technology also need to be adjusted. Figure 4.3 depicts the mechanisms of adjustment and development of an imported technology. Following this route ultimately results in the improvement of technological capabilities. Depending upon the characteristics of the environment, the imported system will at first be exposed to a number of physical and non-physical constraints (Kahen 1995c). The processes of acquisition, adaptation and development of the technology are influenced by factors such as the capability of the country in question to prevail over these constraints, as well as the nature of the technology (that is, whether it is technical-oriented, human-oriented or capital-intensive), the type of technology transferred (energy, health care), its design specifications, its scientific and cultural context, and, finally, the appropriateness level of that technology for the host country or organisation.

The pace of improvement also depends upon the existing constraints and coordination among the four elements comprising the technology system (humanware, technoware, orgaware and inforware) and on their interactions with the techno-social environment

Figure 4.3: The mechanism of technological change and development for an imported technology: improving technological capability

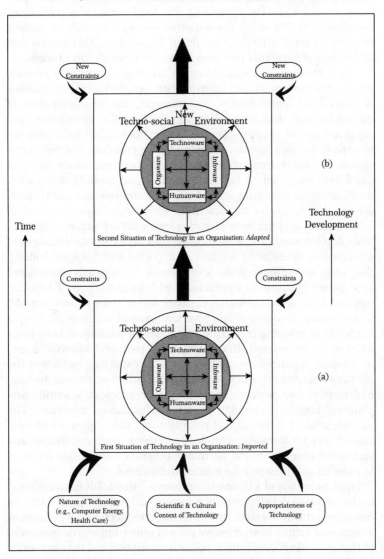

(see Figure 4.3). Movement from the initial state (a) to the secondary situation (b) may bring about new conditions (for example, new constraints, a higher level of technological capability) that can change the previous technology development pathway. Any progress following the implementation and adaptation of the imported system will improve the techno-social environment. This improvement provides a solid basis for expanding the local domain of technology knowledge. At this stage, the imported system is capable of shifting to a higher level (that is, stage [b] in Figure 4.3). This means that technological capability has been improved through this process.

The utilisation of a technology in an organisation or a country with underdeveloped or intermediate technological capabilities is shaped by many factors, for example, the characteristics of the technology and its relationship to scientific knowledge, and organisation- or country-specific factors that affect local abilities to exploit the new opportunities and to appropriate the respective outcomes. Apart from socio-national capabilities, other types of capability also need to be considered. These include acquisitive, developmental, operative and adaptive capabilities, the institutional set-up, the nature of the scientific knowledge base, the level of related skills, and the existence of relevant infrastructures for capability development. These factors are critical in the establishment of a progressive foundation for new or imported technologies. Indeed, the style of technological development increasingly considered appropriate is based on interactions with local systems of capabilities and local socio-economic capacity rather than on intervention from outside. In order to improve and expand technological capabilities in developing countries, two different sources of knowledge need to be considered: first, indigenous technical knowledge and technological capabilities along with local expertise, skills and the people's sciences on which local firms and other organisations have had to rely; and, second, specialised technological, scientific and planning knowledge brought in from industrialised countries. The identification of technological priorities and the implementation of related policies through technology transfer require continuous and successful interaction and partnership between these two forms of knowledge and between the related institutions.

Thus, by means of a systematic process—that leads from adoption to the eventual development of a foreign technology—a country can move from the initial state (in which imported technology behaves as a dominant factor) to an effective state of utilisation and development of that technology. Acquisitive, operative, adaptive and developmental capabilities, backed up by social capability, work together as a dynamic system to cope with the initial domination of foreign-imported technology in the techno-economic system. Figure 4.4 is a stylised representation of interrelated capability elements within the process of

Figure 4.4: Imported technology and the dynamic wheel of a country's technological capabilities

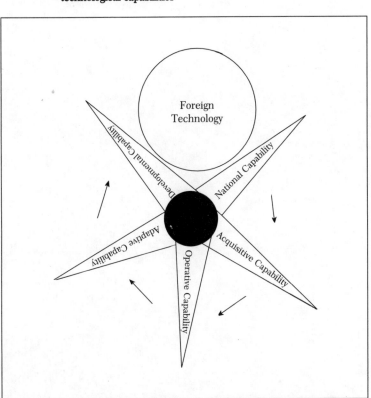

utilisation of imported technology. It depicts the major capabilities involved, and the direction of interchange between them. The discussion of the pyramid of technology transfer along with the analysis of the concept and process of technology diffusion in this chapter leads us to the visualisation of a country's technological capabilities in the form of a dynamic wheel. We shall now turn our attention to the concept of 'appropriateness' of technology and its role in an effective system of technology transfer in the next chapter.

5

APPROPRIATE TECHNOLOGY

RECONSIDERING TARGETS AND KEY-ROLE FACTORS

A careful review of the relevant literature reveals that most earlier studies on the process of technology transfer lack a systematic approach to the problem of effective transfer. These studies fail to identify clearly the dominant components within the process of transfer, focusing mostly on the external or general aspects of the transfer process rather than on the internal or specific aspects. Indeed, in our view, it is these latter factors that may be responsible for causing any technology transfer project to succeed or fail. Here we undertake to identify the major 'key-role' factors responsible for the failure or success of transfer, basing our insights on: (*a*) a review of the theoretical literature on the subject; (*b*) our own examination of real-world examples of technology transfer, such as in the energy, manufacturing and steel industries; and (*c*) the critical reconsideration of the general problem of transfer, undertaken in the course of this research in the light of the philosophical framework adopted here (see chapter three).

Generally speaking, the factors underlying success or failure may be categorised into macro and micro level factors: those involved at the choice of technology stage (at national or sectoral level), and those concerned with the stage of implementation of the technology (at firm or organisational level), respectively. The first group of factors helps guide the process of selection in order to arrive at appropriate choices; the second monitors the effectiveness of implementation, or provides support for technical and technological operations.

The identification of the major components within an effective technology transfer system undertaken in this chapter completes our elaboration of a comprehensive approach to the process of transfer, based on which the relevant criteria and theoretical bases for technology assessment will be reached. This approach will enable us to identify systematically the strengths and weaknesses of a system, recognise the characteristics of a country, and build an appropriate set of assessment criteria. These insights, combined with the characteristics of candidate technologies, provide the requisite inputs for a model of technology assessment, to be developed in the next chapter.

THE CONCEPT OF APPROPRIATENESS OF TRANSFERRED TECHNOLOGY

There is enough evidence that the improper transfer of technology to developing countries causes many social, cultural, political, environmental, regional and economic problems. A good example of this is Thailand, both a user and a supplier of technology. While techno-economic growth over the last 50 years has increased wealth in Thailand, it has brought both benefits and problems to the country. These problems may be identified with increasing imbalances in wealth, among regional economies, and in the ecology. Ecological imbalances have resulted from the introduction of new technologies that caused deforestation, pollution, degradation of water courses and waste production (Akrasanee 1993).

The major premise underlying the concept of 'appropriate' technology is the limited relevance of industrialised country technologies to the structural, socio-cultural and techno-economic characteristics of developing nations. The notion of appropriate technology emerged mainly as a reaction to the failure of growth-maximising strategies for comprehensive development. Although defined differently by different people, the principal goals of such development are to alleviate unemployment and poverty, and to redress the lack or shortage of resources necessary for initial techno-economic and social development. While the issue of technology transfer may be addressed from various perspectives, success in technology transfer is intimately related to the appropriateness of the transferred technology. If the technology that is transferred is not appropriate to the needs and conditions prevailing in the receiving country, it will be rejected no matter how superior or

efficient it may be. In the following sections, we analyse the main elements within the notion of appropriateness of technology.

There are, of course, different ways in which existing technology
can be adapted and made more appropriate to developing country
conditions. Three such methods have been discussed in the literature: (a) downscaling of large-scale technology; (b) upgrading of traditional technology; and (c) adaptation of imported technology
(Bhalla 1979, 1996; Choi 2001; James 1979; Kahen 1995c; Kaplinski
1984, 1990; Stewart 1977, 1987, 1992). It must be remembered that
no single technology can be considered appropriate for all developing
countries: the development of appropriate and adapted technologies
needs to be centred around the given country's existing priorities and
characteristic variables.

Machine-Intensive versus Labour-Intensive Technology

Much of the literature on appropriate technology focuses on the twin
terms 'capital-intensive' or 'machine-intensive' technology and
'labour-intensive' technology. 'Capital-intensive' technology is emphasised in approaches that rely heavily on the infusion of capital, whereas
the 'labour-intensive' strategy places greater emphasis on the human
labour factor. However, such definitions often tend to be confusing
because capital is required in labour-intensive strategies as well.
Conversely, capital-intensive technologies too cannot function without
adequate labour. What a capital-intensive strategy really implies in the
techno-economic approach to development is, in fact, a *machine*-
intensive approach. The machine-intensive approach may be viewed
as a joint paradigm incorporating both engineering and economic perspectives regarding technology (see the discussion in chapter two).

The machine-intensive approach is predominantly an urban-based
strategy centred around large-scale industries that depend crucially
on machines and huge amounts of capital, but requiring little labour
input. Most technologies used in the machine-intensive approach
are not locally produced in developing countries. They have to be
imported from industrialised nations, and are generally purchased
using scarce foreign exchange funds (Kahen & Sayers 1995b). This
might be viewed as paradoxical in view of the huge availability of
human labour in these countries: instead of using the abundant cheap
labour already existing in developing countries, precious capital is
used to buy machines. As Oshima (1976) shows, many nations

employing the machine-intensive approach have run into a number of problems: for instance, persistently high unemployment rates, increasing underemployment and other techno-economic distortions leading to a deterioration in the quality of life. Moreover, the large amounts of capital required for machine-intensive technologies have to be acquired from international agencies and multinational firms, institutions usually controlled by industrialised nations. Capital-intensive technology is also much more sophisticated and more expensive than labour-intensive technology. Despite all these contra-dictions, Third World countries, in order to overcome their various problems, need to be supported by the importation of foreign tech-nology; therefore, they need to reconsider the traditional concept of appropriateness.

The labour-intensive strategy, on the other hand, would allow capital to remain in developing countries, while also providing employment to the great mass of labour available in these countries. But a labour-intensive strategy is also not without problems. It leads to the perpet-uation of a large number of small and traditional units of production, such as workshops, farms and stores. It would seem easier to deal with a small number of big industrial units using capital-intensive technology and located in a few major centres. However, this neglects the complex social structures that exist in non-Western societies.

As mentioned earlier, the literature on technology transfer relies heavily on one-dimensional economic analyses used in the choice of technology. Researchers have set up simple economic or financial models that lack a multidimensional analytical approach to making appropriate/sustainable choices. These perspectives are similar to the one-dimensional (that is, the economic) perspective on the con-cept of technology that we analysed in chapter two. Using the tradi-tional approach, the task of a decision-maker is simply to find the technology that combines the factors of production, usually capital (machines) and labour, in the least costly way. This conventional pro-cedure also offers clear financial predictions of how technology would differ (in terms of complexity, modernity, or substitutability between factors of production) between developing and developed countries. Due to low wage rates, the lack or shortage of hard cur-rencies, and high capital costs, policy-makers in the developing world generally select labour-intensive technologies. The traditional process of choice allows them to focus on technologies that would contribute to solving potential unemployment problems in their countries.

Therefore, the dominant consideration in the choice of technology for developing countries has been the capacity of technology to absorb labour. Contrary to expectations, however, the expanding industrial sectors in developing countries are not creating large numbers of job opportunities. This is partly because the technologies used by factories in low-wage nations are often not significantly more labour-intensive than those used in industrialised countries, so they have done little to relieve unemployment. This is primarily the reason why the predictions of the simple economic theory and of the mono-dimensional approach cannot be appropriate for the multidimensional process of technology transfer to developing countries. It was as a response to these debates that, during the 1970s, the idea of 'intermediate technology' came to be seen as a convenient solution for the unemployment problem. Supporters of this movement defined it as a type of technology that involved less capital and more labour than that generally used in more advanced countries (see Schumacher 1973).

Substitution effects also play an active role in inducing organisations and firms in developing countries to adopt different production techniques from those normally employed by comparable organisations in more developed countries. For example, in Latin American industrial firms, substitution between different types of machinery and/or raw materials, particularly among those of local vis-à-vis imported origin,[1] affects the choice of technology and technique (Katz 1987). As in other developing countries, this has led to the employment of more universal machines, or manual rather than electronic process control devices, less sophisticated maintenance technologies, and more labour-intensive transportation systems within the plant. Accordingly, the majority of case studies in Latin America indicate that local firms normally start their operations with labour-intensive control and maintenance technologies.

THE SCALE OF TECHNOLOGY, GOVERNMENT POLICIES AND APPROPRIATE TECHNOLOGY

With very few exceptions, industrial firms operating in developing countries are just a tiny fraction (between 1 and 10 per cent) of the size of their counterparts in developed nations (Katz 1987). However, it has been shown that more advantages may be derived by importing

---

[1] A result of tariffs imposed on imported goods, quotas, distorted exchange rates, outright prohibition of access to certain inputs and other factors.

large-scale technology than from utilising small-scale technology (this was demonstrated, for instance, by the case of the Korean transfer of petrochemical, machinery and synthetic fibre technologies: see Kim & Kim [2000]; Lee [2000]; Sung et al. [2003]). Therefore, if the potential exists for reaping substantial economies of large-scale production, if imports are not seriously restricted, and if the government is determined to adopt the latest proven technology, it may be profitable for the country to choose a larger-scale technology.

Any transferred technology may experience a cyclical interaction between internal and external forces. Internal forces are represented by indigenous technological capabilities, which consist of the quality and quantity of resources (human resources, financial resources, availability and capability of existing R&D, effective organisations). External forces include the techno-economic environment, the physical and natural environment (including energy resources and geographical conditions), social and cultural environment (represented by education, ethics of labour and entrepreneur, custom and tradition, national consciousness, the preferences of consumers), and the policy system. Each of these forces affects the path and the process by which the transferred technology is utilised and developed within its new environment.

General government policies are extremely important in influencing the choice of technology and the direction of local technological change (see Stewart 1987, 1992; Stewart & Ranis 1990). Policies on price factors (for example, tax incentives for investment, wage policies, workers' insurance premium), the nature of the financial system and credit markets, the structure of international trade, income distribution, and policies on social security and product standards affect the choices of technology, products and techniques made by individual enterprises, and also the composition of units (that is, the proportion of total investable resources controlled by different types of decision-makers).

Experience shows that in many countries, macro policies systematically favour inappropriate technologies (see Colman & Nixson 1978; Gurr et al. 1998; Jafry & O'Neill 2000; Murphy 1985; Stewart 1987, 1992; Stewart & Ranis 1990). Policies that support appropriate products (in the conventional sense) and labour-intensive techniques will lead to a greater use of older, more standardised technologies. These technologies are likely to be more easily accessible for arm's-length transfers, to be available from a wider range of technology sources, including developing country sources, and to be transferred at lower prices than the technologies associated with more capital-intensive strategies. Appropriate technological strategies depend on the stage of development of the country (from both macro and micro perspectives). The least developed countries have no choice but to import technology, often in a packaged form. For countries with more industrial experience, importing technology in unbundled form has considerable advantages from the point of view of inducing learning effects and the creation of technological capacity. Middle-stage developing countries with high levels of education and skills and a significant R&D capacity are in a solid position to exploit the new technologies effectively.

APPROPRIATENESS OF ADVANCED AND MACHINE-INTENSIVE TECHNOLOGIES

Appropriate technology has commonly been defined in terms of the satisfaction of certain criteria or *objectives*: employment, basic needs, environment, etc., and also in terms of the *characteristics* of the technology: simplicity, small scale of operation, labour intensity, low skill requirements, etc. However, the recent rapid rates of technological development witnessed in Southeast Asia serve as factual evidence for the appropriateness of large-scale and machine-based technologies, and provide adequate grounds for enriching the concept of appropriateness to include machine-intensive, and even advanced, technologies.

Labour-intensive and capital-intensive plants generally exist side by side in developing countries. Depending on the country and the circumstances, both have been known to meet with success. For instance, the experience of the Far Eastern countries (viz., Singapore, Taiwan, South Korea, Thailand) shows continuous improvement of capital-intensive technologies, while China, India and some African countries have been comfortable and successful with labour-intensive technologies. However, the results of a study in Thailand that assessed technological capability within three sectors (biotechnology, materials and electronics) revealed that large-scale technologies and firms tended to possess much higher acquisitive and adaptive capabilities than medium-/small-scale technologies (see, for example, Intarakumnerd et al. 2002; Lauridsen 2000; The Technology Atlas Team 1987b).

To cite an example, the acquisition of 'intelligent' equipment through computerisation or the use of information technology is not only labour-saving but also skill-saving. Since developing countries do not possess large, skilled labour forces, the shortage of skills can be overcome by the introduction of intelligent equipment. Computer technology, therefore, should be considered an essential, appropriate technology for the development of developing countries. In this respect, a major problem would be the large amount of investment needed to import high technologies. This is because of the lack or shortage of local capital resources (hard currency, in particular) in these countries. This bottleneck may be tackled by encouraging certain kinds of cross-country cooperation (that is to say, economic convergency) among developing countries to enable them to derive the benefits attainable from the existence of potential convergency in the transfer of information technology (see, for example, Kahen 1997b; Kahen & Sayers 1994).

While the benefits are undeniable, an inevitable effect of the transfer of high technologies such as information technology to developing countries is their potential to change the pattern of technology transfer in a manner that further increases the technological and scientific gap between developed and developing countries. Indeed, the decreasing cost of communications and data transmission and the concentration of information in developed countries means that it is becoming cheaper for institutions and firms in developing countries to have their problems solved for them elsewhere than to develop local research facilities. A further dimension of this process is that the data that provides the basis for decision making will flow towards richer, more developed nations; information reflected in decisions already taken will flow towards poorer, less developed nations. This problem, similar to that of the unavailability of capital sources mentioned before, is a serious threat that can be resolved through an 'inward technical and technological convergency' within developing countries.

One of the major effects of advanced computer technology, as suggested by many scholars, is that technologies depending on computerisation and automation (in other words, highly capital-intensive, labour-saving technologies) are becoming more competitive relative to technologies that rely on the use of cheap labour (see Do Boer & Walbeek 1999; Montealegre 1998). The main reasons for this may be summarised as follows:

1. By decreasing the proportion of direct labour costs in total business cost, automation erodes the advantage of low labour cost and makes possible the manufacture of formerly labour-intensive goods in developed countries.
2. The application of the technology to organisation reinforces the

management, marketing and coordination superiority of developed countries, by increasing the efficiency and lowering the cost of recording, processing and retrieving information.

3. In order to improve products and processes, management in some traditional mass production industries (especially in developing countries) is beginning to promote research and development, and the industries themselves are becoming highly capital-intensive with the introduction of these improvements. In this way, more and more industries are crossing the barrier into the high-technology category where design and quality are essential to the acceptability of products.

4. The technology encourages further industrial and service concentration and vertical (forward) integration, which are accompanied by streamlining in certain sectors and increased efficiency in the use of resources. A different result of this process, however, can be the creation of new opportunities for newcomers who take advantage of the loss of production flexibility and innovative capacity in established firms.

5. The use of microelectronics technology produces a saving in capital per unit of output, but an increase in capital per worker employed and, thus, in capital intensity. Formerly labour-intensive activities are thus becoming capital-intensive, with important consequences for capital requirements and formation.

The preceding discussion has shown how, within the traditional concept of appropriate technology, high technologies can be considered appropriate. Microcomputers, for instance, are not too expensive, they are user-friendly with almost simple skills requirements (even if they are not so simple to build, programme and maintain), they can promote decentralisation, and do not require the sophisticated infrastructure of a modern industrialised country in order to function (Avgerou & Land 1992). By means of advanced technology such as information technology, the time lag between the stages of reporting, evaluating, dispatching and implementing within the process of maintenance can be shortened. This increases efficiency and reduces costs. Such computer applications, together with education of the poor in remote rural areas through computer-based tutoring systems, diagnostic expert systems in health care services (Kahen & Sayers 1997; King & Beck 1990), regional and international microcomputer-based communication systems (Kigada 1991; Networks Group 1992; Rodriguez 1995), and proper exploitation of the potential of information systems to serve planning and improvement of socio-economic development, can fulfil the main criteria for appropriate technology. But there are still difficulties of adjustment and adaptation (Kahen 1995c; Kahen & Sayers 1994). This is because new information technologies drawn from modern and industrialised societies contain implicit cultural values that may be fundamentally different from those of traditional societies, which most developing nations are (S. Hill 1988; Ndebbio 1985). In our view, a technology defined in terms of its four principal elements—humanware, technoware, orgaware and inforware—will be appropriate to a developing country when each of these elements fulfils the criteria for appropriateness within the socio-economic system of that country.

PROPER CRITERIA FOR APPROPRIATE TECHNOLOGY

The experience of successful transfer of high technologies to Latin America (Argentina, Brazil, Chile) and Southeast Asia (Hong Kong, Singapore, South Korea, Taiwan) supports the idea that it is essential to review and enrich the traditional concept of appropriate technology. Rather than using computerised systems for applications of strategic importance (such as global education, health care services, manufacturing, agriculture and research and development), from which real pay-offs may be expected, developing countries use computers mostly for automating large-scale clerical work, a practice that usually is not successful (Jimba 2000; Kahen 1995c; Kaul et al. 1987; Odedra 1990; Walsham 1993; Walsham et al. 1990). The appropriateness of a technology must therefore be determined on the basis of its acceptability, adaptation and institutionalisation in a new organisational setting (Oyomno 1995). According to Ahmad (1977), indigenous technology can at times be inappropriate, and often appropriateness depends on the goals of the society rather than on the functions of technologies. It is widely accepted that 'technology can never be an end in itself: it is appropriate only to the extent that it has a chance of furthering some national objectives' (Avgerou & Land 1992). A technology may be useful and in high demand, and yet be inappropriate for sustained use in an organisation (Brodman 1986; Kiggundu 1989; Pinckney et al. 1982). An important overall objective of appropriate technological choice is the achievement of greater technological self-reliance and increased domestic technological capability, together with fulfilment of other developmental goals such as health care and social development (Kahen & Sayers 1996a).

Despite what has been suggested in the literature about appropriate technology, the experience of the newly industrialising countries of the Far East and Latin America has proved that the notion of appropriateness should not be limited to, or defined exclusively in terms of, elementary and labour-intensive technologies. In other words, the pursuit of appropriate technology does not necessarily mean the employment and adoption of low level technology (Elkington 1986). In our view, an appropriate technology for developing countries, whether low level or high level or even sophisticated technology such as medical expert systems (Elliot 1985; Kahen & Sayers 1996a), should satisfy seven important criteria:

1. Effectiveness: it must work and fulfil its purpose in the circumstances in which it needs to be used.
2. Affordability: it does not have to be cheap, but trade-offs between cost and effectiveness must be considered.
3. Cultural acceptability: it must fit in with the needs and characteristics of local users.
4. Local sustainability: it should not be over-dependent on imported skills for functioning, maintenance and repairs.
5. Efficiency: compared with other available technologies, it should be more efficient.
6. Measurability: its impact and performance need proper evaluation.
7. Political responsibility: it should support political stability in the country, and not alter the existing political balance in ways that might be counterproductive.

To summarise: for a technology to be appropriate in a particular situation, it should meet the technical, socio-cultural, political and economic requirements of that situation. It should also take into account environmental (Kahen & Sayers 1995b, 1996b) and anthropocentric (Kahen & Griffiths 1995) considerations. A successful technology transfer can only be achieved if the technology in question meets all the appropriateness criteria, which means that it needs to be adapted to the requirements of the people who are going to operate it. The traditional concept of appropriateness, however, excludes computer-based technologies (such as expert and information systems) as capital-oriented or machine-oriented technologies (Kahen 1995c). In our perspective, such technologies are categorised as appropriate. Appropriateness requires that a technology be ethically, socially, culturally and economically acceptable and affordable in terms of socio-economic cost–benefit and cost-effectiveness considerations.

KEY-ROLE FACTORS IN AN EFFECTIVE TECHNOLOGY
TRANSFER SYSTEM

THE ROLE AND IMPORTANCE OF INTELLECTUAL PROPERTY
SYSTEMS

The continuous importation of technology without any absorption and development not only accelerates the escape of hard currency from developing countries, it may also reduce the effectiveness of any resources allocation planning. If basic technical and technological infrastructures (S&T, R&D) do not exist, and if the technical human capital base is inadequate to absorb the imported technology, to adapt and employ it effectively, and improve and further develop it so as to keep abreast of the latest developments in the world, then the imported technology will not be fully and effectively utilised. This situation is likely to foster a state of continuing reliance on foreign technology imports, and to keep the country locked into the vicious circle of scientific and technological underdevelopment.

This hazardous situation may be avoided by using the leverage provided by the level of technological capability that a country possesses. However, as pointed out in the previous chapter, techno-logical capability, in turn, is dependent upon the development of well-established technical and technological infrastructures and a skilled human resource base. The lack of appropriate policies and essential infrastructures such as intellectual property systems, com-bined with a complete reliance on foreign technology, will result in reduced investment potential for the improvement of indigenous production systems in the long term.

Those who undertake investment in new technology, however, cannot risk having their new product copied and undercut by others with better resources or cheaper labour who did not invest time and money in the original R&D (Aggarwal 2000; Hodkinson 1990; Hsiao 1997). This is the reason why intellectual property is regarded as the driving force of any business (Sullivan 1995; Yang 2001). Intellectual property implies any concept, device, design or invention which has been conceived or constructed by the innovator and over which he wishes to claim some kind of ownership as his own property. The basic principle is simple: 'keep it secret' (Allen 1992). The intangible nature of intellectual property assets and their significant value, however, pose special problems and require particular sensitivities.

The intellectual property rights embodied in technology constitute the core of the international technology business. The protection of intellectual property almost always causes a range of problems between transferee and transferor. The types of intellectual property rights that generally appear in the context of technology transfer range from confidential information, trade secrets, know-how and patents, to copyright and design rights (registered and unregistered). Since no technology business can afford to ignore its intellectual property rights, the identification of intellectual property rights within the process of technology transfer is a key factor in assessing how best to maximise the 'mutual benefits'[2] between the two parties from the use of the technology.

While a large number of international intellectual property treaties are in force, a single worldwide system does not yet exist. Intellectual property rights have arisen in a piecemeal and inconsistent fashion around the world. They generally reflect the varying priorities of the techno-economic systems of different countries. A cross-country study in Africa (Yankey 1986) shows that an effective patent system as a tool of economic policy plays a useful role in the transfer of technology and the development of indigenous technological capability. Such a system should therefore be integrated into national technology policy and development strategy.

A review of earlier studies leads us to the conclusion that, in order to facilitate effective technology transfer, every receiving country needs to establish a protectional intellectual property system dealing with two principal groups of issues: (a) intellectual property rights regimes enforced by developed countries; and (b) protection of intellectual properties generated in developing countries. The establishment of an appropriate strategy for intellectual property protection is essential for successful technology transfer. It requires direct government involvement, in the mode of other similar responsibilities borne by the government such as allocating resources to the pursuit of different targets and guiding the direction of and strategy for techno-economic development in science and technology. In the case of intellectual property systems, however, developing countries, as follower countries that rely mainly on technology importation and application, are in a very disadvantageous position (Chiang 1995). To ensure effective transfer and to compete with technological forerunners, followers (that is, developing countries) need to establish strong complementary assets. With rapid changes occurring in the

---

[2]We will discuss this issue later in this chapter.

world economy and in the system of international technology transfer, along with the increasing sophistication of technology, these follower countries cannot expect to enjoy the traditional follower's advantage that they did earlier (as, for example, happened in Taiwan and South Korea). Indeed, they may have to engage in the fierce competition for technological development and new inventions, a competition for which they are not prepared.

Successful transfer requires, in the first place, a clear identification of the long- and short-term objectives of the transfer, as well as of the exploitation of the technology or its derivative products, by the national planning system and the national protocol for technology transfer. Second, both transferor and transferee should then select an appropriate legal structure to facilitate an effective transfer process. Past experiences with transfer demonstrate the paramount importance of the selected structure to both parties (Rubin 1995). The chosen legal structure should be the one that most easily enables the parties to achieve their techno-economic objectives throughout the life of their business relationship.

Once recipients are culturally at ease with the new technology, it is possible to foster a sense of innovation and motivation among them, and at this stage training will become self-sustaining. Recipients often feel ill at ease with a 'mothering' relationship, but this attitude is all too often encouraged by the secrecy over certain elements of technological transfer. 'Source coding' and 'patenting' are commercial devices to protect the interests of innovators, but in the area of technological cooperation a relaxation of such procedures would benefit the receiving country/company. This will foster a high level of self-sufficiency in the use and further development of certain innovations and eventually lead to technological change in developing countries.

MUTUAL BENEFITS

MUTUAL BENEFITS AND TRAINING SUPPORTS

As long as one part of the world continues to be very rich while the other part is artificially maintained in abject poverty, it is not possible to envisage a state of continued well-being and peace. It is necessary to take a close look at what development means, and who bears the costs. If sustainable development is to be achieved through technology transfer, both transferor and transferee as well as aid agencies must play crucial roles in improving mutual benefits from the transfer. The

European Community (EC), for example, a major source of aid to developing countries (Roe 1993),[3] has reoriented its aid policy from the provision of straight aid to economic cooperation.

Thus, increasing the mutual benefits of both parties from the transfer is an important goal, apart from the pursuit of techno-economic objectives. Technology transfer can assist in changing environmental attitudes and increasing the standard of living in recipient countries. In the past, however, transfer has often been a 'xeroxing exercise', where donors and developers wish to sell technology and minimise costs by providing a minimal amount of training (Bichage 1993). What is necessary, therefore, is achieving a proper orientation among those receiving the technology and fostering expertise within the host country. This can only happen if technology providers appreciate the socio-cultural milieu of the company or country into which they propose to introduce the new equipment and methods. Appropriate training is thus needed, not only for experts and technicians, but also for the wider community.

The funding of training is usually a costed element in any transfer project, and it is often difficult for businesses to find a mutually agreeable method of costing. The major constraints in the smooth and adequate provision of training are time, patience, money and lack of infrastructure. The fact that many developing countries have illiteracy rates of between 70 and 80 per cent is often the major inhibitor of smooth transfer, with the conveyance of information to the illiterate becoming an important consideration. The executive body that makes the final decisions about the possibility of technology transfer also needs to be educated. Politicians need to become aware of the need and appropriateness of the technology, and this awareness needs to be perpetuated in a 'trickle-down' fashion. Opposition to the transfer at a higher level will retard the process of dissemination and development of the technology. The government's role in this regard should be to promote self-sufficiency rather than reliance on imports. It may be noted in this connection that partnerships between businesses and between governments require different approaches. It is necessary, further, to ensure that training (in order to be mutually beneficial) is continuous and long-term rather than 'one- off'. There is also a need for governments to instil public acceptance of the technology.[4]

---

[3]Member countries contribute approximately half of total world aid.

[4]For instance, in the UK, people were encouraged to support and use clean technology through the channel of school education.

MUTUAL TECHNICAL BENEFITS AND REVERSE TECHNOLOGY TRANSFER

Apart from the financial benefits and economic trade-offs that comprise the major incentives of developed countries for the transfer of technology to developing countries, there exist other benefits that can support the success of transfer. These benefits include any technical outputs or significant findings derived from the host firm's/country's research and development activities. These results are of interest both from the point of view of economic analysis and from the point of view of public policy within both groups of countries.

The nature and intensity of feedback effects on the transferor's or host country's economy will depend not only on the type of technology transferred, but also on the degree of development of industrial structures in developing countries. Evidently, the capacity of firms in developing countries to absorb and assimilate imported technology determines their ability to compete with home countries. In this regard, it has been found (see, for example, Mansfield et al. 1979, 1982) that R&D carried out in the host country tends to emphasise predominantly product and process modifications and improvements, rather than entirely new products and processes. A further example of benefits to the host country from adopting technically advanced projects may be provided by citing the Korean experience again. It has been observed that the demand for foreign technology reflects, in part, recognition by the Korean government and Korean firms that capital can be more easily raised for technically *advanced* projects. In particular, foreign capital is more readily available to those Korean firms that adopt the technology that is generating profits for producers in developed countries.

It has also been found that research and development activities carried out by firms in overseas laboratories tend to be less basic and more focused on development than that carried out by firms in their home laboratories (for the case of software technology in Japan, see Kahen [1999]). For instance, US transferors established overseas laboratories primarily in order to service and adapt product and process technologies transferred to their foreign affiliates (mostly in Canada, England and Germany). These firms perform about 10 per cent of their R&D overseas, but about 47 per cent of their R&D expenditures result in technologies that are transferred back to the US (Mansfield & Romeo 1984). The main reason why overseas laboratories (that is, those established in host countries) transfer so much technology back to the transferor (the home country) is that many of them are no longer devoted solely to the servicing and adaptation of

US technology. What this means is that, as time has gone by, these laboratories have begun generating new or improved products and processes expressly for foreign application. Eventually, some of them have begun to produce technology for application throughout the world, including in the US (Mansfield et al. 1979, 1982). It is interesting that the rate of productivity increase in US-based firms depends much more on overseas R&D than on domestic R&D.

Most research suggests that a smaller proportion of effort is devoted mainly to product innovation in developing countries. A high proportion of world R&D takes place in developed countries, much of it in large companies; less than about 3 per cent of R&D expenditure is located in developing countries (see Annerstadt 1979; Bhalla 1996; Pavitt & Patel 1988). Even data on formal funded R&D for developing countries are rare. With the introduction of structural adjustment measures in many developing countries, and in the face of serious debt situations, government expenditures on R&D are likely to decrease even further in the future, with the long-term pay-offs and uncertain results involved in such expenditure.

Mastering a technology gives the technology holder an advantage over others who do not have the same ability to master the technology. It enables the country or firm to do what others cannot do, or to do it well. The possession of this technological mastery therefore implies a substantial benefit. As an instrument of strategy, technology development is usually planned with a view to ensuring the maximum flow of income in the long run and to supplying the maximum number of markets. At the micro level, therefore, the transfer of technology will only take place when the interests of the firm/organisation (mostly financial and technical interests) are satisfied.

GOVERNMENT POLICIES AND INDUSTRIAL POLICY

In order to help develop technological self-reliance, governmental policy on technology transfer has to play a significant role in the following areas:

- national planning
- evaluation
- resource allocation
- financial support
- sales promotion
- exports promotion
- subvention

Among these, subvention involves a crucial set of protective features for supporting a successful transfer. These include 'technology law', policies on commercial and non-commercial technology and various other infrastructures in the host country.

It is indeed very important that a climate of confidence is established between those transferring the technology and those receiving it. Flows of technology from developed to developing countries may be affected not only by human, technical, orga-managerial and financial shortages constraining the transferee, but also by legal factors. Although such factors are usually of secondary importance, they may have significant side-effects in influencing the direction of flows of technology. A country's legislation may impose heavy obligations on a supplier of technology, and such obstacles to the creation of a viable contractual relationship may limit flows of technology, which may finally result in unsuccessful transfers. A restrictive attitude on the part of the authorities might have unfavourable effects on the flow of technology to that country, particularly if the potential and size of the country's market are not important in the view of firms exporting technology.

The transfer of technology is clearly linked to changes in the world economy. Apart from economic and political factors, including the investment climate and incentive policies in the host country such as free zones, grants, interest subsidies or barriers to entry to the local market, controls and regulations on the transfer of technology play a significant role that may be positive (that is, supportive) or negative (preventive). These factors may be categorised as what we have just referred to as 'technology law' within the host country. The decision to transfer technology is the result of a wide variety of influences on the strategy of the firms involved (those holding and those acquiring technology) and the strategy of the host country. The national legislation of developing countries must therefore be flexible enough in its application in order to provide and promote supportive technology law and to prevent legal obstacles from arising in the course of transfer (as happened in the case of Japan and some of the Southeast Asian countries; see Chiang [1995]).

While industrial policy also plays a key role in techno-economic development, state intervention in this regard (for example, a protectionist policy) is not necessarily always successful. The crucial questions that should be addressed here are: under what circumstances and to what extent is state intervention likely to be successful, and what factors determine the effectiveness of industrial policies? The greater success of the East Asian countries (compared to the Latin American) has been attributed to extensive state intervention and an

inward-oriented strategy of techno-economic development
(Aggarwal 2000; Balassa et al. 1986; Enos 1984; Jenkins 1995; Lin
1988; Mahmood & Singh 2003; Putranto et al. 2003b; Ranis 1985;
Trajtenberg 2001). Other reasons cited for this difference in perfor-
mance include differences in the relative autonomy of the state and
in the degree of politicisation of the bureaucracy in East Asia and
Latin America (see Anglade & Fortin 1990; Jenkins 1991; White &
Wade 1988).

The experience of these newly industrialising countries (NICs) in
East Asia and Latin America points to a number of factors, at both
macro and micro levels, that contribute to the effectiveness of state
intervention (Jenkins 1995; Rueschemeyer & Evans 1985). At the
macro level, three major factors may be identified: (*a*) effective intervention requires a certain degree of state autonomy; (*b*) it requires a
high degree of state unity, in the sense of a minimum level of coherence and coordination within and among different state organisations; and (*c*) the state must have at its disposal appropriate policy
instruments (such as financial incentives). While these macro level
factors affect the capacity of the state to formulate and implement
policies effectively, at the sectoral level a further factor may be identified that may influence the effectiveness of policy: the 'congruence'
between the objectives of the state and those of leading actors within
the sector.

South Korea, which among the NICs has been consistently the most
successful in automobile technology transfer and industry development, has been the most distortionary in terms of its use of highly
discretionary policies to determine who will produce what in the
industry (that is to say, the state has consistently shown a high degree
of autonomy and unity). Conversely, Taiwan, which has come closest
to intervening in a non-discriminatory fashion, has been the least
successful in this regard. This was despite its well-established state
policies devised and implemented for technology transfer into such
strategic industries as steel, electronics and petrochemicals (Arnold
1989). Conflicts and internal divisions within the Mexican government (which resulted in a lack of coherence in policy) weakened its
ability to formulate effective policies for the transfer and development
of car manufacturing technologies (Jenkins 1995). Thus, the lack of
autonomy and unity and the presence of conflicts within the state
apparatus may contribute significantly to the failure of transfer.

Inter-regional dichotomies may also act as a barrier to effective
industrial policy making and technology transfer. Moreover, comparisons of industrial policy in South Korea and Taiwan (Wade 1990)

show that conflicts of interest between the state and the private sector have been more common in Taiwan, and that state unity has been less marked here than in South Korea, making government leadership of the private sector more difficult in Taiwan.

However, Taiwan's economy is an example of appropriate industrial planning, with its rational policies for technology transfer, a strong record of economic growth over more than 30 years, and an average GDP growth rate of 8.5 per cent a year over the period 1956–90 (Fan 1991). Taiwan's success may be attributed in large part to its adoption of an economic policy that reversed the strategy of import substitution, and laid the foundations for the island nation's high level of export-led growth. This policy has been implemented through three systematic, planned stages: development of industry for export markets in the 1960s; development of heavy industry in the 1970s; and the promotion of high-technology and skill-intensive industries in the 1980s.

The lack of clear understanding of the options and opportunities for applying indigenous capabilities and for employing external technology lies behind the different perceptions of technological change within the developed and developing worlds. For example, in Indonesia, a developing country, existing industries

> will have to attempt the difficult task of survival in an open economy on the basis of upgrading their production facilities (technologies) through imports. But they find that, exporting raw-materials and primary goods to pay for imported machinery and process know-how, is a losing business, because the purchasing power of these commodities has steadily fallen while that of machinery has continuously risen over the last two decades (N. Sharif 1994b; see also N. Sharif 1994a).

Furthermore, technological choices at the national level in developing countries have become so interwoven with cultural, political and social processes that the domain and criteria for decision making have moved from the engineering and economic spheres towards non-techno-economic spheres.

In this respect, even world agencies prefer to support technological projects in countries where governments encourage the private sector and see it as playing a supporting role in techno-economic development. A basic policy of the World Bank with regard to providing aid to developing countries has been that sufficient resources for small- and medium-scale investments are made available from private sector investors, both domestic and foreign (Stern 1993). When it comes to social expenditure on human capital, such as health and education, the Bank prefers financing to take the form of grants directed towards the training of doctors and teachers.

FINANCIAL INFRASTRUCTURE: A DYNAMIC FINANCIAL SYSTEM

According to Gurley & Shaw (1960), a country cannot reach a high level growth path without the presence of a dynamic financial development system. Such a system is based on the process of financial *deepening* (Saltzman & Duggal 1995; Shaw 1973), which begins with monetisation of the economy and eventually contributes to technological improvement in the techno-economic function of production. Financial deepening is measured by the level of monetisation rather than by the amount of money balances (real or nominal). A poorly functioning financial mechanism would become a constraint upon the processes of technology transfer and technological improvement. Saltzman & Duggal (1995) conducted an empirical study to understand and analyse the role of this constraint in the process of technological change through technology transfer during 1968–88 in Korea. Not only was a direct link established between the monetisation variable and technological development, but this linkage was also found to be strong and significant. A dynamic financial system therefore acts as supportive infrastructure for the process of technology transfer.

TARGETING TECHNOLOGY(IES)

An integrated technology strategy provides any given developing country with the tools for improving its industrial (or even services) sectors. 'Technology targeting' is one such tool within an integrated strategy for technology. In the field of manufacturing, for instance, a sustainable strategy for advancing the entire process of technology transfer in a country requires that the development of an industry involve two key transitions: from assembly to full manufacturing, and from production exclusively for the domestic market to achieving significant exports.[5] The targeting of technologies, as a principal element of industrial strategy, serves as a support for the national system

---

[5]For instance, these two key transitions have been traced for the different phases of development of the automobile industry in Brazil, Mexico, South Korea and Taiwan (see Jenkins 1993).

of policy making and planning for socio-economic and technological development. Targeting of technology may be achieved by establishing a set of priorities or means in relation to industrial and technological policies. Thus, the targeting of technology is based on the practice of *industrial* targeting, which forms a part of the national techno-economic strategy and development plan.[6] It has been observed that when the priorities and the means have both been appropriate, the policy has generally succeeded (as for instance happened with the Korean system of technology transfer and development, as well as those of the Far East Asian countries).

On some occasions, the policy has failed because of flaws in the means, even though the priorities were more or less appropriate. However, when the priorities established have themselves been inappropriate, the policy has almost invariably ended in failure because the means devised for carrying out the priorities merely magnified the error. The practice of targeting technology, if it is seen as essential initially, should be addressed through feasible and appropriate objectives; otherwise it can prove to be harmful. It is widely believed that the policy of industrial targeting in Japan in the 1960s brought prosperity to the country. But it is by no means clear that it was industrial policy, in the sense of industrial targeting, that made Japan's experience so successful. Some industries did succeed, but many others failed despite policy emphasis (Okimoto 1989). It must be noted that the role of the government, that is, the central decision-making authority and planning system, is crucial in this respect (in terms of setting priorities and implementing them).

The experience with technological targeting in developing countries has ended in disaster in many cases (Soon 1994). A notable example of this is Brazil, which tried to foster domestic technology by discouraging imports of foreign technology, a policy that finally ended in failure. It is hence crucial that a government maintain a neutral outlook in this regard. However, a review of the literature suggests that an appropriate policy for targeting technology can bring about effective technology transfer. The success of transfer depends heavily on the policy-making and planning systems, which ought to facilitate and support a competitive industrial environment. This would allow the market to induce appropriate transfer and development of technology. It is vital that the government's role in formulating

---

[6]Examples include the targeting of heavy and chemical industries in Brazil, China, India, Korea and Mexico (see Auty [1994] for examples of technology and post-war diffusion in the NICs).

and implementing policies for targeting technologies be properly understood. An appropriate targeting policy should be based on a comprehensive evaluation of national techno-economic and socio-cultural capabilities (we analysed these various types of capability in chapter four). The government should maintain a broad outlook with respect to its policy on industrial development, and evolve systems and institutions that are fair to all and that provide all actors and sectors within the techno-economic system with fair and equal opportunity. It should restore industrial balance where necessary, and encourage technological change and innovation across industries.

THE COUNTRY'S FOREIGN EXCHANGE REGIME AND ITS MANAGEMENT

The foreign exchange constraint faced by developing countries has been one of the major bottlenecks in the process of technological and economic development (Kahen & Sayers 1995b). Inappropriate exchange rate policies and allocations pursued by some developing countries have not only set back the trend of technology transfer to these nations and damaged their national techno-economic systems, but have also contributed to the international debt crisis (Brodsky et al. 1981; Findlay 1984; Gulhati et al. 1986; O. Johnson 1984; Kiguel & O'Connell 1994). Inappropriate foreign exchange regimes may, further-more, decelerate the pace of technology transactions and technological relationships between the developed and developing worlds.

Problems such as these stem from the fact that most developing countries are heavily dependent upon foreign exchange earnings from exports to finance their imports of technology—imports that are important determinants of capital formation and techno-economic growth within these countries. To cite examples, Taiwan, which desired rapid economic development, adopted the managed foreign exchange regime to prevent capital flight (Fan 1991) and to facilitate transfer of technology. On the other hand, in Iran since 1979, the mismanagement of foreign exchange, an inappropriate economic structure and an unstable exchange rate, combined with various political and social factors, have drastically decreased both private and foreign technological investments in the country.

STRUCTURAL BOTTLENECKS

'Structural bottlenecks' do not refer to the short-term problems that arise inevitably in any economy due to the fixed structure of productive capacities in the short run. Rather, structural bottlenecks are the outcome of social, political and technical conditions of production in particular sectors of the economy, as well as of the overarching economic and political institutions that limit and condition both effective economic intervention by the government and the operation of the market mechanism. For instance, the lack or shortage of 'absorptive capacity'[7] in developing countries in general, and in the oil-exporting less developed countries in particular, may be referred to as a 'structural bottleneck' (Karshenas 1990). Various factors can lie hidden behind a structural bottleneck in a country (for example, the political institutions within the Islamic government of Iran since 1979).

Any candidate technology that is initially selected as a principal target for transfer must be subjected to examination with regard to whether it can solve existing structural bottlenecks, or if it has the potential to cause new bottlenecks. This is a serious question that should be carefully taken into account within a comprehensive process of technology evaluation.

A major structural bottleneck results from uncertainty surrounding technological investment due to political conflicts in a country, such as in the case of Iran. In general, the long historical experience of development creates different types of bottlenecks at different stages of the process of techno-economic development. Studies on a number of Latin American countries with semi-industrialised mixed economies reveal that four broad institutional factors are mainly responsible for causing structural bottlenecks in their techno-economic systems:

1. food supply deficiencies arising from backward conditions of production in the agricultural sector (that is, a non-industrialised agriculture sector);
2. lack of integration in the manufacturing sector resulting in heavy reliance on imports of capital goods and intermediate manufactured goods;
3. lack of diversification and relatively slow growth of exports arising from technological backwardness and inefficiencies in the manufacturing sector; and
4. a rigid state fiscal structure that lacks the necessary flexibility to keep up with mounting public expenses in support of the

---

[7]This concept in the development literature refers to the organisational and human skill capacities for undertaking new technological and investment projects (see, for example, E. Eckaus 1972; Fontes 2001a; Lewis 2000; Marris 1970).

techno-economic process (Diamand 1978; Fitzgerald 1978, 1983; Furtado 1970; Kaldor 1978; Kalecki 1976; Jin & Zou 2002; Seers 1962; Taylor 1983; Wells & Malan 1984; Zhang 1996).

These are structural factors that cannot be corrected in the short to medium term. They appear mostly due to an unstable economy, an ineffective technological system, political problems, social pressures and the lack of flexibility in the fiscal structure of the state. Socio-political factors and the shortage of absorptive capacity are the most common bottlenecks within underdeveloped economies. Limited markets and the shortage of foreign exchange can also cause structural bottlenecks; these factors are related to the inefficiency of the manufacturing sector and its inability to export during the early stages of industrialisation.

THE ROLE OF CAPITAL TECHNOLOGY AND LOCATION FACTORS

The capital goods sector or heavy industry has played a crucial role in industrialisation and technological transformation in developing countries. Acting as the embodiment of technology, it has served as the most powerful instrument for the generation and diffusion of technical change. Capital goods production has been the dynamic agent in accelerating technological change in many societies (Patel 1983). Electronics technology, the most important of the frontier technologies, has been relevant to the development of the capital goods sector (Kahen 1995b, 1995c), and, hence, to techno-economic development in several developing countries (particularly in Korea, China, India and Brazil).

Technology transfer from developed to developing countries has tended to concentrate on the transfer of industrial technology (Bell & Pavitt 1993a). This is owing to the dominant tendency of developing countries to import industrial technologies rather than agricultural ones. The significance attached to industrial technologies relates to the perceptions regarding the prerequisites for technological development. It has also been recognised that there are difficulties in transferring agricultural technologies from industrialised to developing countries. Indeed, the basic processes of technological accumulation, change and development differ fundamentally between the agricultural and industrial sectors in less developed countries. The main reason is the 'location-oriented' nature of agricultural technologies:

industrial technology is less location-specific than agricultural technology. Developing countries prefer to focus more on the scope provided by industrial transfer than on that of agricultural transfer, in order to achieve benefits from the international diffusion of high-productivity technologies. This also affects patent distribution around a country (see Sun 2000).

The import of technology should support a balance between rural and urban regions. If imported technology does not have positive effects on the existing balance between the two regions (rural and urban) as well as between sectors within the country's techno-economic system (agriculture and industry), it can create a conflict situation in the country. This situation has been addressed in a number of studies (Gar-on & Wu 1999; P. Kuznets 1977; Madon 1992). It is believed that the Iranian crisis during 1978–79 was to a large degree the result of huge and rapid changes occurring within the Iranian techno-economic system. In Korea, the apparent conflict between achieving self-sufficiency in foodgrains and building an industrial base was settled in favour of the latter. The technological plan, rather than emphasising economic growth, attempts to expand regional development and achieve improvement in the quality of life.

POLITICAL FACTORS AND THE ROLE OF POLITICAL STABILITY

The government's role in promoting technological development is by no means limited to direct funding schemes, but extends to more indirect measures that influence the general techno-economic climate, affecting the individual inventor, entrepreneur and established technology-oriented firms. Generally, however, the government's role is regarded as being restricted to producing a favourable climate for industrial innovation by means of appropriate measures (Gee 1981). But, as E.L. Jones (1988) points out, political factors have frequently played a key part in determining whether or not technological, social and economic growth occur. Jones's argument that cultural and other institutional factors are of less importance in this regard is, however, debatable, particularly when one reviews cases in which religious sentiments, guilds and caste issues have been involved. The significance of cultural and social factors such as national consciousness, self-understanding and traditional notions of hard work within the Japanese experience of transferring and developing technology does not support Jones's position. (For further discussion of this point, see Hayashi 1990; Kahen 1995b, 1999.)

The importance of political regimes in determining rates of techno-economic growth may be underlined by citing some recent examples. Little (1979) undertook a comparison of the economic performance of the rapidly growing countries of the Far East (South Korea, Japan, Taiwan, Hong Kong and Singapore), and came to the conclusion that 'part of any explanation must come from government and economic policies'. By contrast, many Sub-Saharan African governments failed to build up sustainable techno-economic systems during 1945–80 (Fieldhouse 1986). These governments (in Ghana, Nigeria, Senegal and Zambia) used their powers to divert income into the hands of their supporters, for example, by taxing farmers and subsidising favoured industries, or by paying relatively high public sector wages.

Experiences with effective technology transfer (such as in South and North Korea, Brazil, Japan, Taiwan, Thailand and Argentina) also demonstrate a significant link between political climate and techno-economic development (see Easton 1965, 1975). On the one hand, the achievement of economic development is unthinkable without a certain amount of political and legal order. On the other hand, techno-economic development can contribute to stabilisation of the political system. However, due to the operation of various external and internal key-role factors, technological progress and economic development cannot by themselves safeguard the survival of a regime, as was demonstrated under particularly spectacular circumstances in Iran and the Philippines in the 1970s. Conversely, it is not merely the continuation of a particular form of government that guarantees techno-economic and social development. Indeed, the interrelations are more complex than they appear. Political stability is a necessary condition for techno-economic development (as in the case of Kenya), and in the absence of political stability there is no possibility of any enduring techno-economic and social development (as is the case in Uganda; see, for example, Berg-Schlosser & Siegler 1990).

It is now recognised that political stability is a prime prerequisite for growth. It needs to be accompanied by policies that at least do not stop growth in its tracks, whether through unduly heavy taxation or by inhibiting technological investment or rendering it grossly inefficient in other ways. Indeed, democracy or no democracy, some degree of national consensus on social goals and strategies seems imperative for progress. Again, the case of Iran since 1979 is relevant in this connection. The phenomenon of ethnic, cultural and religious divisions leading to unrest and war and economic decline is of great concern for technological and economic development. No society can expect to transform itself without improving the quality of thinking of its citizens, as the people who man and manage institutions, people who generate new ideas and implement them.

LOCAL AND ENTERPRISE CULTURE

Industrialisation and techno-economic growth in developing countries are complex and multidimensional processes. They involve quite a number of different factors, some of which may facilitate and others retard the process of growth. Many studies (for example, Chatterji et al. 1993) show that, in addition to the influence of savings ratios, human capital, levels of education and government spending programmes, non-economic variables such as the degree of political freedom and local or enterprise culture affect the process of technological growth, in two conflicting ways.

First, on the positive side, a liberal political climate and the free exchange and dissemination of ideas can encourage a technological environment that promotes innovation activities. On the negative side, a harsh political regime imposes greater discipline on human resources in order to extract higher labour productivity (this represents the lowest degree of political freedom). A quantitative study involving 85 countries reaffirms the role of political freedom in facilitating techno-economic growth (Chatterji et al. 1993). These results suggest that nations with a greater degree of political freedom have higher long-run equilibrium levels of real GDP per capita than those with less political freedom.

Second, examination of the potential role of enterprise or local culture through measuring specific geographical factors in the process of technological progress and socio-economic development reveals the existence of certain encouraging and supportive elements for the foreign investor and technology aid agencies. These cultural forces vary systematically across nations, and so they can provide different techno-economic opportunities in different cases. For instance, some countries may have good international reputations in respect of the characteristics of their people, justice systems, political environments and production systems (in other terms, they may be reputed for having a high degree of political stability, social conscience, and for being productive and safe havens).

Cultural environment plays a fundamental role in the process of technology transfer and management (see Hofstede 1998; Ross 1999). The existing culture within a given society contains subcultures related to various groups' values and beliefs, depending on their special life experiences or circumstances. Major cultural values and beliefs in a society are expressed not only in people's views of themselves, of others, organisations and society, but in their views regarding nature and the cosmos (Kotler 1994). Any new technology has potentially negative impacts on both the 'core beliefs' and the 'secondary beliefs'[8] that form the basis of local cultural values in a given country. People in developing countries are, however, usually persistent in respect of their core values; technological change and new technology generally only effect changes in secondary values. Even in the long term, the transferred technology has very little chance of changing core values. It may even cause a strong social impact that could stop the process of technological change and of application of the new technology. Thus, in order to reduce the potential conflicts that could result from technological change in a developing country, getting a form of *public acceptance* is crucial before any implementation. This acceptance is based on public awareness, which can be created and supported by public communications through official (the educational system, mass media such as radio, television, press and the Internet) or unofficial (common and traditional) channels.

Geographical factors are related to enterprise and organisational culture in a variety of ways (for instance, through environmental and climate factors, quality and quantity of land). The results of a quantitative model (Chatterji et al. 1993) to study the effect of culture related geographical factors on techno-economic growth show that geographical characteristics and enterprise culture do have a vast effect on growth in developing countries. These results were confirmed by formulating a model of techno-economic growth in developing countries over the period 1960–85. According to this study, the sign of the variable implies that the more politically free countries have higher rates of growth; thus, Africa and Latin America have lower growth rates than Asia. Further, uneven development is

---

[8]Core beliefs include the strongest values held by a people (such as nationalism, certain ideological orientations, religion) that are passed on from generation to generation and are reinforced by major social institutions. Secondary beliefs are embodied in different social modes and processes that reinforce the core values (such as health care and safety formalities, marriage age).

observed to be a characteristic of relatively liberal regimes, and appears to be a common phenomenon in Asia.

The geographical and cultural distance between the transferor and the host country is another factor to be considered in the process of transfer. Since technology transfer is a process involving close inter-actions between the staff of the transferor and that of the transferee, such distances can affect the success of transfer. The effect of this factor may be witnessed in the experience of technological change in South Korea, Singapore and other Far Eastern countries that are geographically close to Japan. If the recipient is located in a distant country, more executive time needs to be spent by the transferor, which entails further costs.

THE IMPORTANCE OF INTEGRATING HOME AND HOST COUNTRY FACTORS

Technology encompasses much more than machines and belongings; it also includes bodies of skills and knowledge that are essential to ensure the effective and efficient use of the machine. Technology may best be conceptualised as a system with particular characteris-tics (see Hannay & McGinn 1980; Szyliowicz 1981), as discussed in chapter two. From the point of view of technology transfer, therefore, the notion of a technological system contains an important implica-tion: the entire system can never be transferred, only certain of its elements. This situation emerges because of the constraints that belong to the domain of general factors in the technology transfer process: controlled and uncontrolled factors; qualitative and quanti-tative factors; and strategic and tactical factors.

All these factors may be further categorised into internal (host) and external (international) elements that inevitably affect the process of transfer. With some notable exceptions, technology trans-fers have generally not been successful owing to the interplay of these factors. A major external factor is the transfer of inappropriate technology to developing countries (Forsythe et al. 1980; Madu 1989; Prasad 1986; Todd & Simpson 1983; UNCTAD 1975). The lack of an appropriate planning authority and inadequate socio-cultural considerations may be categorised as internal factors affecting the transfer process. Policy making for technological change, it should be recognised, involves more than just one or two technical dimensions, and it is clear that a strategy for technology is much more than a policy for R&D that is generally evolved in developed countries (Craig 2000; OECD 1988; Roobeek 1990).

Many works treat aspects such as the attitude of governments in developing countries, the degree of political stability of these governments, the prospects of market growth, threats to investment, national mall-leadership and mismanagement as major concerns in the process of transfer. In the case of technological direct investment, one of the major technology transfer modes, 'the dangers posed by threats of political action, expropriation or arbitrary changes in ownership or remittance polices, and lengthy bureaucratic procedures are ... significant deterrents in particular areas' (Lall & Streeten 1977). However, in many cases, cost considerations, tax incentives or short-term gains are often seen as no less significant by both local and foreign technological investors.

A major determinant of the ability of a developing country to absorb an imported technology is the preferences of its government, reflected in the terms that it imposes on foreign suppliers (Enos 1985). If these terms are output- and employment-oriented, the country's ability to absorb the technology will be enhanced. On the other hand, if these terms are profit- and publicity-oriented, the country's ability for absorption will be reduced. What the Korean government has generally done, for example, is to perform four tasks:

1. to keep fully aware of the progress of the absorption of the technology;
2. to ensure that all the different branches of government (viz., those making national or sectoral decisions, those issuing import licences, those granting permits, those training individuals, etc.) synchronise their activities;
3. to establish a system of incentives and penalties (such as prices for, and allocations of, inputs needed by the new operating firm and the products manufactured by it); and
4. to instil in all the non-governmental bodies the same sense of purpose that the government itself has.

The governments of many developing countries often fail to perform the first and last of these tasks (Enos & Park 1988).

Generally speaking, the literature often ignores the impacts of home country factors as well as international factors on the process of technology transfer, or it almost always looks at home and host country factors separately. As these factors are concerned with two different environments, their impacts may be expected to be different, as also, for instance, in relation to the types of industries (import substitution or export promotion) or sectors for investment (energy generation, computerising information, raw material industries such as petroleum and agriculture, manufacturing and services). Any discussion should, however, integrate both types of factors.

THE ROLE OF FOREIGN INVESTMENT

The type and the source of investment in technology also influence the effectiveness of the process of technology transfer, and should hence be taken into account in any technology assessment model. It is evident that the transfer of technology through foreign investment in developing countries has had both positive and negative developmental impacts (see, for example, Amirahmadi & Wu 1994; Cable & Persaud 1987; Craig 2000; Jungnickel 1993; Lall & Streeten 1977; Lall & Mohammed 1983; Moran 1986; Morisset 1989; Reuber 1973; Rothgeb 1984; Xu 2000). These impacts can be seen in economic, cultural, political and social sites. As far as positive impacts are concerned, IBM in Mexico, for example, has made an important contribution in terms of technology production and exports within three years of its establishment. A number of studies have also described the negative non-economic effects of MNCs in developing countries.

Mattelart (1983) addresses the issue of fostering cultural dependency through the control of cross-border data flows, international advertising, the diffusion of news and the production of books, magazines, television programmes and motion pictures. Controlling the perceptions, values and tastes of people in host countries through these means may lead to a risk of deculturation: the destruction of local cultures. In Kenya, foreign enterprise—through its influence on central government ministries—was able to prevent the emergence of a strong, independent labour movement in the country (Leys 1975). In Mexico, multinational drug firms used their networks of local suppliers as well as national business organisations against a state enterprise that tried to raise the price of a raw material used in the production of steroid hormones. Despite all these findings (see also Chitrakar 1994), it should be understood that technologies transferred through MNCs are highly adaptive social agents. Accordingly, the degree to which they help or hurt the host country depends on the latter's own policy choices. Each developing country, depending upon specific and well-defined national goals and interests, therefore needs to devise its own policies in an appropriate manner.

The results from a survey of 500 major corporations investing in developing countries showed that 'guaranteed remittance of earnings' and 'protection from expropriation' are the two most critical positive factors resulting from transfer for foreign investment from overseas. In contrast, threat of war/hostilities and unfavourable investment laws may be regarded as the two most critical negative factors (Wallace 1990). Market growth, host tax laws and industrial policies and pricing controls are some other major factors.

The requirement most frequently encountered by foreign investment is conformity with the objectives of development policies and national economic planning in a given developing country (Chitrakar 1994). This conformity entails meeting requirements with respect to local content, exports, imports, technology transfer and appropriate technologies, training, local human resources and management utilisation, health and safety or the protection of environment. Factors that affect the transfer of technology and foreign investment motivations in developing countries vary from country to country. However, these factors may be categorised broadly into three groups: firm-specific, sectoral, and national or country-specific factors.

ERGONOMICS AND THE ROLE OF HUMAN–TECHNOLOGY INTERACTION

A main concern in developing technological capability is the design of any type of technology, which reflects the design system and cognitive background of the designer and his understanding in relation to the proposed technology. In order to assess the appropriateness of any candidate technology, we must evaluate the 'cognitive triangle' of tasks, users and tools, which forms the basis of technological system design. Technological systems here involve both sides: the characteristics of humans (users of technology) as well as those of technology. The cognitive triangle, then, is actually integrated into a system: the human–machine system. Therefore, provided we understand the underlying cognitive systems, we can apply the transferred technology effectively and eventually develop designs that enhance the performance of operational systems. Through such an approach, criteria of appropriateness can be met satisfactorily, ultimately leading to the development of technological capabilities in a productive manner.

Western technology transferred to developing countries without any modification would prove to be inappropriate (Kahen & Griffiths 1995). A poor fit between technology, technology users and the operating environment leads to low productivity, poor quality of work and, in manufacturing and heavy industries, high rates of injury and accident. We may cite many cases in which imported technologies did not fit the conditions in the recipient country or firm, and produced harmful effects (see, for example, Abeysekera & Shahnavaz 1987; Ahassan & Benincasa 1999; Ito 1986; Jafry & O'Neill 2000; Kroemer 1975; Lanza 1985; O'Neill 2000).

A number of studies address the transfer of non-sustainable and inappropriate technology as common behaviour in developing countries (Gurr et al. 1998; Shahnavaz 1992; Wisner 1984). In order to learn from these mistakes and avoid similar problems in the future, it is necessary to consider and evaluate the specific needs, ergonomic characteristics and conditions of each country at the outset of any technology transfer. To be effective, a technology being transferred should be evaluated in such a way as to avoid the following mis-transfers:

1. 'Incomplete transfer', which results from not considering all aspects of the technology during the transfer process (for instance, leaving out the transfer of maintenance capability).
2. 'Imperfect transfer', which is the consequence of not considering the user's characteristics (that is, human factors) in the transfer process (such as by not providing appropriate manuals and instructions to local users). Basic ergonomic aspects that need to be considered are anthropometry, physical working capacity, physical working environment, managerial styles, cultural institutions at work, etc.
3. 'Inadequate transfer', which results from not considering the environmental conditions of the recipient country, such the climate, societal infrastructure, finance, technology and culture (for example, transferring products such as protective clothing not appropriate to local climatic factors, or employing certain colours in monitoring control systems that work differently in the host country or organisation).

Technology transfer without the consideration of micro- and macro-ergonomics is doomed to failure (Meshkati 1989a, 1989b). On the micro-ergonomic level, we must consider not only workplace design issues (anthropometry, strength, etc.), but also the cognitive aspects of work (stereotypes, the concept of mental models, information processing and decision making). On the macro-ergonomic level, the effect of socio-cultural variables on technology transfer needs to be taken into account. These include attitudes towards work and towards technology, orga-managerial characteristics, group dynamics and motivation within the technology receiver. The impact of socio-cultural and individual differences should be considered when selecting technologies for experiments, system testing and evaluation (Moroney & Reising 1992).

FIRM-SPECIFIC, SECTORAL AND COUNTRY-SPECIFIC FACTORS

Firm-specific factors refer to location, ownership and internalisation elements. Location elements include resource endowments (natural, human or both), proximity to markets, infrastructure (commercial, legal, transportation), government policies and physical distances (Dunning 1979). Ownership factors are concerned with the advantages possessed by the enterprise (proprietary technology, management skills, natural resources information), and the advantages associated with size, established position and geographical spread. Internalisation refers to the benefits accruing from any decision to exploit an advantage within the firm, such as market control, reduction of transaction and negotiating costs, assurance of stability, protection of proprietary and technical skills and the economies associated with vertical and horizontal integration.

Among the most important *sectoral* factors affecting transfer are costs of production and sectoral growth rates in the host country (which may help to reduce inflation and maintain realistic exchange rates), trade barriers, investment incentives/disincentives, the availability of skilled manpower, and the existence of export processing zones (for export-oriented investment).

A country's natural resources represent one of the most important *country*-specific factors attracting foreign investment (for example, in the cases of Malaysia [see Onn 1989], Mexico and Saudi Arabia). Also relevant are factors like socio-political stability (for the case of Singapore, see Wong & Khan [1991]); the openness of the financial system (almost unrestricted remittances of funds into and out of the country); strategic location (see Miranda [1991] for the case of the Philippines); access to relatively cheap local raw materials (as in Thailand: see Patarasuk [1991]); an unprotected domestic market, in the sense that multinational corporations are present even in domestic consumption sectors like consumer durables, clothing, footwear, and food and beverages; an abundant supply of young and skilled labour (such as the disciplined labour force in Singapore: see Wong & Khan [1991]); a good infrastructure system (comprehensive network of roads and railways and utility facilities); and an environment conducive to innovations and new technologies. These various factors may usefully be considered under three broad headings (Giese et al. 1990):

1. Economic and strategic factors (minimisation of labour, capital and resource costs; and trade barriers, differences in economies of scale, and differences in technological know-how)
2. Transactional and intangible assets (technology and patents, skilled labour and extensive transportation and communication systems), and also non-production activities (R&D, advertising and marketing)
3. Political factors (stable government and a laissez-faire attitude)

Despite the extensive body of literature on technology transfer, empirical studies at the level of the user (the micro level) have been a much-neglected area of research. Although a number of factors at this level are responsible for ineffective transfer (such as working conditions, the ideologies of individuals, channels of communication, and lack of compatibility between the education system and the level of individual knowledge expected or required of the technology user), unstable technology management plays a crucial negative role in this respect (Walker 1988). Historical reasons are also frequently cited as responsible for attracting or not attracting foreign investment into a given country (Brinkerhoff 2000; Tambunlertchai 1989). For instance, refusal to adopt the language of any major economy results in a disadvantageous situation for the recipient nation (as, for example, in Thailand) in the conduct of business across international boundaries.

Conflicts and Resistance to Change

Installation of a transferred technology may be seen as a complex shift to new systems. There is, therefore, a need to gauge the readiness of people and of the industry or organisation to accept and support what could be a hurried and risky switch. Resistance to change (technically and orga-managerially) is an important socio-cultural aspect of transfer and should be given serious attention. Such resistance may be demonstrated at the levels of the individual, organisation and society.

The level of resistance depends on the nature of the technology, people's attitudes, social and organisational structures, capabilities for change, political situation, and so on. Although a great deal of organisational literature (for example, Greenfield 1973; Laurent 1986, 1991; Pascal & Athos 1981) has been devoted to the issue of resistance to change, few such studies relating to technology exist. It has been observed that the negative reaction of an organisation to a transferred technology and to technological change is weaker than that of individuals or even societies. This means that organisations have a much greater capacity for change than smaller organisms like the individuals who populate them or larger entities like the societies and cultures that constitute their environment (Laurent 1991). This is because *relationships* between structural entities are more amenable to change than the structural entities themselves. Therefore, compared with individuals and societies, the acceptance of a new technology within the organisational context seems to be faced with less resistance.

Both individuals and societies may be viewed as fairly stable structural entities, whereas organisations may be construed as temporary systems of relationships and transactions between individuals and their environment. This perspective provides policy-makers with an avenue for identifying the appropriate procedures to initiate a new technology and to reduce resistance to technological change within the process of technology transfer. We know from the evidence provided by cross-cultural studies that levels of resistance to technological change caused by the transfer of Western technology to the techno-economic and social systems of developing countries vary from country to country. Comparative research (Au 2000; Hofstede 1980, 1998; Laurent 1983) demonstrates that different national cultures hold different conceptions and assumptions about organisations and their management. We may reasonably claim that people from different national cultures (see Newman & Nollen 1996) react differently to transferred technology, to its nature and its orgamanagerial aspects.

The process of change that occurs in a firm, organisation or industry in which the imported technology is initiated is a dynamic one. The dynamics of this change are based on the role of human resources within the technological system. This human element moves through a 'resistance change curve' (Dauphinais et al. 1995), which provides the basis for assessing the dynamics of change within any technology transfer project. The process of change may be perceived as a chain, whose elements (namely, the stage of introduction of a foreign technology, the initial behaviour of change, tackling reorganisation, the formation of new values, widespread change in users and in organisations, creation of technological change) interact in a sequence. Technological change leads eventually to cultural change; therefore, cultural effects (appearing in the form of support or resistance to change, culturally and technologically) should be viewed as a crucial constraint in the process of technology transfer.

ENVIRONMENTAL ASPECTS OF TECHNOLOGY TRANSFER

Technological development through the transfer of foreign technology is a part of the dynamic process of socio-economic development. Environmental issues in this regard do not fundamentally change the nature of the problem, but alter the criteria used in selecting technologies. An extreme example is that of the disaster at the Union Carbide Chemical Plant in Bhopal, India. As has been stated, 'the real cause of the Bhopal tragedy is *blind* technology transfer' (Lanza 1985, emphasis mine). Most technology transfer projects focus only on the immediate economic benefit, and neglect any detrimental side-effects on the environment (see Kahen 1997a, 2001b, 2001c). It is evident that when technology is implemented under conditions of extreme scarcity, it tends rapidly to deplete the resources present, and places an enormous burden on the productive segment of the society to sustain its cost.

'Soft' technologies may be seen as: (*a*) clean and simple technologies; and (*b*) involving design skills, orga-managerial knowledge, information and expertise that complement the transfer of 'hard' technologies. Hard technologies also may be considered as: (*a*) complex technology; and (*b*) involving physical systems, machinery and equipment. Sustained effort is required to build up 'soft' capacity in the indigenous techno-economic system: this has proved difficult in the past, but ways and means should be found and evaluated for the future. Given the rapidity of technological movement and change, it is surprising that the resulting environmental changes and severe long-term impacts in developing countries are rarely assessed. Sometimes, contradictory consequences have been produced in different countries (for the case of Mexico, see Cole & Mogab [1987]).

In the 1970s, the need to integrate environmental variables into development planning and technology transfer came to be widely perceived. For example, in 1971, the Founex Report clarified that 'development' and 'environment' were two sides of the same coin:

It is quite likely that future technological developments in the developed world will be influenced by their current preoccupation with non-pollutive technology. It is also obvious that some of this non-pollutive technology would be quite costly for developing countries .... Its export to developing countries under tied credits will further reduce the real content of foreign assistance (UNEP 1981).

This was followed by Recommendation 108 in 1972: 'it is recommended that the Secretary General of the UN be asked to ... find means by which environmental technologies may be available for adoption by developing countries under terms and conditions that encourage their wide distribution without constituting an unacceptable burden to developing countries' (UN 1972; UNEP 1981). Despite this, the majority of developing countries suffer from the absence of integration of technological development and environmental factors.

Transfer of clean, low-waste and pollution-control-led technologies was put on the agenda when UNEP introduced its *Environmental Perspective to the Year 2000 and Beyond* in 1987 (UNEP 1987). In this global plan, the transfer of safe technology was given the main attention. In view of the proliferating environmental impacts of transfer of unclean and hazardous technologies to developing countries and the new threats being posed in the process, another important recommendation was made by the Governing Council of UNEP, which called upon the Executive Director 'to promote the identification of ways and means to facilitate access by and transfer of technology to developing countries in respect of cleaner production methods, techniques and technologies' (Tolba 1992; UNEP 1992). The many attempts and suggestions made by international agencies and organisations have led to the establishment in several countries (mostly developed countries) of some procedures to screen emerging and imported technologies from the standpoint of their environmental significance and impacts. But in developing countries, attention is rarely paid to environmental considerations regarding technology.

Environmental departments in many developing countries tend to have tiny staffs and budgets and insufficient financing for ordinary activities, particularly for technology assessment. Nature conservation or environmental protection often falls far below the standards calculated as the minimum to qualify for deficiency (Leader Williams & Albon 1988). Furthermore, no examples of any 'technology assessment models' can yet be cited (Tolba et al. 1993; see also Choi 2001; CSTD 1991; Green 1999; Heaton et al. 1991; Kahen 1997a; Kahen & Sayers 1995b, 1996b). But, generally speaking, techno-economic growth and development are perfectly consistent with environmental protection, as is trade liberalisation. It is clear that technology by itself will not lead to the necessary environmental upgrading (Goldin & Winters 1995; Touche Ross 1991). Indeed, we should emphasise that technology alone is not sufficient to meet environmental and social objectives, or to promote health and a

Figure 5.1: **System for effective technology transfer and its environment**

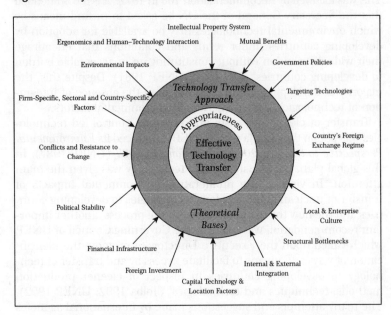

better quality of life. Unless the transferees and even ordinary people in developing countries are involved, systems will not be maintained correctly and are likely to fail. It is now understood that for the successful transfer of environmentally sound technology, the different but interrelated components of health enhancement, social acceptability, technical, economic and financial viability, institutional support and environmental awareness, all need to be considered and evaluated prior to transfer.

EFFECTIVE TRANSFER OF TECHNOLOGY

Since the transfer of technology is a multifaceted phenomenon, the success of transfer is affected by both macro and micro level factors within the techno-economic and socio-cultural environments of a country, as well as by various external factors (such as the international economic environment). We have referred to these factors in this chapter as a set of key-role factors that should be given adequate weight within the technology transfer system of any developing country. As shown in Figure 5.1, the effectiveness of this system is a function of the appropriateness criteria for a given country. The key-role factors play crucial roles in the process of investigating and defining the relevant elements and criteria needed for a model of technology assessment.

6

TECHNOLOGY PLANNING

IDENTIFICATION, EVALUATION AND DECISION MAKING IN A GENERIC INTEGRATED MODEL

The technological planning process may be broken down into four major stages:

1. Identification and classification of development goals (macro as well as micro objectives) in developing countries
2. Defining technology development objectives within the national planning system
3. Establishing the structure of a national system of technology transfer
4. Modelling technology assessment quantitatively within such a technology transfer system, at: (a) national and sectoral levels; and (b) the micro or organisational level (at this level, defining priorities is not only crucial but a prerequisite for any action)

It is evident that these stages should all be backed up by a system of technology transfer control and evaluation. This chapter defines the major issues involved in a technological policy planning system. With this background, we shall elaborate a conceptual model of technological planning for technology transfer.

In the majority of cases in industrialised countries, large technological projects (such as in manufacturing, energy and other resource-based industries) are sponsored by individuals, a private company or group of companies. They are guided by clear-cut objectives, and are accustomed to making decisions on the basis of well-established criteria. In developing countries, however, such projects are commonly initiated by the transfer of technology from the industrialised world and undertaken on the basis of government sponsorship. International institutions frequently attempt to guide some of these developments. So, the planning process for technological utilisation and development in the two worlds is carried out in two different environments, and is thereby affected in each case by different variables and constraints.

In developing countries, social and political parameters (in particular) inevitably influence the planning structure. The planning process, therefore, in accommodating these, must give full recognition to such parameters, and also manage the strength of these influences. In fact, the planning process for technology transfer or for a techno-logical project sponsored by government seeks to generate questions and answers in many areas that would not normally be of concern to the private sector. In order to overcome this incompatibility in develop-ing countries, the planning system should provide comprehensive and appropriate guidelines to be followed by both private and governmental transferors. Additionally, the planning process should take account of the need for 'education' of the decision-makers. On the one hand, decision-makers must be knowledgeable or educated in key aspects of the technological project; on the other, professionals involved in the technology planning process must seek to obtain adequate under-standing of existing national policies.

In general, the actual planning process for technology transfer begins with the definition of the direction and environment for techno-economic development by the national planning system. An appropriate organisational structure should be determined for the transfer process. The planning process is a continuous one; a key element is effective communication between the political directorate and the experts and professionals involved in the process. Whether it is a technological development within a ministry, a development agency, a sector or an organisation, clear lines of communication are needed for the 'educa-tion' element of the planning process. Various sources may generate the first interest or indicate the starting point (or identify a priority) for the process of technological planning, or of planning for a technology trans-fer project. The most common sources of such initiatives include:

1. The identification of a priority in a national plan or similar government policy statement (for instance, the potential use of an available natural resource in energy technology)

2. The targets of some sponsored projects, the requirements for specific technological development, or regional plans addressed by international agencies such as the World Energy Agency, the World Health Organisation and the World Bank
3. Proposals based on studies conducted by or on the specific interest of a local development agency within the government or private sector

Within the process of technological planning, the generation of interests by national policy-makers or key advisers to such persons should be taken into account. Investment bodies or 'foreign participant parties' for the transfer of technology also play a crucial role in this process. Participant parties can come from international development agencies, independent consultants, technology suppliers, interested financial agencies, potential joint venture partners, raw material suppliers, etc. Coordination of the various efforts of all these parties is inevitably complex; hence, what is required is a multidisciplinary approach to technological planning.

POLICY PROBLEMS AND GOVERNMENTS

Developing countries have been largely peripheral to the world system of technological development and innovation, with respect to their institutional features as well as the resultant technologies. The serious problems within the socio-economic systems of developing countries, along with the absence or shortage of technological foundations and institutional requirements, mean that a laissez-faire approach will not obtain the best results: an active technological strategy is necessary. Developing countries contemplating technology transfer are faced with an intrinsically imperfect production system; they also usually need to develop their own system of government interventions aimed at promoting and protecting technology-creating activities.

Each country has a unique and complex set of policies determined by multiple objectives, by the resources and technologies used to produce different services and commodities, what is imported, what is exported, what is not traded, and its presence in different world markets: large in some markets, small in others. It is generally accepted that the assessment and selection of technologies should be carried out in ways that maximise the national objective function, subject to certain constraints. Income goals, distribution goals and stability goals, along with environmental, political and other considerations, may be seen as the major objectives.

Constraints may be classified into 'domestic' and 'international' constraints. Domestic constraints pertain to resources (land, capital and human capital and their distribution among various agents, available technologies, fiscal resources, foreign exchange reserves), political factors (power wielded by producer vis-à-vis consumer groups, stability of government, election campaigns), and institutional factors (infrastructure, market structure, educational system). International constraints relate to world prices and market conditions, international transfer of technology, capital flows, trade in goods and services, international political pressures, etc. The assessment of candidate technologies to be transferred into any given sector needs to be considered within the national policy pyramid. Three sets of issues (discussed in chapter three) should, therefore, be taken into account: industrial policy issues relating to the specific sector, national policy issues and international policy issues (see Figures 3.2 through 3.8).

PLANNING AND THE TECHNOLOGY TRANSFER CONTINUUM

We may define technology transfer as 'a continuous process that involves planning, decision making about technological options and choice of the most appropriate technology in the light of local characteristics and available resources, and the utilisation and development of this technology with the aim of achieving particular goals and objectives at some time in the future'. It is important to emphasise that, especially in less developed countries, planning for technology transfer, similar to other types of planning, cannot be considered in isolation from the socio-cultural, administrative and, in particular, the political environment in which technology has to operate. Thus, the interrelationships between planners, policy-makers, implementing authorities and politicians or the political system need careful consideration. Political factors have direct as well as indirect impacts on the role, method, content and organisation of the technology transfer planning system, with the result that enormous variations among countries are inevitable. The political environment also affects both the character of the planning body as a whole and the role of the individual planner. It limits the ways in which they can operate, the types of proposal they can incorporate in their plans and the impact they are able to generate on the course of events. The

Figure 6.1: The technology transfer continuum

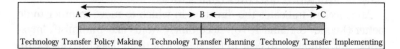

profound influence of political issues on the organisational structure within which technology transfer planning operates in developing countries means that the selection of candidate technologies often does not take place through a reliable, factual and effective evaluation process. This may be considered one of the main factors responsible for the failure or ineffectiveness of many transferred technologies in developing countries.

Professional planners are frequently frustrated by what they often regard as 'political interference' and by their inability to achieve meaningful results because of the nature and distribution of socio-economic and political power. This situation, in some cases, leads to a crisis of conscience for the individual planner, to the point at which the technology transfer planner has to decide whether to continue in his present role or seek other ways of achieving his objectives.

The process of utilisation of foreign technology may be seen as a *continuum*, in which three points are significant and affect one another (points A, B and C in Figure 6.1). Each point represents one of three interdependent stages within the process of transfer: technology transfer policy making, technology transfer planning and technology transfer implementing. It must be understood, however, that although it is useful to distinguish technology transfer *planning* from technology transfer *policy making* and its implementation, the three activities are closely interrelated and neither technology transfer planning nor technology transfer planners can operate in isolation.

OBJECTIVE SETTING AND EVALUATION

What is the major objective of transferring a technology? Clearly, objectives will differ depending on the situation of a country and its characteristics (its technological capabilities, regional factors, economic system, socio-cultural constraints or advantages). The first step in technology evaluation for transfer is to state clearly what decisions need to be made. This step dispels any ambiguities produced by the situation or by the country's techno-economic context. Introducing some reasonable definitions at this point will help us understand the stage of structuring objectives (goal setting).

An *objective* indicates the direction in which to move in order to do better (Keeney & Raiffa 1976). Accordingly, words like 'minimise', 'maximise' and 'improve' appear in the statement of an objective (for example, 'improve' technological capabilities, 'increase' GNP, 'maximise' productivity). Objectives may never be achieved completely; it is the degree of their achievement that is important. It is evident that all objectives cannot be achieved simultaneously. For example, it may not be possible to improve technical abilities and GNP while reducing local or foreign investments at the national level, or to maximise productivity while minimising technological change at the firm or sectoral level. This means that trade-offs may exist among objectives, which should be taken into account in order to achieve a reliable and effective structure of objectives. Objectives may also be broken down into sub-objectives and related attributes. The word 'attribute' is synonymous with the often-used terms 'measure of performance' and 'measure of effectiveness' (Bodily 1985).[1] The process of developing objectives and attributes is a creative one that cannot be formalised into rules and procedures. Usually, this process begins with a single, general, often ill-defined objective. We suggest that the source of appropriate objectives be a *panel of experts*, individuals with both experience and special skills relating to the area of concern. Objectives may also be found in the literature on the problem under consideration, or in the practice of similar countries or institutions (that is, by means of case studies). The specification of goals, objectives and their relative importance establishes the desired state of affairs. In the enumeration of technology options, an attempt can be made to establish various ways of achieving some or all of these goals.

THE TECHNOLOGY PLANNING PROCESS AND CRUCIAL ISSUES

A definite structure for the planning of technological projects has to be evolved over time in developing countries. As stated earlier, this structure must accommodate the social and political parameters that affect the various stages of the technology transfer process: including technology assessment and selection, technology operation, adaptation, development and innovation. In the following discussion, we shall

---

[1] Indication of the unit of measurement and a description of how the attribute is to be measured are generally a part of the definition of an attribute in each situation.

identify the major areas that require adequate attention during the planning process (in both private and public sectors).

When the planner considers the future, it is essential for him to draw clear distinctions between what *could* happen, what *should* happen and what *will* happen (Jones & Twiss 1978). Evidently, the planner is interested in what 'will happen', for this determines the socio-economic and political environments in which the proposed plans will come to fruition. A precondition, of course, is that this state is feasible—that it *could* occur. The essential step between a *feasible* outcome and what *actually* occurs involves a complicated network of human decisions most of which are taken by other people (for example, the politician). Here we consider, first, the important issue of choosing the technology to be transferred.

The distinctions just mentioned are vital for the planner who must recognise that assessors of technology are usually technologists primarily concerned with technological potential. Technologists often surrender to a dangerous tendency to oversimplify the inputs into their assessments, by assuming that cultural, social, political or economic influences will not change sufficiently to invalidate their conclusions. Our proposed methodology for the assessment of candidate technologies, therefore, takes into account the views of various experts (economists, sociologists, politicians, ergonomists, environmentalists) as well as those of engineers or technologists. Technology planners must also take into account value judgements likely to influence others whose decisions affect the process of technology transfer, as well as the environment in which technological change would happen (in other words, both macro and micro levels). Another important aspect of technology assessment consists in the recognition of threats and opportunities. But recognition of the role of all these factors must be followed by evaluation. This implies the quantification of the effectiveness or appropriateness of the process of technological change that will be achieved through the transferred technology. Technology planning, therefore, initially entails the quantification of technology assessment, for which we shall develop an approach in this book.

TECHNOLOGICAL PLANNING, TECHNOLOGY CHOICE AND STRATEGIC CONSIDERATIONS

The critical policy question for most developing countries is the manner in which the needed foreign technologies can be acquired while reducing technological dependency (mostly on MNCs) and the costs that such dependency entails. Pursuit of these dual objectives necessitates the incorporation of policies on foreign technology within the framework of a comprehensive technology plan that is fully integrated with national plans for economic and industrial development.

Most developing countries have adopted a system of industrial planning for the achievement of economic and industrial objectives. Planning in these countries has also been regarded as critical to the reduction of existing imbalances in their economies, such as inadequate growth of machine-building industries and the limited local processing of natural resources (Marton 1986). Of course, the scope and detail of national industrial plans vary considerably among countries. However, only a few of these countries have recently accorded a much greater emphasis to technology plans covering various aspects of technological development and application. Even in these cases, technology plans have not been integrated with industrial plans, nor have the elements of technology planning been linked with the achievement of industrial targets. We argue that close co-ordination of technology planning with industrial plans and targets is essential if industrial development and technological development are to progress in harmony and according to identified objectives.

It is a function of the technology plan to assess the technological requirements for achieving sectoral targets, and to identify technological linkages among various industrial sectors. Such a plan must also deal with the development of technological infrastructures, which includes the development of human resources and the promotion of indigenous R&D by domestic industry and specialised research institutions. Technology plans would also have to identify the explicit and implicit measures necessary for the growth of local managerial and entrepreneurial capabilities, so as to reduce the dominance of MNC subsidiaries and affiliates. Notwithstanding the existence of both physical and human resource constraints in developing countries, technology planning must be regarded as an essential element of techno-economic development.

In this connection it may be remembered that international issues in the transfer of technology include trans-border data and information flows, access to technology, risks of new forms of technological dependency and the role of international aid agencies and governmental and non-governmental donors. National and techno-economic issues in this domain include:

1. the development strategy, general policy approach and institutional framework, ranging from a market-oriented, completely laissez-faire attitude to a rigid, highly planned framework with centralised control;
2. impacts on economic growth, productivity and employment (Fransman 1986; Mansfield 1977; Ndebbio 1985);
3. socio-cultural effects of the transferred technology (Hill & Still 1980; Jimba 2000; Kahen & Griffiths 1995; Kahen & Sayers 1994; Kedia & Bhagat 1988; Newman & Nollen 1996; Ross 1999); and
4. international (side-) effects.

All these considerations must be taken into account in elaborating an adequate technology plan.

The tendency of developing countries to see technology transfer in a *political* light, and to view their dependency on industrialised countries—for both technology and the information it manages—as a political problem, has important consequences. It frequently leads them to overlook the importance of national technology planning and the potential role that an appropriate technology assessment system can play in coping with their developmental problems.

Modelling for Strategic Technological Choices

There is a need to build a quantifiable evaluation model for technologies to be transferred to developing countries in order to facilitate a reliable and appropriate process of decision making. This model should take into account as many relevant facts as possible, and show how those facts apply to the process of decision making. As the decision about transferring technology deals with many relationships among things that affect the outcomes that are of interest in this regard, our model should incorporate these impacts over a sufficiently long period of time; it should not respond only to the most obvious short-term considerations. A model such as this should be capable of providing the national, sectoral or organisational decision-making body with sufficient insights into the subject of transfer in general, or regarding a particular piece of technology. Decision-makers involved in the process of technology assessment should be able to explore the relative weights of and trade-offs among the various factors that enter into the decision, and should be able to understand the structure of transfer (that is, the relationships among the various elements involved).

This type of modelling approach proceeds by deconstructing the case into its various constituents, and then reassembling them in order to understand the 'anatomy' of the process in question. Complex systems, such as the process of technology transfer, behave non-intuitively; we therefore require the model to give us insights into these non-intuitive aspects of behaviour that originate in the interactions of the factors involved. Our model should then provide us with intuitions about the whole, starting with intuitions about the parts. For adequate clarity and communicability, the proposed model should be easily understood and should accurately reflect the assumptions of an expert body such as the technology transfer decision-makers at macro (national and sectoral) and micro (organisational or firm) levels.

Strategic planning is that component of strategic management that aims at the formulation of (a firm's, sector's, industry's, non-governmental institution's, or national organisation's) strategy. Strategic technological planning is the determination of long-term technological goals, the definition of courses of action and the opti-mum allocation of resources necessary for achieving these goals at national, sectoral or organisational level. In developing countries, technology management is deeply affected by the transfer of foreign technology. And, as we pointed out earlier, the process of transfer involves several complex and mostly unstructured stages. Consequently, it is essential to provide support to the technology management system for effectively performing these tasks, in the manner clarified by the theoretical approach developed in this book.

Our purpose in this volume has been to emphasise the need to develop an integrated system that can support the management of technology, from strategic planning through to strategic evaluation and implementation of technology in developing countries. Among these various phases, that of technology assessment may be regarded as crucial. Technology assessment should be carried out on the bases provided by the strategic technological planning system as a whole.

SYSTEMATIC MODELLING AND THE TECHNOLOGY ASSESSMENT SYSTEM

Although cost–benefit analysis is a valuable quantitative assessment technique, there is still a need to develop an assessment model enabling decision-makers to assess technology on both quantitative and qualitative bases simultaneously. While using the cost–benefit approach, which can be applied at the micro or project level as a tool for comparing, for instance, construction and energy technologies, we would need to ensure that all direct and indirect impacts (such as socio-cultural and environmental impacts) have been taken into account at the stage of strategic technology development planning. This is in complete contrast to what happens, in some countries at least, when policies are established by political authorities without regard to expert advice.

It needs to be emphasised again that policy making should be 'expert-oriented'. It is rational that the political authority should involve qualified experts and make use of their proposals in reaching decisions regarding any sector or any technology in a developing country. An expert-oriented modelling approach would offer a basis for rational policy making that achieves reliability, reduces the risk of arriving at damaging decisions and limits the potential of future losses. Such a framework of decision making is vastly at odds with the irrational and mechanistic modes of technological planning and decision making that characterise the highly politicised decision-making processes of the majority of developing countries.

In the realistic modelling approach that we propose here, the functional levels of systematic planning and operations are appropriately integrated. Technological planning, following the formulation used for the purpose of structuring the tasks of any planning, is conceptualised as comprising three functional levels (see Ozbekhan 1969, 1970): policy planning or policy-making functions, goal setting or strategic planning functions, and operational or tactical orga-managerial functions (Kahen 1995c). Any technology development system should involve the analysis of, and establish control over, the total integrated system, including: policy making or planning, assessment and decision making, implementation, control and evaluation (see Figure 6.2). Technological planning and technology assessment constitute two fundamental subsystems within this integrated framework, and thus they comprise the major concerns of this study. The system of assessment of any given technology, industry or sector, apart from its role in facilitating the analyses carried out in each of the other subsystems, involves the analysis of interrelationships between the functions of its six subsystems. Therefore, we propose a 'chain' type analysis of any candidate technology, including: strategic analysis, technological/technical analysis, economic analysis, socio-cultural analysis, political analysis, and environmental analysis (Figure 6.3). Without due consideration of the level, type, infrastructure, compatibility and sensitivity of the individual society or organisation, a new technology is likely to be ineffective.

Figure 6.2: Management of technology development based on a typical system of technology transfer

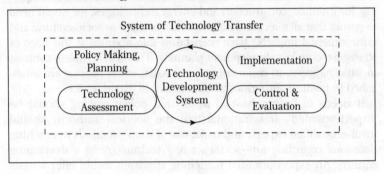

Figure 6.3: The technology assessment system with its six subsystems, outcomes, interrelationships and linkages with the system of national planning for technology development

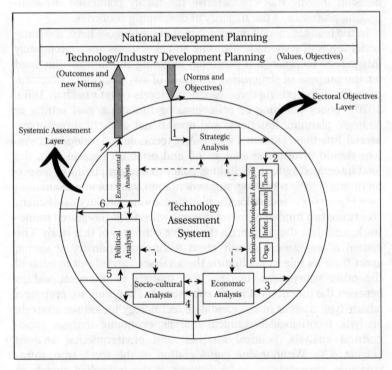

To reiterate, we propose a systematic assessment approach to facilitate the thorough analysis and evaluation of candidate technologies. This system of assessment contains six subsystems, which are rational and based on the existing realities of any given country. Of these six subsystems, the first two (strategic and technological analyses) cover the questions of feasibility of the candidate technology and its general desirability in terms of furthering national and sectoral goals. The third (economic analysis) establishes the economic outcomes and financial profitability (so as to choose an optimum option) of the technological project. The subsystems dealing with socio-cultural, political and environmental analyses concern the assessment of global or external aspects of the project, the risks that it involves and its evaluation in non-financial criteria/terms. Each subsystem, therefore, copes with a number of specific and related functions (Kahen 1997b). It may also be pointed out here that the technological subsystem, as per our conceptualisation of technology, involves four components that interact dynamically with each other: humanware, technoware, inforware and orgaware. The environmental subsystem concerns two main groups of factors: local impacts (at the national level), and global impacts (at the regional or cross-boundary level). In this respect, one or more relevant techniques related to the Environmental Impact Assessment (EIA) scheme could be applied (Carrol & Turpin 2002; UNEP 2002).

This formulation of technology decision making in terms of functions within six subsystems opens up the possibility of assessing a variety of candidate technologies and also evaluating feasible technologies. Technologies may be treated as strategic options for achieving given functional values and objectives. The interrelations existing among the subsystems provide the crucial flexibility needed in the process of technology development planning. Through this integrated approach to technology development planning, the capability of national and sectoral plans may be extended. It must be remembered that the outcomes of a selected technology, or a selected strategy for the development of a function, vary according to other technologies or strategies (Kahen 1997c) introduced into the overall system, although with different degrees of sensitivity.

In order to take into account the major objectives defined at the technology development planning level within the assessment system and all its subsystems simultaneously, we propose their conception as a circulating layer: the 'sectoral objectives layer' (see Figure 6.3). The analytical results arising from each of the six subsystems will also be transmitted into the technology development planning level, through what we may term the 'systemic assessment layer'. This layer enables the circulation of feedback (in terms of outcomes and new norms) that may be applied for the revision of the plan, the establishment of new values and objectives, and final decision making.

The variables within each subsystem (for instance, in the case of energy technology, these would include negative environmental effects within subsystem 6), representing the predicted impacts of a given technology, require to be given suitable weights so that they may be compared with other measures within the assessment system. The identification of adequate and relevant measures, as well as their quantification, are issues that still need to be addressed.

Having recognised the importance of technology as a necessary component of national development, and having determined to make it an integral part of national development plans, policy-makers first need to define clear objectives, standards, needs and capabilities. The next stage is the identification of criteria and dependent relationships. The influence of these criteria on technological decisions becomes apparent when experts clarify how these criteria influence the social system. The next crucial step is the identification of potential technologies. It is possible that different technologies are available that are able to satisfy these criteria. Obviously, experts and consultants may identify several criteria as well as technologies. These lists must be narrowed down to include only the significant ones. The ranking of technology types will be undertaken next. The basic principle behind assessing different technologies in this manner is ensuring that only the most appropriate technology is transferred.

THE PERSPECTIVE OF ASSESSMENT

For the purpose of needs assessment, the 'determinants' of technology assessment may be categorised into: (a) macro determinants (national and sectoral factors); and (b) micro determinants (firm, organisation factors). Clearly, macro considerations depend upon sector-, industry- and firm-specific determinants. The assessment of technology may also be considered at the macro level (wherein candidate technologies are evaluated on the basis of national priorities or interests and the fundamental objectives of strategic planning and development), and at the micro level (where technology is assessed in detail at the firm or organisational level).

It may be pointed out here that, while the selection of technology at the macro level is not simply a matter of choice of tools for technological development in the narrow sense, from the firm's perspective (that is, at the micro level) also, choosing a technology is more than just arriving at a method for producing something in conformity with expected costs, benefits and engineering norms. From the technological point of view, it may be said that by these means, the capabilities that can be acquired from experience with the technology are also chosen simultaneously. Such capabilities may enable a firm or a country to move on to new technological activities and developments that may be used elsewhere (sector or region) in the economy.

CRITERIA FOR CHOICE

Choosing the right technology by means of a systematic evaluation framework involves simultaneously optimising the 'static' and 'dynamic' elements of choice. Let us first consider the static elements involved in selecting a technology. On the basis of the analyses undertaken in earlier chapters, we may highlight the following issues:

1. identifying local needs, interests and conditions at national, sectoral and organisational levels;
2. collecting information to broaden the field of technological possibilities for the assessment of options;
3. highlighting barriers (economic, technical, social, cultural, political, environmental, anthropocentric) that need to be taken into account in the process of technology assessment;
4. devising relevant criteria for each set of factors in accordance with needs and conditions, and with the type of technology involved; and
5. evaluating the benefits (that is, returns) and costs, and not only by economic analysis, of different choices of technology in order to yield the highest benefits, both social and economic.

Dynamic elements, on the other hand, are concerned with evaluating future possibilities and outcomes from a preferred technology. Thus, the investigation of dynamic factors allows us to assess the various possibilities that different technologies might open up—in terms of acquiring added capabilities or modifying the technology in order to increase national productivity. The focus, clearly, should be predominantly on choosing technologies that can open up the most possibilities and enable the development of additional capabilities at the national level as well as at the level of industry (sector), firm or organisation (in other words, at both macro and micro levels).

CRITERIA CLASSIFICATION AND TECHNOLOGY IDENTIFICATION

On the basis of the analysis undertaken in chapters three, four and five in particular, the criteria that specifically influence the selection of a technology may be said to fall into two categories:

1. Intrinsic criteria:

    • technological capabilities
    • the ability to identify technology from the perspective of its four major components (humanware, technoware, inforware and orgaware)
    • resource requirements and availabilities
    • the past experience of the country or organisation in managing technology
    • the decision-making system and decision-makers' attitudes
    • existence of research and development institutions
    • the time horizon of the technological project

2. Extrinsic criteria:

    • government policies and interests
    • the techno-economic climate
    • the risk/return ratio
    • the economic system and the market environment
    • regulations and technology law (including the legal system of intellectual properties)
    • the socio-cultural environment
    • legal and technological implications

As far as technology identification is concerned, it needs to be emphasised here that the identification of options (that is, of candidate technologies) needs to be carried out with the utmost care, because unless technology options are suitably identified, it is impossible to utilise the resources available to the country, sector or organisation in an effective way. In fact, a decision is, at most, as good as the options or solutions evaluated. Hence, unless the decision team ensures that all the best options are identified, it will be unable to make the right choice. This is why it is important for us to reiterate that the proper identification and evaluation of feasible technological options has a crucial bearing on the choice of technology.

THE STRUCTURE OF A CONCEPTUAL MODEL

The process of evaluation of candidate technologies for transfer may be explained with the help of the simple input–output model depicted in Figure 6.4. What is required for this process is information concerning the sector's or country's needs, based on the objectives delineated by the national plan for techno-economic and socio-cultural development, or plans for specific technological change (for example, the development of a particular sector or industry) in a developing country, regionally and locally.

Figure 6.4: The systemic process of evaluating candidate technologies for transfer

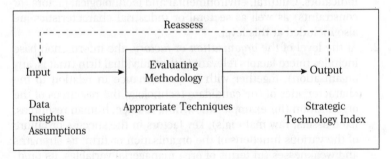

To be useful, the outputs of evaluation should be quantified. But here we are confronted with several types of difficulty. It is simply not possible to be wholly informed about a technology or about a sector or country; furthermore, as mentioned before, there is always a lack or a shortage of reliable data in developing countries. Consequently, an element of 'judgement' must enter into the process of evaluation. This means that the evaluation process should be supported by a valid 'subjective' evaluation methodology. The subjective evaluation must follow logically from what is fed into the evaluation process. Apart from various factors concerning specific technologies and those involving the country/sector, the main parameter in this process is the intellectual calibre of the evaluator: his insights and his ability to identify significant factors that need to be considered.

Another crucial factor in this respect is the *information base* upon which the plans for technology transfer, technological and socio-economic development in a country are founded. The information base is extensive, and its contents bear a close relationship to the fundamental objectives and interests of the country, sector or organisation (see Figure 3.6). It is also affected by the national protocol for technology transfer, as depicted in Figure 6.5. Essentially, information bases (that is, objective and subjective data) deal with the status of the country in all aspects of the local environment in which the technology will operate. In this respect, information bases should be considered at two levels (see Figure 6.5):

1. At the *higher* (national) level, these data relate to broad external or macro factors such as economic, sociological and political indicators (both international and national) or fiscal and monetary indicators. Cultural, environmental and technological factors (or constraints) as well as sectoral or industrial characteristics are also included at this level.

2. At the level of the *organisation* or *factory*, the information base includes micro factors relevant to the individual firm (that is, any organisation), together with its performance in relation to the characteristics of the candidate technology, the resources of the organisation (for example, know-how, finance, human resources, fixed assets, raw materials), key factors in the success or failure of the various functions of the organisation or firm, its strengths and weaknesses (in terms of orga-managerial variables, its products or services and processes, and its divisional and functional departments), the situation of the organisation within the relevant sector compared to similar organisations, and competitors' activities in common fields of interest.

The evaluation of technology, at more than one level and as illustrated in Figure 6.5, is not only important for technologically based concerns (that is, those heavily oriented to the country's technological

Figure 6.5: A basic schematic model defining the objectives of technological planning and technology evaluation for effective technology transfer

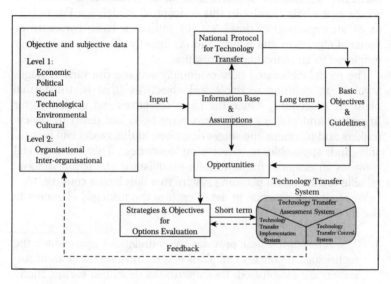

capabilities), it is important also to the users (intermediary and end users) of technology. A country/organisation that uses the imported technology is naturally interested in the changes and improvements (Kahen 1997b; Kahen & Sayers 1995b) that the new technology can bring about, since these, in turn, form part of the information base for its own planning system. For instance, technological change and development caused by technology transfer can affect human resources institutions, managerial styles or financial systems, in respect of procedures, computerisation, job performance, communication channels and methods, human–technology interactions, office equipment, etc. The implications of such changes for the concerns supported by policy-makers and planners should not be ignored.

Figure 6.5 depicts the evaluation inputs feeding into the information base of a basic planning model. This model is based on, and is an improvement over, the conceptual model for technological policy issues and technology transfer developed in chapter three (see Figures 3.4–3.7). It is important that the trends of technological change initiated through the transfer of technology be analysed at various levels. Also, depending on the nature of these trends, conclusions must be drawn and decisions made; this is because evaluation can: (a) indicate opportunities for or threats to a country or sector as a whole (level 1 in this conceptual model; see Figure 6.5) or to an organisation (level 2); (b) influence basic corporate or national objectives and policy; and (c) directly affect the technology employed in an individual organisation.

The model elaborated here essentially sets out the various stages involved in defining technological objectives (that is, the formal planning procedure). Once the basic objectives and guidelines for importing and utilising technology have been laid down by policy-makers and planners, the stages described in this model will be suitable and applicable to developing countries. This basic model provides an essential framework for establishing an appropriate and reliable technological planning system in a developing country.

We shall now describe in detail each of the principal elements in the model:

1. The *information base* provides the foundations upon which the technological policies and plans of a country, sector or an organisation are established. Its contents, as described earlier, therefore bear a close relationship to the basic objectives of a national techno-economic or developmental plan. To put it differently, the information base deals with the status of the efforts and activities of a given organisation or sector within which the transferred technology will be utilised. It is concerned with all aspects of the new environment in which the candidate technology will be operated: at the macro or national level, as well as at the micro or organisational level.

2. *Opportunities* are stated within the information base, and describe the existing technological and socio-economic potential for development in a given country, sector or firm. They represent the local advantages and performance levels towards which the country or firm can direct its capabilities (see the discussion in chapter four) and its efforts. Ordinarily, opportunities represent the maximum benefits and outcomes that can be gained through technology acquisition and utilisation in the long and the short terms.

3. *Objectives* are defined in the technological, socio-cultural and economic arenas, and should satisfy the requirements of the national protocol for technology transfer. Objectives may be construed as levels of activity that are taken as goals. They preferably

lie beyond past performance levels but within the limits prescribed by the opportunities. Objectives are believed to be within reach of the planned resources of the country or firm.

4. *Strategies* follow on the basis of the chosen level of objectives. Strategies are the means proposed in order to reach the level of objectives set within the upper limit of possibilities represented by opportunities.

Once these essential elements have been determined, the basic interests and objectives, priorities and guidelines for technological change and transfer of foreign technology are brought into the fold of the technology transfer system. This system consists of three inter-related subsystems: a system of technology assessment, a system of technology implementation, and a system of technology control and feedback. The defined overall objectives, policies and priorities, which are established in conformity with the national protocol for technology transfer, along with the characteristics of candidate technologies provide a solid basis for the stage of technology evaluation within the technology transfer system (see Figure 6.5). Clearly, the stages of implementation, defining action programmes, budgeting, monitoring and control, as consequential procedures, follow the final stage of evaluation (that is, technology selection) at the operational or project level.

The lack of effectiveness or failure of many imported technologies in a number of developing countries is due to the fact that they are almost always chosen at random. Accordingly, a crucial objective of this research has been to understand the key factors and criteria within an appropriate approach to technology transfer, which enables a technology to be evaluated and selected within a restricted spectrum of opportunities.

The evaluation of technological options is a crucial task for strategic planning systems in developing countries. Due to the inherent complexities of the evaluation process and the lack of structured information, evaluation is also a difficult task. The evaluation process must consider both *external* opportunities and threats, and *internal* strengths and weaknesses. Following the approach developed in this book, an attempt should be made to define and analyse the leading 'internal' factors within a quantitative model. Due to the lack of reliable data in developing countries, however, we cannot define an absolute quantitative model. Therefore, the establishment of a qualitative methodology or approach as a supportive tool of measurement will facilitate the fulfilment of the task.

TOWARDS AN INTEGRATED MODEL OF
TECHNOLOGY TRANSFER

The conceptual elaboration of a technology transfer planning system offered here provides a solid basis for the development of a complementary 'integrated model' in any given developing country. Such a model would comprise a quantitative decision-making framework for technology assessment and selection within the process of technology transfer to developing countries. The proposed model is based on a decision-making methodology specifically evolved for technology transfer. Assessment and decision models may be classified into two categories: the 'small model', which provides insights and structures for thinking, and the 'general model', which allows the synthesis of a variety of phenomena (Boer 1987). The small model identifies relevant issues in the decision, forcing users to provide plausible inputs to satisfy model queries. General models, on the other hand, provide a structure for assembling measurements and criteria from a variety of sources to solve a given problem. The 'integrated technology transfer model' should be classified as a general synthesis model because of its flexibility in accounting for country- or sector-specific issues as well as rapidly changing technology alternatives from the perspective of sustainable technology transfer.

Decision making for the assessment of a single technology or a group of technologies for transfer should ideally be a structured process. In general, decision-making processes span the continuum from highly structured to highly unstructured processes (Dalal & Yadav 1992; H. Simon 1960). Structured decisions deal with routine and repetitive problems for which standard solutions exist, whereas unstructured decisions involve complex problems for which there are no clear solutions (especially in developing countries). In unstructured problems, due to the lack of data and intrinsic knowledge of the problem, the information needed for the solution cannot be described in detail before making the decision. The evaluation and selection of technology for transfer may be regarded as a 'human decision-making process', which may be divided into three phases: intelligence, design and choice. The intelligence phase involves searching for conditions and situations that call for a decision. In the design phase, possible courses of action (for example, criteria, attributes, effective factors) are devised, developed and analysed. The choice phase entails selection of a course of action from the options generated.

In an unstructured decision, none of these three phases is structured. This situation is typical of decisions to adopt transferred technology into a new environment. A viable model for technology assessment and adoption decisions would guide users through these three phases of the decision sequence. A complex set of options must initially be analysed with respect to both qualitative and quantitative criteria in order to determine the options that would best meet the needs and requirements of a specific country or sector. An integrated decision model such as that proposed here would help achieve an appropriate ranking of options for this multi-criterial decision. It is important that the decision-making group consist of experts in related fields and in the techno-economic system of the country. The social dimensions of the authorised expert group, it must be remembered, affect the process of assessment and decision making. The group of experts must work through the system, discovering specific criteria relevant to the country, sector or firm, and ranking options with respect to these criteria. To complete the loop, the preference evaluation model is incorporated; this will ensure that the chosen option meets the performance requirements identified for the country or sector.

The component set for carrying out the process of technology assessment should therefore include: (a) a set of multiple criteria for the analysis of options; (b) the specifications of the technology options being considered; and (c) the performance results of the option ultimately chosen. The integrated technology assessment model allows the analysis of several criteria and facts simultaneously or concurrently (see Kahen 1997a, 2001b, 2001c). These criteria may be either quantifiable, such as economic variables (hard currency, costs, national capacity), or non-quantifiable, such as environmental impacts, cultural impacts or level of service. Quite often, the criteria under consideration are in opposition with each other; the achievement of one criterion is accomplished at the expense of another.

Such a multiple criterion model takes into account decision-makers' subjective evaluations, most often accomplished through pairwise ratings and ranking sets and through subjective estimation. Integrating both qualitative and quantitative factors, the authorised expert decision-making group addresses a range of issues, from the determination of relevant criteria and of the reasons why the transfer of a technology is important for the process of techno-economic development (which is based on the national strategic planning system of the country, as discussed earlier; see Figures 3.6–3.8), to the consideration of which option to select, and finally the evaluation of how the technology adopted can affect the socio-cultural and techno-economic systems of the country (that is, the identification of technological opportunities and threats). This integrated approach also allows the national protocol for technology transfer to be established through the three rational steps in decision making described earlier. In investigating why a candidate technology (or technologies) is needed, the 'intelligence phase' of the decision process is completed. The consideration of options with respect to country- or sector-specific criteria concludes the 'design phase' of the decision process, while the tracking of the impact and performance of the chosen option represents the 'choice phase' of the decision.

To recapitulate the main points of our argument, a multi-criterial decision process requires the analysis of both non-quantitative and quantitative factors, and must also consider subjective evaluations. An integrated decision model allows users to rank criteria and options. The decision-making body consists either of 'knowledgeable' governmental authorities or a set of individual experts. The integrated model of technology transfer provides a thorough, systematic process for decision making, which is accomplished through the integration of three independent decision models. The integrated system also ensures smooth transitions between decision phases, and a more complete analysis of the technology option that is selected and implemented.

STEPS IN THE PROCESS OF TECHNOLOGY ASSESSMENT

As we have argued, the process of technology transfer must be viewed as a dynamic system, which affects and is affected by all levels of a country's techno-economic system. Assessment of candidate technologies should therefore be carried out at both 'macro' and 'micro' levels, and should be subjected to a 'structured decision process'. The structure of the decision process is based on the macro planning system and on the national protocol for technology transfer analysed in previous chapters. It involves a logical, systematic and comprehensive procedure for selecting technology(ies) that will achieve the country's or firm's objectives, and consists of the following seven steps:

1. Recognition of interests and priorities and problem definition
2. Specification of the goals to be achieved by employment of the technology and their relative importance

3. Enumeration of technology options
4. Definition of criteria and their relative weights
5. Evaluation of each option
6. Selection of the optimum option(s)
7. Controlled implementation (from physical technology transfer to technology development)

The integrated technology assessment model prescribes an appropriate theoretical basis, appropriate techniques for each stage of decision making, as well as quantifiable frameworks for the strategic choice of technology for any given developing country.

7

GLOBALISATION AND TECHNOLOGY TRANSFER

POST-WTO AND A NEW PERSPECTIVE

The world economy is undergoing fundamental structural changes. These changes are driven by the globalisation of business as well as by the revolution in information and communication technology (Kahen 2001a; Pohjola 2002; Rao 2001). Nations have entered the new millennium with this powerful technology in hand, fundamentally transforming the way in which business is conducted around the globe. The removal of restrictions in international trade, further, has enabled countries to have easy and ready access to one another's domestic markets. At the beginning of the 21st century, a new reform movement has emerged, more techno-economy-centred, more market-conscious, and more influenced by the policy shift towards deregulation.

Over the last 50 years, trade expansion has made a major contribution to development. The promotion of techno-economic growth and development is a fundamental objective of the World Trade Organisation (WTO) and the multilateral trading system, as recognised in the WTO Agreement. For developing countries to benefit from this open, rules-based system, they need comprehensive assistance (for instance, through the WTO or UNCTAD) in order to address capacity deficits and supply-side constraints. Building on its past efforts, the WTO has evolved a new strategy for technical and technological assistance that integrates trade into overall development strategies. This necessitates the development of an integrated approach to the management of technology transfer and capacity building for development and economic reform. If such an approach is to be successful, it is crucial that technology and trade related activities generate mutual benefits for both parties involved in these transactions. Mutuality is an important strategic element within the process of technology transfer in the post-WTO era. Information technology, too, plays a key supporting role in the new technical assistance strategy of the WTO. It brings into cross-border relations a stronger presence of 'scales' in trade that were once local or sub-national. The WTO has created for this purpose a network of 104 computerised information centres ('reference centres'): 41 in the least developed countries, 42 in developing countries and 21 in regional and subregional organisations (WTO 2001a).

THE WTO AND DEVELOPING COUNTRIES

The WTO provides the framework for the conduct of international trade in goods and services and for the protection of intellectual property rights (Das 1999). The WTO superseded the General Agreement on Tariffs and Trade (GATT) in 1994, when GATT 1947, the older version of the GATT Agreement, was replaced by GATT 1994 (the new version of the General Agreement incorporated into the WTO), which governs trade in goods. The WTO administers the implementation of a set of agreements that contain disciplinary measures relating mainly to governments and also to some enterprises. In the pre-WTO period, most firms in developing countries functioned under restrictive regimes in terms of both investment and trade in technology, services and goods.

It is evident that no nation has ever attained development and affluence through isolation, and this is why acceptance of the principles of free trade and globalisation has been encouraged in most developing countries. In the debate on the costs and benefits to both private and state-owned companies from accession to the WTO by a developing country, different views exist. On the one hand, accession to the WTO by a developing country would break the monopoly of indigenous firms and severely hurt national interests. On the other hand, WTO membership would initiate a new round of institutional reforms that would alter the economic as well as the political rules of the game in fundamental ways. However, there is evidence that developing countries that have opened their markets to trade in technologies, goods and services

Figure 7.1: Delivery of WTO technical assistance by region in 2001

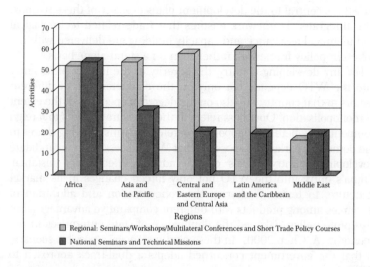

Source: http://www.wto.orgenlishres

have prospered much more than those that have not. The former's technological needs, trading experiences and capacities have been extremely diverse, and so WTO technical assistance efforts essentially consist of two core activities: providing legal and economic advice, and providing training in the purpose and implementation of WTO agreements. Figure 7.1 presents a general overview of WTO technical assistance activities to developing countries by region.

In many developing countries, pro-market reforms have encouraged faster growth, diversification of exports, and more effective participation in the multilateral trading system. While export growth in these countries rose from 4.3 per cent a year in the 1980s to 6.4 per cent in the 1990s, GDP growth per capita increased from 0.4 per cent per year to 1.5 per cent per year over the same period (WTO 2001c). Accordingly, the average non-weighted tariff applied by major trading partners to developing countries' exports fell from 10.6 per cent to 6.9 per cent in the first quarter of 2001. In addition, the Integrated Framework (IF)—the joint technical assistance programme for least developed countries (LDCs) involving the IMF, ITC, UNCTAD, UNDP, the World Bank and the WTO—has been redesigned, and is now in operation on a pilot basis in a number of these countries. The IF will help ensure the growth of trade, which, as an engine of continuous improvement in the process of technology transfer and growth, is central to the development plans of many of these nations. The Integrated Framework ensures that trade related technological and technical assistance and capacity building are delivered within a coherent policy framework rather than on a stand-alone basis.

For any developing country, the severity of the impact of its entry into the WTO depends not only on the characteristics of different sectors in that country, but also on the degree of openness or the extent of monopolisation. Openness refers to the exposure of firms to foreign competition, whereas monopolisation refers to firms' existing shares in the domestic market. It is possible that WTO accession by a candidate developing country entails certain adverse effects. For instance, China's entry into the WTO not only forced changes in its market structure, in terms of altering the concentration and allocation of resources among products with different comparative advantages, but also profoundly weakened the dominance of state enterprises in the economy (A. Chen 2000). In these circumstances, a possible scenario is that the government concerned adopts a dual-track approach to WTO accession, by implementing one set of game rules for foreigners and another set for domestic players (in other words, enforcing different rules for domestic and foreign businesses). Given the enormous gap between most developing countries' current political scenario and the game rules in force in these countries on the one hand, and WTO rules on the other, this scenario is more than likely to occur in many cases. By virtue of this dual-track approach, foreign companies may engage in international trade without trade licences, whereas domestic firms would be required to obtain them. Such a situation may exacerbate inefficient and unequal income distribution, institutionalise state corruption, lower moral standards, and increase social tension, factors that destabilise a country's political system. It is true that the WTO's operating principle of liberalisation can cause dislocation and is misleading for many developing countries. Many NGOs (see Khor 2000; LeClair 2002) have concluded that some clauses in the WTO Agreement have no place in a trade organisation that is supposed to promote liberalisation, and not protectionism over technology.

GLOBALISATION AND ITS IMPACT

Society in the 21st century is being shaped by new and powerful forces. The most important among these include the globalisation of

Figure 7.2: Shift in market strategy from local presence to the global market

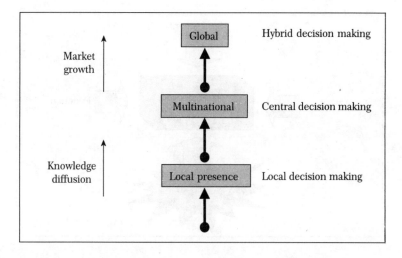

economic activity (Reiko 2001), the growing importance accorded to knowledge and high technology as prerequisites for participation in fundamental human affairs, and the increasing democratisation of socio-political systems. Globalisation has occurred both in terms of economics and the diffusion of knowledge. It may be defined as the process of compression of the world and the intensification of the consciousness of the world as a whole (Robertson 1992). The new global concept is the new world order represented by a global economy.

Several forces drive the present global business landscape. In terms of management, traditional organisational boundaries defined by formal functions, positions, titles and procedures are no longer sufficient for supporting high-performance, globally distributed work. Companies in developing countries find themselves seeking a rapid growth in international markets, expanding from local presence to multinational (or multi-local) presence and eventually the global market (see Figure 7.2). A major feature of this strategic change is the change in the type of decision making, which varies in orientation from 'local' to 'central' and finally 'hybrid' decision making. The new global strategy, based on the WTO Agreement, yields various advantages, such as economies of scale, higher levels of competition, knowledge diffusion, excellent innovative practices, diversification, and easy-to-change products. An organisation's ability to acquire and manage knowledge from around the world determines

Figure 7.3: New world trade and geography as an active dimension in organisational balance

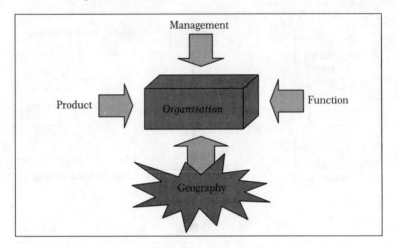

the level of its competitive advantage. 'Geography' now appears as an important factor in maintaining organisational balance in the new trade era (Figure 7.3). In other words, in addition to management, function and product—the three principal elements previously responsible for forming a balanced organisational structure—the active 'geographical' dimension has opened a new global window for both international business and technological management. It provides fresh insights into balancing the traditional elements as well as related strategies for working effectively with people of different cultures. Technological infrastructures by themselves tend to overwhelm workers with information without providing them the means to make sense of the various worlds they work in.

Intergenerational issues between the ageing developed societies and the young and maturing, developing and emerging economies will continue to frame issues related to business and work. As workers in emerging economies continue to complete higher levels of education, they will become part of the skilled global workforce. In the new century, more than half of the employees in MNCs will be from developing country affiliates (Saveri 1999). This trend will continue to emphasise the need for cross-cultural management and work practices. There will be no single context for global work. A new consumer is also emerging globally—with a higher level of income, education and familiarity with information and communication technology. New technological developments emerge and diffuse more rapidly throughout society at a global level, changing the context for defining work, relationships, identities and organisational assumptions.

With the advent of globalisation, free trade and market competition will provide the context for the integration of the world (Wen 2000). Three principal forces drive globalisation. The first is the explosive growth in low-cost technology (that is, information and communications technology) that is connecting people and places and promoting a greater awareness of international economic opportunities (see Amesse & Cohendet 2001; Fagan 2001). The steady dismantling of the trade barriers erected just before and during the Great Depression of the 1930s has been the second major driving force behind globalisation. Finally, widespread economic restructuring and liberalisation have wrought changes in the landscape of competition. Globalisation, it is true, does not benefit every nation equally and automatically. 'Creative destruction' is the term economists use to describe the ultimate engine of growth in a market economy (Acs et al. 2001). It takes vision and foresight to see the fundamental trend underlying this unfolding process. Indeed, globalisation demands hard work and wisdom in finding flexible institutions to adapt to this precarious historical process socially and institutionally before a nation can benefit from it. In other words, globalisation raises the stakes. It demands deeper cross-boundary collaboration among people from diverse contexts—social, cultural, technical and organisational— with shorter deadlines, higher investments and wider social and organisational impacts. Given the high stakes involved in such collaboration, organisations in both developed and developing countries need a new social infrastructure.

Economic globalisation is seen by many as a driving force of global techno-economic growth (Tisdell 2001). While opinion is divided about the benefits of this process, as highlighted by the WTO meeting in Seattle in late 1999, it is clear that globalisation will affect the nature, mode and quantum of technology transfer. The precise nature of this impact is difficult to predict (Siddharthan 1999), but it would seem that along with better protection for intellectual property and an increase in foreign direct investment, the role of MNCs in transferring technology and international trade will increase.

Apart from its technological and socio-economic implications, globalisation might be expected to have a positive environmental impact. Many believe that the WTO and the trend towards economic globalisation also have positive implications for economic efficiency and sustainable development (Hansen 1990; Sebastian & Alicbusan 1989).

Environmental pessimists, however, argue that the impact of globalisation-induced growth on resource use can be expected to more than offset any efficiency gains in resource use. They warn of possible negative consequences for the environment and for sustainable development (K. Anderson 1998; Greenpeace 1997; Lang & Hines 1993; Tisdell 1999, 2001; WWF 1999). However, the fact is that an adequate stimulus to techno-economic growth generated by economic globalisation will produce a positive impact on the environment, provided the economic growth is large enough. In the post-WTO era, the economic growth of developing countries may even stimulate the development of new resource-saving technologies (Ramirez et al. 2001; Tisdell 2001). With further growth, existing technology may be replaced more quickly by the new technology, which, in general, is likely to promote greater efficiency in resource use and to be more environment-friendly.

The role of the WTO in relation to global environmental polices and the goal of sustainable development remains unsettled (Tisdell 2001). It seems unlikely that the WTO will be able to avoid greater policy involvement in these areas in the future, although given the current international institutional arrangements in which the WTO plays an important role, it is probable that global economic growth stimulated by trade liberalisation and globalisation will indeed promote sustainable economic development. However, it might be idealistic to expect the general political support of WTO members given developing countries' preferences, environmental priorities and related issues. In this regard, it is now evident that any conceptual and methodological issues in technology transfer should also emphasise the multiple levels of collaboration required between governments, NGOs and private entities to ensure the adoption of environmentally sound technology. Contingently, however, the ISO 14000 series of environmental management standards can foster a greater ecological conscience in industrial sectors, and thus enhance the quality of technology transfer (see, for example, Morrow & Rondinelli 2002; UNCTAD 1997).

One of the reasons why economic globalisation may accelerate an increase in the ratio of 'man-made capital' over 'natural capital' is that it has facilitated foreign direct investment and increased the scope for expansion of MNCs. The fact that WTO rules are designed to encourage international investment has considerable consequences both for technology transfer and for the economic systems of developing countries. Although sustainable development is mentioned in the preamble to the WTO Agreement (Halle 2000), the stated objective of GATT and WTO is to provide a secure and predictable international trading environment for the business community, and to ensure a continuing process of trade liberalisation in which investments, job creation and trade can thrive. This environment is governed by the new knowledge-based economy, and driven by rapid innovations in technology, process and organisation. It will eventually shift the focus away from regional competition in existing markets towards targeted collaboration in order to create new markets. It may be mentioned in this connection that negotiation on geographical indications[1] was one of the WTO issues that appeared on the agenda of the Doha WTO 2001 Ministerial Conference. Geographical indications are a multilateral system for notifying and registering place names or names associated with a place, used to identify the origin and quality, reputation or other characteristics of products.

TECHNOLOGY TRANSFER POST-WTO

The main provisions of the WTO that influence technology transfer and global competition are included under the following sections: Trade Related Aspects of Intellectual Property Rights (TRIPs), Trade Related Investment Measures (TRIMs), Subsidies and Countervailing Measures (SCMs) and the Information Technology Agreement (Siddharthan 1999). The Doha WTO 2001 Ministerial Conference ended with an agreement on a new programme, spelt out in two declarations—the main declaration, and one on intellectual property and public health—and one decision on developing countries' difficulties in implementing current WTO agreements. As the majority of WTO members are developing countries, the Conference sought to place their needs and interests at the heart of the work programme adopted in its Doha declaration. This represents an attempt by the WTO to help developing countries secure beneficial and meaningful integration into the multilateral trading system and the global economy. Therefore, a better public understanding of the WTO and of the benefits of a liberal, rules-based, multilateral trading system needs to be promoted at the national and multilateral levels in these countries. There is no doubt that technology will appear at the heart of such a system. The Conference also strongly reaffirmed WTO commitment to

---

[1] A part of the WTO's intellectual property arrangements or, more accurately, of its programme on Trade Related Aspects of Intellectual Property Rights (TRIPs).

the objective of sustainable development, as stated in the preamble to the Marrakech Agreement (WTO 2001b). Accordingly, it is now recognised that sustainable development must be 'mutually supportive', and that, under WTO rules, no country should be prevented from taking measures for the protection of human, animal or plant life, or health, or of the environment at the levels it considers appropriate.

In the pre-WTO regime, foreign firms were required to source components and materials from the host country. This resulted in the parallel transfer of technology to component manufacturers and improved the designing capabilities of firms. The increasing share of developing countries in world trade will be complemented by the opening up of large sectors of their economies to global competition, which may further improve the effectiveness of technology management in these countries. Entry into the WTO will give them a further boost by breaking down restrictive barriers and opening the channels for direct investment and technology transfer from outside. As a matter of fact, further economic liberalisation and integration into the global economy will undoubtedly be a stimulus to regulatory, institutional and cultural change within developing countries. In the post-WTO regime, the main competition will come from technology and diversified new products. Competition will then depend on the easy and instant access of organisations and nations to the Internet and to electronic commerce (e-commerce).

As highlighted by the Doha Conference, market access and technical assistance form the main focus of the WTO's efforts to improve the condition of developing countries within the multilateral trading system. A major problem developing countries face is the implementation of current WTO agreements. This requires, on the one hand, action to promote more effective implementation of technology transfer provisions in general, and, on the other, a greater stress on developed countries' obligations to provide incentives for their enterprises and institutions to transfer technology to the least developed countries in particular. Clearly, developing countries acceding to the WTO also have to learn and to understand how the WTO works. They need to draft domestic laws that comply with WTO rules, establish mechanisms for enforcing those rules, and negotiate suitable conditions of entry into the WTO with existing members. This will eventually remove restrictions on the free flow of information among sectors and organisations in developing countries, enabling them to remain in business and be competitive. As we said earlier, import–export restrictions in the pre-WTO period compelled MNCs to transfer technology to component manufacturers in the host countries (Siddharthan 1999). But it is now profitable for them to import the whole product and sell it in the host country. This may mean that, in the post-WTO regime, knowledge transfer from developed to developing countries is significantly reduced. Such a situation may be avoided by evolving a mutually beneficial context for technology transfer.

One of the broader implications of the post-WTO era for developing countries is the delivery of significant market access opportunities specifically for these countries by the WTO. The current technological context is more knowledge- and information-intensive, and concomitantly less natural-resources-intensive or materials-intensive. In order to facilitate strategies of technological transformation, the urgent need of the hour is to improve infrastructure, introduce administrative reforms and accountability, and ensure transparent decision making for efficiency-seeking foreign investment in these countries. Entry into the WTO also entails diverse individual and systematic impacts on each of the three major sectors: industry, agriculture and services (Blouin 2000). Apart from the implications for other sectors, physical trade and the less visible trade in services require a financial infrastructure in the same way 'that new buildings need plumbing and electrical wiring' (Yam 2001). Thus, WTO entry also entails a surge in the banking business in these countries. Two main issues in this connection are: (a) the greater demand for banking services, resulting from the growth induced by the effects of WTO accession; and (b) the financial deepening stimulated by more rapid financial liberalisation, greater banking competition, and product innovation induced by the terms of WTO accession. The WTO is also an appropriate enabler for offering assistance to make the best use of the intellectual property systems of these countries. The WTO's Integrated Framework, based on the 'mutual beneficiary' approach, provides a supportive and constructive leverage for technology transfer to developing countries.

The phenomenon of economic globalisation has meant that national economies are being increasingly subsumed into a global economy (Dudley 1998). The discipline of international markets and money markets, rather than national, social and political priorities, increasingly determines public policy. As a result, policies require states to reduce public spending, encourage deregulation and enforce cutbacks in welfare intensity. The management of technology transfer is no exception to this process. Less public money, particularly in developing countries, is available for highly technical training and education. The new budget tends to be concentrated on technology, science and market related fields. Globalisation stimulates changes in R&D and higher education practices, making the situation more techno-science-oriented and more sensitive to industrial policy and intellectual property strategies (see the discussion in chapter five of this volume). Moreover, international technology alliances represent a new form of internationalisation of technological activity (Rao 2001; Saggi 2000), a development quite consistent with the trend towards decentralised R&D under the integrated network type of organisation. If developing countries are to take full advantage of increased trade, the liberalisation of trade and of foreign investment policies needs to be complemented by appropriate policy changes with respect to education, R&D and human capital accumulation.

In relation to the WTO's policies, the diversification and institutionalisation of technology transfer management are viewed as emerging requirements in the current context. These processes contribute to the development and stimulation of developing countries' techno-economic systems. International trade and division of labour among nations open up an unlimited horizon for individuals and nations in their pursuit of enhanced welfare. A thriving New Economy for developing countries requires a high degree of diversity in institutions, investments and forms of control through both economic planning and technology management. In order to achieve diversification in technology transfer and dynamic socio-economic development, four interrelated reform measures are required:

1. cultivation by an organisation or a country of the ability to pursue its own ends
2. greater flexibility in the systems of techno-economic planning, research and education
3. responsible strategic management of decision making and implementation
4. establishment of a manageable pluralist evaluation system

On the basis of the supportive mechanisms engendered by the WTO, the first and second of these reform measures may promote national or organisational autonomy. The success of the third and fourth types of reform and of technology policy depends on the presence of a considerable degree of 'steering' and 'accountability' within the country's socio-economic infrastructure. The cultivation of the ability by a nation/organisation to pursue its own ends is necessary in a future intelligence-oriented society. Moreover, while an advanced, appropriate and diversified techno-economic planning system tends to promote more developmental, research-oriented technology transfer, diversification also leads to the establishment of local and professional technology management. The mutual beneficiary approach to technology transfer would also ensure autonomy for the concerned country or organisation.

Responsible decision making and implementation improve administrative structures so that sectors and organisations in developing countries can quickly and flexibly respond to the demands of society. The establishment of a plural evaluation system is considered necessary to enable countries/organisations to be more independent and to continually improve both their management of technology transfer and their research and development efforts. Technical and institutional socio-economic assessments at the country level are crucial prerequisites for determining the potential for success of a particular technology and its products in the free trade context. Thus, a new third-party evaluation system should be added to the conventional self-monitoring and self-evaluation systems. Given that a major problem in most developing countries is the shortage of resources (for example, hard currency), such an evaluation system can also make for an efficient allocation of resources.

Regional free trade agreements provide another context for trade promotion and techno-economic development, and as such have consequences for strategies of technological transformation. These are agreements made within a region in order to expand trade, which directly and indirectly affect the process of technology transfer both within these regions and in the world as a whole. Recent times have witnessed an increasing trend towards regionalisation, especially with the formation of new regional integrations outside the triad markets, particularly in East Asia, South America and southern Africa (Proff 2001). These are 'open' rather than 'closed' or isolated regionalisations. While in 1995, 76 per cent of worldwide GDP (World Bank 1997) was generated in the triad markets (6.1 per cent in the new integration areas), this proportion is predicted to fall to 62 per cent (OECD 1997) by the year 2020 (8.2 per cent in the new integration areas). Consequently, the new regional integrations formed by hitherto developing partner-countries are considered attractive fields of operation for all MNCs. These regionalisations also constitute a further step towards globalisation. The path of technology transfer too may be described as proceeding from an ethnocentric (home country) orientation, via a polycentric (national) orientation, towards a geocentric (global) orientation. The current 'region-centric' orientation may be considered as an intermediate stage between the polycentric and geocentric stages. The management of technology transfer, in parallel with the present international economic orientation, is now substantially market- and product-driven. It requires the re-understanding of technology transfer from the perspective of the knowledge-based economy in which countries or organisations manage the co-evolution of their absorptive capabilities and their knowledge transmission strategies.

A PROGRESSIVE MUTUAL BENEFICIARY FRAMEWORK

It is now accepted in most developing countries that their national economies should be based on the principles of dynamic comparative advantage and increasing returns to scale. These nations are willing to face the challenges that a dynamic international division of labour will pose to their national pride and to the vested interests of some domestic economic groups. By accepting the rules and regulations of the WTO, each developing country is committed to following suit and levelling most of its trade and investment barriers against other countries within a certain time period. There is no doubt that accession to the WTO will bring many opportunities to developing countries in both the technological and the socio-economic spheres. As a developing country allows foreign technology or capital gradually to enter its various sectors, such as its heavy or soft industries, agriculture (Rolle & Satin 2002), telecommunications (Blouin 2000; Tarjanne 1999) and financial sectors, the rest of the world too will further open its markets to that country's products. Therefore, in order to generate a mutual beneficiary context for the new trade system, developing countries will have to take further steps to liberalise their economies and provide intellectual property protection as per the provisions of TRIPs, which also leaves enough scope for member nations to develop their own intellectual property rights laws so as to promote their national interests.

Multinationals have emerged as the major drivers of trade and techno-economic activity in developing countries. As these activities become more and more globalised, MNCs will have to reconsider their roles in this process. In terms of technology transfer management, MNCs influence the operations of local firms as well as the definition of economic development and industrial policies in these countries. It is clear that MNCs (as the main technology suppliers to developing countries) have different goals from the national goals of developing countries. In a mutual beneficiary scenario, an MNC may be regarded as effective if, along with maximising its own economic benefits, it attempts systematically to improve the host country's technological capabilities. Not only the mode of technology transfer but the rate of transfer and the direction of the benefits from transfer for a developing country depend upon MNCs' behaviour and upon the existence of the potential for trade as well as the existing levels of technological and managerial capabilities in that country.

In the new world economic order, developing countries are no longer willing to be passive recipients of technology without the promise of longer-term sustainable growth and the transfer of skills. The recent history of technology transfer shows that the conventional processes of transfer earn profits for MNCs but often leave the host country depleted in resources and lacking in modern technological knowledge. A rational system of technology transfer through MNCs necessitates the development of a complementary framework that would establish a 'mutual' network of developmental, technological, managerial and economic benefits for both parties involved in the process of transfer. Mutuality of benefits, in our view, is the dynamic element that will make for progressive transactions in the global techno-economic order and in world trade. The basic principle underlying this approach is to balance the interests of various contrasting parameters.

In terms of the general system of technology transfer with its three subsystems introduced in chapter three, S_3, or the third subsystem (that is, the MNC as primary technology supplier), is the part of the model that requires adjustment in the post-WTO era (see Figure 7.4). (To recapitulate briefly, the model provides a comprehensive perspective on transfer by incorporating three subsystems, viz., the national and international subsystems and MNCs, in the following manner: S_1 comprises the developing country's system for technology transfer; S_2 the international support system including organisations such as the WTO, UNCTAD and the UNDP; and S_3 represents the MNCs as major international technology suppliers.) The reforms prescribed by the WTO necessitate changes in the country's national planning system (S_1) towards the achievement of an open, rules-based trade system. Similarly, a revised framework is also needed on the supplier side (S_3). This framework provides a new perspective for the achievement of an effective process of technology transfer in the post-WTO era of globalisation.

Figure 7.4: The post-WTO era and the adjustment of two subsystems within the general system of technology transfer

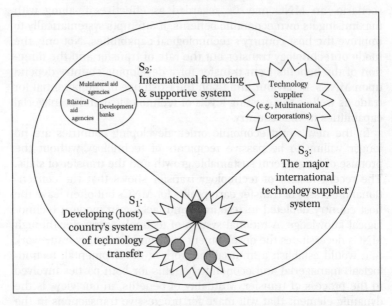

The problems regarding benefits generated from R&D produce some of the most important conflicts between MNCs and developing countries. In an effective process of transfer, MNCs (as technology suppliers) who base their activities on the principle of mutuality of benefits cannot exclude ethical considerations, represented by WTO agreements, values, notions of appropriateness and financial behaviour, in their interactions with host nations. The structure selected for monitoring these interactions should be the one that most easily enables the parties involved to achieve their trade related and techno-economic objectives throughout the life of their business relationship. It is possible both to increase the MNC's own economic benefits and to improve the host country's technological and production systems through convergency in a particular field (see, for example, Sedaitis 2000). In order to choose the best market and technology strategies for firms in developing countries, it is necessary for them, first, to change existing business strategies in order to enter the new international market, and, second, to adapt to changing conditions with respect to the company's particular product or service. Multinational firms supplying technology must also find a suitable market strategy for their products or services in a particular country.

This includes the way both parties (the developing country and the technology supplier) plan their operations on a worldwide basis for higher productivity.

Post-WTO, governments and MNCs may be expected to formulate stable processes for technology transfer. This means that MNCs will be forced to develop a more balanced approach to their global policies that makes all countries where they operate equal partners and stockholders in their enterprises. This two-way (bilateral) process entails technical and economic benefits for all parties. For developing countries, the major benefits from future equitable trade include a substantial market combined with the long-term promise of growth.

Towards a New Perspective

Many developing countries have opened their markets to foreign providers of high technology, banking, insurance and telecommunication services because they want to attract much-needed expertise and foreign investment. In the new world trade system, any monopoly-oriented, single-beneficiary perspective on technology transfer is unacceptable. The rationale of the post-WTO regime and of economic globalisation is firmly rooted in the promise of mutual beneficiality from international trade. The establishment of a fair and market-oriented trading system is now essential in each developing country in order to prepare it for the new arena represented by globalisation. The strategic policy backbone of this new international system is aimed at promoting technology management and the economic growth of trading partners along with the development of developing countries. These goals are directly and indirectly addressed by the supportive initiatives of the WTO in regard to facilitating and sustaining the process of technology transfer to developing countries for enhanced technical assistance and capacity building. The supportive role played by the WTO also includes policy analysis and development for a more rigorous evaluation of the implications of closer multilateral cooperation for the development policies and objectives of developing nations, human and institutional development in these countries, as well as the enhancement of the mutual supportiveness of trade and technology management.

The challenge now is for the international trading system to address comprehensively the issue of transfer of technology to developing countries in order to ensure that the latter become equal partners in the global effort towards world prosperity. This will require strengthening the provisions in WTO agreements that seek to promote developing countries' access to modern technology. In our view, an effective framework should initially adopt a global outlook with regard to technology demand and the consumer market in developing countries, for improving local economic and technological capabilities as well as enhancing world trade.

It is also necessary to emphasise strongly the need for a multilateral framework that will help to secure stable and predictable conditions for long-term cross-border investment, particularly foreign direct investment. Any framework should reflect in a balanced manner the interests of technology suppliers, home and host countries. On the basis of a mutual beneficiary approach, this framework will provide a supportive and constructive leverage for technology transfer to developing countries. Cooperation with other intergovernmental organisations, including UNCTAD, may provide strengthened and adequate resource assistance to respond to relevant needs. To this end, steps have been taken with the mandate of the WTO to increase flows of technology transfer to developing nations. In addition, the delivery of WTO technical assistance should be designed to assist developing countries that are in the process of transition to adjust to WTO rules and disciplinary measures: for instance, by helping them to derive the benefits of an open, rules-based multilateral trading system. Clearly, the process of technology transfer to developing countries is now dominated by the multilateral trading system and trade related technology management.

Conclusion

Indicators for a Successful Technology Transfer Process

The development of developing nations consists in socio-economic growth, which is spurred in most cases by industrial growth. The latter, in turn, depends on technological development, most readily achieved through the medium of technology transfer from developed country sources. However, the history of technology transfer has not been one of unqualified success. Many failures have occurred, for reasons that have not always been clear. The aim of the present book has been to help reduce such failures by formulating a practical approach or methodology that will make it possible for planners to improve the chances of success of a process that is extremely important for many developing countries.

A critical review of the literature suggested that various factors of evident importance in the process of transfer have not always been paid due attention. We concluded that a careful reconsideration of all relevant issues was justified. Thus, the present volume investigates the process of technology transfer by starting out from first principles: an exploration of the nature of technology itself. Four aspects (or components) of technology are observed to be involved in the transfer process: we refer to these as technoware, humanware, orgaware and inforware. Each comprises vital elements that must be addressed in reaching decisions about technology transfer. Further, these aspects generate the criteria that form the basis for the most critical stage in the transfer process: the selection of a suitable technology in the light of national circumstances (that is, given the characteristics of the national techno-economic system).

Technology transfer suffers from the lack of systematic study and comprehensive quantitative modelling—lacunae that this book has attempted to bridge. We approached the task by identifying important 'missing' factors, generating a realistic and suitable model of the demand side of technology transfer to developing countries that takes into account these various factors, and establishing how best to handle them. Based on this understanding, we offfered a consistent, general approach to technology transfer to developing countries. A major problem, it may be noted, is acquiring the necessary information on which rational decisions—and technology selection—can be based. Few developing countries have the resources to acquire data of adequate reliability and, in any event, much of the essential information cannot be expressed in quantitative terms.

Adoption of the strategic modelling approach presented in this book, we believe, will enhance the probability of transferring viable and appropriate technology. The receiver of technology should, of course, be able to sustain and maintain the transferred technology. For this reason, the technology assessment function is among the most difficult tasks that recipients of foreign technology encounter, especially given the high rate of technological proliferation and the increasing activism concerning issues of socio-cultural change in the world today. Apart from this, the rapid trend towards globalisation at the turn of the new millennium, as highlighted in chapter seven, has necessitated intensive structural changes in all aspects of development and the process of technology transfer.

With appropriate policy making and an effective techno-economic planning system in place, technology transfer can provide a unique opportunity for developing nations to accelerate their development efforts. The fundamental objectives underlying the transfer and utilisation of advanced technology coincide with general national socio-economic and technological goals: improving standards of living, and bettering the quality of social welfare.

INDICATORS FOR A SUCCESSFUL TRANSFER PROCESS

A number of conclusions may be drawn from our analysis. In the first place, except for some common technologies, it is not possible to consider technology as a product or as a physical tool. Thus, transfers do not respond to 'inducements' arising from a technology market, but usually depend on the objectives of the countries or organisations transferring and acquiring technology. Further, while it is relatively easy to identify changes brought about by transfers of production capacity that have direct and immediate effects on the techno-economic system, it is rather more difficult to record all the consequences of the gradual acquisition of know-how in the long term, except in the most general way.

There are serious difficulties in defining significant indicators that could measure the effectiveness of any particular mechanism of technology transfer. As an investigation of the Japanese style of technology transfer and development showed (Kahen 1995b, 1999), the effectiveness of any technology transfer also depends on local cultural institutions and indigenous management perspectives.

The following factors were identified in our analysis as likely to inhibit successful technology transfer:

- a limited general understanding of the concept of technology, and the lack of a consistent framework for its study
- lack of systematic planning for technology transfer in developing countries or the misunderstanding of its underlying philosophy
- lack of bilateral scientific/technological advantages in the process of technology transfer (mutual benefits)
- lack of a systematic and integrated engineering and socio-economic approach to the technology transfer process
- lack of a relevant quantitative framework/approach to the analysis and evaluation of technology transfer to developing countries
- the failure to include ergonomic aspects in technology transfer or to accord sufficient value to the human-machine interface variable of the transferred technology, or the failure to adjust the technology to the existing socio-cultural system
- inattention to environmental considerations and technology impact assessment
- failure to determine whether a national consensus and orientation exists for a transfer
- failure to recognise the local potential (cultural and economic) for adoption of the candidate technology (that is, failure to determine the availability of social and economic infrastructures)
- failure to determine if the existing national productive capacity is adequate to support the application of the transferred technology (technical and technological potential and infrastructures)
- restricting the feasibility study of technology transfer to financial assessments (mostly cost—benefit analysis)

- lack of any universally accepted perspective on relevant socio-economic as well as technological infrastructures in the process of technology transfer (commercial, legal, transportation, utilities and communication networks)
- absence of any substantial effort to review and utilise the potential of technological interchange and socio-technical collaboration for technology transfer between developing countries
- misunderstanding of the concept of technology appropriateness, hitherto confined to only small and non-capital-intensive technologies
- the presence of ethical problems within the technology transfer process
- failure to evaluate or consider 'conflict causing' factors pertaining to the transferred technology. These factors can be categorised into:

  1. 'sectoral conflict factors': conflicts that can arise within the techno-economic system
  2. 'rural–urban conflict factors' arising because of spatial (that is, regional) imbalances in the distribution of physical resources needed for a specific industry in the long term (for instance, sacrificing the existing production institutions in an area in order to initiate a new, imported, mostly large-scale technology), leading to
  3. factors 'disturbing the socio-cultural balance' that operates within the social system:

- due to the nonconformity of the transferred technology with the available potential, and with the inherent objectives of development policies and national techno-economic plans in developing countries; and
- due to the lack of specific software and any other sophisticated supportive tools for technological planning and technology assessment within the technology transfer framework.

Factors that we regarded as vital to understanding the process of transfer were represented by major variables in our heuristic framework for scrutinising the transfer process. For instance, in the discussion of technology undertaken in chapter two, we categorised technology components into the technoware, humanware, orgaware and inforware aspects of the technology transfer process. This enabled us to show how technology assessment may be undertaken within the integrated engineering—economic framework.

The approach we have evolved will prepare technology transfer decision-makers in developing countries to take up an unstructured problem, decide the important variables and attributes, structure the influences among these variables, apply their own or a group's (even politicians') preferences to the problem, exercise the systematic model, and make a proper decision.

FUNDAMENTAL ISSUES

The systematic methodology provided here can be applied at many levels of technology policy making—at the national, sectoral, organisational or specific technology level. We also pointed out that technology development may be accelerated and learning capability improved through *regional convergence* efforts. The existence of common problems, similar bottlenecks and common interests together with complementary potentials and shared ideologies within a group of developing countries could be a basis for establishing a convergence strategy for the transfer of a specific technology and its development (see Kahen & Sayers 1994). Previous experience in another country with similar beliefs and circumstances should provide a country with already identified, acceptable technological options, which can lead to quick technology assimilation. Furthermore, regional cooperation in telecommunications, communication and power utilities, and the availability of certain types of indigenous capabilities for infrastructure development in countries within a region, can also provide a convenient context for rapid progress in the transfer of particular technologies from country to country.

Assessment of any particular technology for transfer to developing countries should be carried out at two major levels: the micro and the macro levels. Improvement of an imported technology system in a given country, from an initial state to the subsequent state, is a function of its appropriateness, the coordination existing among the four components of technology within the imported system, and their interactions with the technological and social environments. For this reason, and in the light of existing constraints to the transfer and development of any particular technology in developing countries, it is proposed that in the first stage, transfer of the system's development methods, techniques, the bases of human-machine interactions and orga-managerial practices be given the highest priority. The transfer of technoware (machinery and technical know-how, hardware or, for instance, generic packaged software for information technology) may be teckled at the second stage of initial transfer.

Humanware[1] is another major factor with a crucial role to play in the dynamic process of technology transfer. Particular incentives should be offered to encourage utilisation of national human resources. *Risk evaluation* and the impact of emerging technologies on individuals and on the national techno-economic system are other concerns within the process of choice. According to the literature, much of risk assessment currently is based upon the impact on the behaviour of individual employees when new technologies are introduced. Consequently, there is a need to focus on the impact of new imported technology on the national techno-economic system (which differs according to the socio-cultural context of a developing country).

A public is required for the establishment of incentives for R&D as a fundamental support for technology transfer at the national and regional levels. A very important requirement is the development of a scientific infrastructure on a regional rather than simply a national basis, inasmuch as a growing number of productive activities will depend on scientific knowledge and not only on technological know-how. In fact, the realities of current and future technological change would indicate that a *national* approach to the production of equipment is clearly insufficient, and that a broader *regional* approach is required. In short, regionalism can play a significant role in successful technology transfer in the less developed world. The first steps in this respect are: setting uniform standards, development of local (for example, inter-province) scientific and technological information links, pilot regional programmes, and educational techniques for technology utilisation.

RECOMMENDATIONS

As stated earlier, this approach is applicable mostly at a national or an industry (or sectoral) level, where it may be used towards achieving national goals and in arriving at a good compromise solution. The choice of technology, however, depends not only on national goals or on government support, but also on other factors, such as a

---

[1] Consisting of both human resources and human factors (that is, human–computer/machine interactions).

company's or firm's profitability, knowledge management, financial ability and manager willingness. Therefore, it is necessary to develop a complementary model for the assessment of candidate technology in terms of beneficial (non-governmental) factors at the firm or organisational level.

As described in chapter five (see also Kahen 1996c, 1997c; Kahen & Griffiths 1995), one of the major factors responsible for the effectiveness of the process of technology transfer is the aspect of human factors engineering. We emphasised the necessity of incorporating relevant indicators for measuring ergonomic aspects within the model of comprehensive assessment of a technology for transfer.

As far as the energy industry (Kahen 1995a, 1997a, 2001b, 20001c; Kahen & Sayers 1995a, 1996b), the health sector (Kahen & Sayers 1996a, 1997), information technology (Kahen 1995b, 1996a, 1996b, 1999; Kahen & Griffiths 1996; Kahen & Sayers 1994, 1996a) and techno-economic resources allocation (Kahen & Sayers 1995a) are concerned, this book offers an opportunity for the development of a strategic technology assessment approach.

As pointed out in chapters five, six and seven (see also Kahen 1995b, 1996b, 1997b, 1999), institutional or behavioural obstacles constitute a major constraint on technological efficiency in developing countries. This constraint may be reflected in the inability to produce relevant information and to specify appropriate criteria at different levels (sectoral, organisational and national) in the process of technology assessment. However, the methodology developed here is able to overcome these difficulties by improving planning and managerial abilities to deal with a complex technological problem, and indicating an appropriate solution procedure in the environment of developing countries.

SUGGESTIONS

When applying this systematic assessment approach in developing countries, the following requirements/conditions must be met:

- technology analysts in a developing country must ensure that both *qualitative* and *quantitative* criteria have been considered when selecting technologies for industrial development
- preliminary feasibility studies for any technology transfer project (for example, with respect to communication, energy, health care,

information technology) should be conducted before applying this integrated multi-criterion approach
- the technologies selected should be subjected to a feasibility study for the stage of 'implementation'

As reflected in Figures 3.4–3.7 and in Figure 5.1, further work needs to be done to define the different types of information essential for the application of this approach. The technological planning system of the country should be fully understood, along with national development targets and systemic sectoral or organisational elements, as also the candidate technology system (see the discussion in chapters three and four). This would help in identifying the 'key factors' and 'constraints' on decision making as well as the limitations of existing resources for effective technology transfer. Defining objectives and constraints and potential resources is also necessary for the decision-making process involved in the technology assessment methodology developed in this book.

Chapters four, five, six and seven provided conceptual and theoretical frameworks useful for the development of an appropriate decision-making approach towards an effective process of technology transfer. This knowledge may be used as input in any appropriate quantifiable model of technology assessment in a given country.

The generality and usefulness of the approach presented here can be seen in terms of the concepts, theories and methods developed. They describe various aspects of the technological decision-making process, such as industrial or organisational effectiveness, the characteristics of the national or sectoral system of technology development, the appropriateness and effectiveness of technology transfer and bases of an individual, multi-criterion decision-making process. The soft system methodology incorporated in this approach is also quite general in its applicability. It provides a rigorous method that may be applied for defining problems in ill-structured situations (a common circumstance in developing countries), as well as a framework for evaluating potential solution procedures for the transfer and development of sustainable technology.

Our recommended modelling approach can help the concerned technology management authority collate and clarify various types of information systematically. This procedure could overcome any possible biases in the judgement of decision-makers. Finally, the approach can be useful for the optimum allocation of resources, and for choosing between technology proposals on the basis of the most relevant criteria so that capital can be committed to feasible, as well as profitable, ventures. This will also addresss the effect of the emerging move towards gloabalisation and post-WTO trends in international technology management and development in general, and in technological change in developing countries in particular.

Certain key variables in the decision-making process for technology transfer are identified and eleborated by the approach presented here, based on interactions with a developing country's environment and its context for technological change. This comprehensive study of the technology transfer process has been founded on the development of a 'joint engineering—management' approach to technology assessment. The technical and theoretical components of the approach comprise appropriate tools for analysing the multidimensional process of technology transfer. We also critically analysed the concept and paradigm of technology transfer and the system of technological development. The decision domain of technology *assessment,* however, is so complicated that questions such as what constitutes the optimum decision set and how to go about arriving at these decisions, or, in other words, which models and information (subjective and objective) are to be used, are matters that are still open to discussion.

REFERENCES AND SELECT BIBLIOGRAPHY

Abeysekera, J.D. & Shahnavaz, H. (1987) 'Ergonomics of Technology Transfer', *International Journal of Industrial Ergonomics*, Vol. 1, No. 1, pp. 265–72.

Abramovitz, M. (1956) 'Resource and Output Trends in the United States since 1870', *American Economic Review*, Vol. 46, No. 1, pp. 5–23.

Acs, A.J., Morck, R.K. & Yeung, B. (2001) 'Entrepreneurship, Globalisation and Public Policy', *Journal of International Management*, Vol. 7, No. 2, pp. 235–51.

Adeboye, T.O. (1977) 'International Transfer of Technology: A Comparative Study of Differences in Innovative Behaviour', unpublished D.B.A. dissertation, Harvard University, Cambridge, Massachusetts.

Aggarwal, A. (2000) 'Deregulation, Technology Imports and In-house R&D Efforts: An Analysis of the Indian Experiences', *Research Policy*, Vol. 29, No. 9, pp. 1081–92.

Ahassan, M.R. & Benincasa, T.G. (1999) 'Technology, Society and Human Factors', in: Straker, L. & Pollack, C. (eds.), *CD-ROM Proceedings of CybErgonomics*, Perth, Australia.

Ahmad, A. (1977) 'Dilemmas of a Developing Society', *Futures*, Vol. 9, No. 3, pp. 259–62.

—— (1986) 'Western Science and Technology in Non-Western Cultures', *Science and Public Policy*, Vol. 13, No. 2, pp. 101–5.

Akrasanee, N. (1993) 'The Developing Country Experience of Successful Technology Co-operation', Proceedings of the Global Technology Partnership Conference, 23–25 March, Birmingham, UK.

Allen, J.C. (1992) *Starting a Technology Business*, London: Pitman.

Amabile, T.M. (1988) 'A Model of Creativity and Innovation in Organisations', in: Staw, B.M. & Cummings, L.L. (eds.), *Research in Organisational Behaviour*, Vol. 10, pp. 123–67, Greenwich, Connecticut: Jai Press.

Amesse, F. & Cohendet, P. (2001) 'Technology Transfer Revisited from the Perspective of the Knowledge-Based Economy', *Research Policy*, Vol. 30, No. 9, pp. 1459–78.

Amirahmadi, H. & Wu, W. (1994) 'Foreign Direct Investment in Developing Countries', *Journal of Developing Areas*, Vol. 28, No. 2, pp. 167–89.

Andersen, E.S. & Lundvall, B.A. (1988) 'Small National Systems of Innovation Facing Technological Revolutions: An Analytical Framework', in: Freeman, C. & Lundvall, B.A. (eds.), *Small Countries Facing the Technological Revolution*, pp. 9–36, London: Pinter.

Anderson, K. (1998) 'Agricultural Trade Reforms, Research Initiatives and the Environment', in: Ernst Lutz (ed.), *Agriculture and the Environment*, Washington, D.C.: World Bank.

Anderson, W.T. (1999) 'The Two Globalisations: Notes on a Confused Dialogue', *Futures*, Vol. 31, Nos. 9/10, pp. 897–903.

Anglade, C. & Fortin, C. (1990) 'Accumulation, Adjustment and Autonomy of the State in Latin America', in: Anglade, C. & Fortin, C. (eds.), *The State and Capital Accumulation in Latin America*, Vol. 2, pp. 238–54, London: Macmillan.

Annerstadt, J. (1979) *A Survey of World Research and Development Efforts*, Anselm: UNESCO.

Archibugi, D. & Pietrobelli, C. (2003) 'The Globalisation of Technology and Its Implications for Developing Countries: Windows of Opportunity or Further Burden?' *Technological Forecasting and Social Change*, in press.

Ariga, M. (1981) 'Restrictive Business Practices and International Control on Transfer of Technology', in: Sagafi-nejad, T., Perlmutter, H.V. & Moxon, R.W. (eds.), *Controlling International Technology Transfer*, pp. 177–91, New York: Pergamon.

Arnold, W. (1989) 'Bureaucratic Politics, State Capacity and Taiwan's Automobile Industrial Policies', *Modern China*, Vol. 15, No. 2, pp. 178–214.

Artemiev, I.E. (1981) 'Comments', in: Sagafi-nejad, T., Perlmutter, H.V. & Moxon, R.W. (eds.), *Controlling International Technology Transfer*, New York: Pergamon.

Attinger, E.O. (1991) 'Assessment and Cost-Effectiveness in Technology Transfer', WHO Meeting of Regional Advisers on Technology Development, Assessment and Transfer, 17–21 June, Geneva.

Au, K.Y. (2000) 'Intra-cultural Variation as Another Construct of International Management', *Journal of International Management*, Vol. 6, No. 3, pp. 217–38.

Ausubel, J.H. (1991) 'Rat Race Dynamics and Crazy Companies: The Diffusion of Technologies and Social Behaviour', in: Nakicenovic, N. & Grubler, A. (eds.), *Diffusion of Technologies and Social Behaviour*, pp. 1–17, Berlin: Springer-Verlag.

Auty, R.M. (1994) *Economic Development and Industrial Policy*, New York: Mansell.

Avgerou, C. & Land, F. (1992) 'Examining the Appropriateness of Information Technology', in: Odedra, M. & Bhatnagar, S.C. (eds.), *Social Implications of Computers in Developing Countries*, pp. 26–42, New Delhi: Tata McGraw-Hill.

Baer, W. & Kerstenentzky, H. (1963) *Inflation and Growth in Latin America*, Homewood, Illinois: Irwin.

Balassa, B. (1986) 'Intra-industry Specialisation: A Cross-country Analysis', *European Economic Review*, Vol. 30, No. 1, pp. 27–42.

Balassa, B., Bueno, G.M., Kuczynski, P. & Simonsen, M.H. (1986) *Toward Renewed Economic Growth in Latin America*, Washington, D.C.: Institute for International Economics.

Baranson, J. (1975) *Intra-national Transfer of Technology*, Tokyo: Asian Productivity Organisation.

Barber, J. & White, G. (1987) 'Current Policy Practice and Problems from a UK Perspective', in: Dasgupta, P. & Stoneman, P. (eds.), *Economic Policy and Technological Performance*, pp. 24–50, Cambridge: Cambridge University Press.

Barnett, H. (1953) *Innovation: The Basis of Cultural Change*, New York: McGraw-Hill.

Barquin, R.C. (1992) 'Macro-Ethics: Toward an Ethical Framework for Macro-Engineering', in: Davidson, F.P. & Meador, C.L. (eds.), *Macro-Engineering: Global Infrastructure Solutions*, London: Ellis Horwood.

Bartlett, C.A. & Ghoshal, S. (1990) 'Managing Innovation in the Transnational Corporation', in: Bartlett, C.A., Doz, Y. & Headland, G. (eds.), *Managing the Global Firm*, pp. 215–55, London: Routledge.

Bar-Zakay, S.N. (1970) 'Policymaking and Technology Transfer: The Need for National Thinking Laboratories', P-4497, The Rand Corporation, Santa Monica, California.

Batstone, E., Gourlay, S., Levie, H. & Moore, R., (eds.) (1987) *New Technology and the Process of Labour Regulation*, Oxford: Clarendon.

Begg, D., Fischer, S. & Dornbusch, R. (1991) *Economics*, London: McGraw-Hill.

Behrman, J. & Wallender, H., (eds.) (1976) *Transfer of Manufacturing Technology within Multinational Enterprises*, Cambridge, Massachusetts: Ballinger.

Bell, M. (1984) 'Learning and the Accumulation of Industrial Technological Capability in Developing Countries', in: Fransman, M. & King, K. (eds.), *Technological Capability in the Third World*, pp. 187–209, New York: St. Martin's.

Bell, M. & Pavitt, K. (1993a) 'Accumulating Technological Capability in Developing Countries', Proceedings of the World Bank's Annual Conference on Development Economics, pp. 257–81, World Bank, Washington, D.C.

Bell, M. & Pavitt, K. (1993b) 'Technological Accumulation and Industrial Growth: Contrasts between Developed and Developing Countries', *Industrial and Corporate Change*, Vol. 2, No. 2, pp. 157–210.

Bell, M., Ross-Laison, B. & Westphal, L.E. (1984) 'Assessing the Performance of Infant Industries', *Journal of Development Economics*, Vol. 16, Nos. 1/2, pp. 101–28.

Bennett, D. & Sharpe, K. (1985) *Transnational Corporations Versus the State: The Political Economy of the Mexican Auto Industry*, Princeton, New Jersey: Princeton University Press.

Bennett, D., Vaidya, K. & Hongyu, Z. (1999) 'Valuing Transferred Machine Tool Technology', *International Journal of Operations and Production Management*, Vol. 19, Nos. 5/6, pp. 491–514.

Berg-Schlosser, D. & Siegler, R. (1990) *Political Stability and Development: A Comparative Analysis of Kenya, Tanzania, and Uganda*, Boulder, Colorado: Lynne Rienner.

Bessant, J. & Lamming, R. (1985) 'The Technical and Operational Context', Units 2/3, Implementation of New Technology, Milton Keynes Open University, SERC Manufacturing Program, Milton Keynes, UK.

Bhagavan, M.R. (1990) *The Technological Transformation of the Third World: Strategies and Prospects*, London: Zed.

Bhalla, A.S. (1979) *Towards Global Action for Appropriate Technology*, Oxford: Pergamon.

——— (1987) 'Can High Technology Help Third World Take-Off?' *Economic and Political Weekly*, 4 July, pp. 1082–85.

——— (1996) *Facing the Technological Challenge*, London: Macmillan.

Bichage, C. (1993) 'Training', Proceedings of the Global Technology Partnership Conference, 23–25 March, Birmingham, UK.

Bienayme, A. (1986) 'The Dynamics of Innovation', *International Journal of Technology Management*, Vol. 1, No. 2, pp. 133–59.

Bienefeld, M. (1984) 'International Constraints and Opportunities', in: Fransman, M. & King, K. (eds.), *Technological Capability in the Third World*, pp. 161–73, London: Macmillan.

Blau, P.M., McHugh, F.C., McKinley, W. & Tracy, P.K. (1976) 'Technology and Organisation in Manufacturing', *Administrative Science Quarterly*, Vol. 21, No. 1, pp. 20–40.

Blauner, R. (1964) *Alienation and Freedom*, Chicago: University of Chicago Press.

Blaut, J.M. (1977) 'Two Views of Diffusion', *Annals of the Association of American Geographers*, Vol. 67, No. 3, pp. 343–49.

Blennerhassett, R. (1992) 'Planning for Information Technology in the Health Service', M.B.A. thesis, Imperial College, London.

Blomstrom, M. (1986) 'Foreign Investment and Productive Efficiency: The Case of Mexico', *Journal of Industrial Economics*, Vol. 35, No. 1, pp. 97–110.

Blouin, Chantal (2000) 'The WTO Agreement on Basic Tele-communications: A Re-evaluation', *Telecommunications Policy*, Vol. 24, No. 2, pp. 135–42.

Bodily, S.E. (1985) *Modern Decision Making*, New York: McGraw-Hill.

Boer, G. (1987) 'Decision Support Systems for Management Accountants', National Association of Accountants, New Jersey.

Bohn, R.E. (1994) 'Measuring and Managing Technological Knowledge', *Sloan Management Review*, Vol. 36, No. 1, pp. 61–73.

Bolwijn, P.T. & Kumpe, T. (1990) 'Manufacturing in the 1990s: Productivity, Flexibility and Innovativeness', *Long Range Planning*, Vol. 23, No. 4, pp. 44–57.

Borden, M. (1983) 'From Transfer to Acquisition of Technology: A Study of the Industrialisation Process in Tanzania', Linkoping Studies in Management and Economics, Dissertations No. 7, Linkoping University, Sweden.

Bosworth, D. & Yang, D. (2000) 'Intellectual Property Law, Technology Flow and Licensing Opportunities in the People's Republic of China', *International Business Review*, Vol. 9, No. 4, pp. 453–77.

Braautigam, D. (1993) 'South–South Technology Transfer: The Case of China's Kaatawee Rice Project in Liberia', *World Development*, Vol. 21, No. 12, pp. 1989–2001.

Branscomb, L.M. & Thomas, J.C. (1985) 'Ease of Use: A System Design Challenge', *IBM Systems Journal*, Vol. 23, No. 3, pp. 224–35.

Brinkerhoff, D.W. (2000) 'Democratic Governance and Sectoral Policy Reform: Tracing Linkages and Exploring Synergies', *World Development*, Vol. 28, No. 4, pp. 615–61.

Brodman, J. (1986) 'Microcomputer Adoption in Developing Countries: Old Management Styles and New Information Systems', Development Discussion Paper No. 219, Harvard Institute for International Development, Cambridge, Massachusetts.

Brodsky, D., Helleiner, H. & Sampson, G. (1981) 'The Impact of the Current Exchange Rates System on DCs', *Trade and Development: An UNCTAD Review 3*, Vol. 34, Winter, pp. 47–82.

Brooks, H. (1966) 'National Science Policy and Technology Transfer', Proceedings of the Conference on Technology Transfer and Innovation, National Science Foundation, US Government Printing Office, Washington, D.C.

———— (1968) *The Government of Science*, Cambridge, Massachusetts: MIT Press.

Brooks, M.Z. (1986) *International Management: A Review of Strategies and Operations*, London: Butchinson.

Brown, L.A. (1979) 'Innovation Diffusion: A New Perspective', Studies in the Diffusion of Innovation, Discussion Paper Series, Department of Geography, Ohio State University, Columbus, Ohio.

Bruland, K. (1989) *British Technology and European Industrialisation: The Norwegian Textile Industry in the Mid-nineteenth Century*, Cambridge: Cambridge University Press.

Bruton, H.J. (1972) 'The Elasticity of Substitution in Developing Countries', *Research Memorandum*, No. 45, April, Williams College Centre for Development Economics, Massachusetts.

Buchanan, D.A. & Boddy, D. (1983) *Organisations in the Computer Age*, Aldershot: Gower.

Buchanan, D.A. & Huczynski, A.A. (1985) *Organisational Behaviour*, London: Prentice-Hall.

Buckley, P.J. & Casson, M. (1976) *The Future of the Multinational Enterprise*, London: Macmillan.

Burgelman, R.A. & Maidique, M.A., (eds.) (1988) *Strategic Management of Technology and Innovation*, Homewood, Illinois: Irwin.

Burns, T. & Stalker, G.M. (1961) *The Management of Innovation*, London: Tavistock.

Burton, H. (1977) 'A Note on the Transfer of Technology', *Economic Development and Cultural Change*, Vol. 25, No. 4 (Supplement), pp. S234–44.

Cable, V. & Persaud, B. (1987) *Developing with Foreign Investment*, London: Croom Helm.

Cairncross, A.K. (1967) *Factors in Economic Development*, London: George, Allen & Unwin.

Caloghirou, Y., Constantelou, A. & Karounos, T. (2000) 'Learning from Technology Transfer in the Greek Context', *Journal of Technology Transfer*, Vol. 25, No. 1, pp. 59–74.

Cannice, M.V., Chen, R. & Daniels, J.D. (2003) 'Managing International Technology Transfer Risk: A Case Analysis of U.S. High-technology Firms in Asia', *Journal of High Technology Management Research*, Vol. 14, No. 2, pp. 171–87.

Cant, J.W., ed. (1989) *Technological Innovation and Multinational Corporations*, Oxford: Blackwell.

Carrol, B. & Turpin, T. (2002) *Environmental Impact Assessment Handbook: A Practical Guide for Planners, Developers and Communities*, London: Thomas Telford.

Centre for Science and Technology for Development (CSTD) (1991) 'Environmentally Sound Technology Assessment', CSTD, New York.

Chamarik, S. & Goonatilake, S. (1994) *Technological Independence: The Asian Experience*, Tokyo: United Nations University Press.

Chan Kim, W. & Hwang, P. (1992) 'Global Strategy and Multinationals' Entry Mode Choice', *Journal of International Business Studies*, Vol. 23, No. 1, pp. 29–53.

Chatterji, M. (1990) 'Innovation, Management and Diffusion of Technology: A Survey of Literature', in: Chatterji, M. (ed.), *Technology*

Transfer in the Developing Countries, Chapter One, London: Macmillan.

Chatterji, M., Gilmore, B., Strunk, K. & Vanasin, J. (1993) 'Political Economy, Growth and Convergence in Less-Developed Countries', *World Development*, Vol. 21, No. 12, pp. 2029–38.

Chen, Aimin (2000) 'The Impact of WTO Entry on the Changing Structure of Chinese Industry', *China Economic Review*, Vol. 11, No. 2, pp. 409–13.

Chen, K. (1979) 'International Perspectives on Technology Assessment', *Technological Forecasting and Social Change*, Vol. 11, No. 3, pp. 213–33.

Chiang, J.T. (1995) 'Technology Policy Paradigms and Intellectual Property Strategies: Three National Models', *Technological Forecasting and Social Change*, Vol. 49, No. 1, pp. 35–48.

Child, J. (1985) 'Managerial Strategies, New Technology and the Labour Process', in Knights, D., Willmott, H. & Collinson, D. (eds.), *Job Redesign*, pp. 107–41, Aldershot: Gower.

Chitrakar, R.C. (1994) *Foreign Investment and Technology Transfer in Developing Countries*, Aldershot: Avebury.

Choi, J.P. (2001) 'Technology Transfer with Moral Hazard', *International Journal of Industrial Organisation*, Vol. 19, Nos. 1/2, pp. 249–60.

Clark, J. & Staunton, N. (1989) *Innovation in Technology and Organisation*, London: Routledge.

Clark, N. (1990) 'Development Policy, Technology Assessment and the New Technologies', *Futures*, Vol. 22, No. 9, pp. 913–31.

Clark, R. & Winters, L.A. (1995) 'Energy Pricing for Sustainable Development in China', in: Goldin, I. & Winters, L.A. (eds.), *The Economics of Sustainable Development*, pp. 200–35, Cambridge: Cambridge University Press.

Cohen, S., Teece, D.J., Tyson, L. & Zysman, J. (1984) 'Competitiveness', Berkeley Roundtable on the International Economy, Berkeley, California.

Cohen, Y.S. (1972) 'Diffusion of an Innovation in an Urban System', Research Paper No. 140, Department of Geography, University of Chicago, Chicago.

Cole, W.E. & Mogab, J.W. (1987) 'The Transfer of Soft Technologies to Less-Developed Countries', *Journal of Economic Issues*, Vol. 21, No. 1, pp. 309–20.

Collins, T.M. & Doorley, T.L. (1991) *Teaming up for the 90s: A Guide to International Joint Ventures and Strategic Alliances*, Homewood, Illinois: Business One Irwin.

Colman, D. & Nixson, F. (1978) *Economics of Change in Less Developed Countries*, Oxford: Philip Allen.

Contractor, F.J. (1979) 'The Cost of Technology Transfers in Overseas Licensing', Ph.D. dissertation, University of Pennsylvania, Philadelphia.

Cornford, T., Doukidis, G.I. & Forester, D. (1994) 'Experience with a Structure, Process and Outcome Framework for Evaluating an Information System', *Omega*, Vol. 22, No. 5, pp. 491–504.

Cornwall, J. (1976) 'Diffusion, Convergence and Kaldor's Law', *Economic Journal*, Vol. 85, June, pp. 307–14.

——— (1977) *Modern Capitalism: Its Growth and Transformation*, London: Martin Robertson.

Craig, S.G. (2000) 'The Forward and Backward Flow of Technology', *Technovation*, Vol. 20, No. 8, pp. 403–14.

Crawford, M.H. (1985) 'Asia's Brains Are Heading Home', *Fortune*, 13 May.

——— (1987) 'Technology Transfer and the Computerisation of South Korea and Taiwan', *Information Age*, Vol. 9, No. 1, pp. 10–16.

Creative Problem Solving Group (1992) 'Climate for Innovation Questionnaire', Buffalo, New York: Creative Problem Solving Group.

Cressey, P. (1985) 'The Role of the Parties Concerned in the Introduction of New Technology', Consolidated Report, European Foundation for the Improvement of Living and Working Conditions, Shankill, Dublin.

Cusumano, M.A. & Elenkov, D. (1994) 'Linking International Technology Transfer with Strategy and Management: A Literature Commentary', *Research Policy*, Vol. 23, No. 2, pp. 195–215.

Daft, R.L. (2000) *Management*, Fort Worth: Dryden.

Dahlman, C.J. & Sercovich, F.C. (1984) 'Exports of Technology from Semi-industrial Economies and Local Technological Development', *Journal of Development Economics*, Vol. 16, Nos. 1/2, pp. 63–99.

Dahlman, C.J & Valadares Fonseca, J. (1987) 'From Technological Dependence to Technological Development: The Case of the Usiminas Steel Plant in Brazil', Working Paper No. 21, Vols. 1 and 2, IDB/ECLA/UNDP Programme, Buenos Aires.

Dahlman, C.J. & Westphal, L.E. (1981) 'The Meaning of Technological Mastery in Relation to Transfer of Technology', *Annals of the American Association of Political and Social Sciences*, No. 456, pp. 12–26.

Dahlman, C.J., Ross-Larson, B. & Westphal, L.E. (1987) 'Managing Technological Development: Lessons from the Newly Industrialising Countries', *World Development*, Vol. 15, No. 6, pp. 759–75.

Dalal, N. & Yadav, S. (1992) 'The Design of a Knowledge-Based Decision Support System to Support the Information Analyst in Determining Requirements', *Decision Sciences*, Vol. 23, No. 6, pp. 1373–88.

Daly, H. (1990) 'Toward Some Operational Principles of Sustainable Development', *Ecological Economics*, Vol. 2, No. 1, pp. 1–6.

Das, Bhagirath Lal (1999) *The World Bank Organisation*, London: Zed.

Dauphinais, G.W. et al. (1995) *Better Change*, New York: Irwin.

Davidson, F.P. & Meador, C.L., (eds.) (1992) *Macro-Engineering: Global Infrastructure Solutions*, London: Ellis Horwood.

Davies, B.T. (1983) 'Why Ergonomics for Developing Countries?' Proceedings of the First International Conference on Ergonomics of Developing Countries, 16–17 June, Lulea University, Lulea, Sweden.

Davis, F.D., Bagozzi, R.P. & Warshaw, P.R. (1989) 'User Acceptance of Computer Technology: A Comparison of Two Theoretical Models', *Management Science*, Vol. 35, No. 8, pp. 982–1003.

Dearing, J.W. (1993) 'Rethinking Technology Transfer', *International Journal of Technology Management*, Vol. 8, Nos. 6/7/8, pp. 478–85.

de Janvry, A. (1977) 'Inducement of Technological and Institutional Innovation', in: Arndt, T.M., Dalrymple, E.G. & Ruttan, V.W. (eds.), *Resource Allocation and Productivity in National and International Agricultural Research*, pp. 551–63, Minneapolis: University of Minnesota Press.

—— (1978) 'Social Structure and Biased Technical Change in Argentine Agriculture', in: Binswanger, H.V. & Ruttan, V.W. (eds.), *Induced Innovations*, pp. 297–323, Baltimore: Johns Hopkins University Press.

Denison, E.G. (1962) 'The Sources of Economic Growth in the United States and the Alternatives before Us', Supplementary Paper No. 13, Committee of Economic Development, Washington, D.C.

Derakhshani, S. (1980) 'Structuring International Transfer of Technology: Lessons from Iran', Ph.D. dissertation, Harvard University, Cambridge, Massachusetts.

Desai, A. (1980) 'The Origin and Direction of Industrial R&D in India', *Research Policy*, Vol. 9, No. 1, pp. 74–96.

Desai, M. (1985) 'Indigenous and Foreign Determinants of Technical Change in Indian Industry', *Economic and Political Weekly*, Vol. 20, Special No., pp. 2081–94.

—— (1987) 'Comments on Sukhamoy Chakravarty: Marxist Economics and Contemporary Developing Economies', *Cambridge Journal of Economics*, Vol. 11, No. 2, pp. 173–78.

Devon, M.D., Adams, E.J. & Adams, T.I. (1987) 'Government Supported Industry–University Research Centres: Issues for Successful Technology Transfer', *Journal of Technology Transfer*, Vol. 12, No. 1, pp. 27–37.

Diamand, M. (1978) 'Toward a Change in the Economic Paradigm through the Experience of Developing Countries', *Journal of Development Economics*, Vol. 5, No. 1, pp. 19–53.

Do Boer, S.J. & Walbeek, M.M. (1999) 'Information Technology in Developing Countries', *International Journal of Information Management*, Vol. 19, No. 3, pp. 207–18.

Doctors, S. (1967) *The Role of Federal Agencies in Technology Transfer*, Cambridge, Massachusetts: MIT Press.

Doeleman, J.A. (1988) 'Social Determinism, Technology and Economic Externalities', in: Tisdell, C. & Maitra, P. (eds.), *Technological Change, Development and the Environment*, pp. 288–321, London: Routledge.

Doh, J.P. & Ramamurti, R. (2003) 'Reassessing Risk in Developing Country Infrastructure', *Long Range Planning*, Vol. 36, No. 4, pp. 337–53.

Dore, R. (1984) 'Technological Self-reliance: Study Ideal or Self-serving Rhetoric', in: Fransman, G. & King, K. (eds.), *Technological Capability in the Third World*, pp. 65–80, London: Macmillan.

Dosi, G. (1988) 'Sources, Procedures, and Macroeconomic Effects of Innovation', *Journal of Economic Literature*, Vol. 26, No. 3, pp. 1120–71.

Dosi, G., Pavitt, K. & Soete, L., (eds.) (1992) *The Economics of Technical Change and International Trade*, London: Harvester-Wheatsheaf.

Dowrick, S. & Gemmell, N. (1991) 'Industrialisation, Catching up and Economic Growth: A Comparative Study across the World's Capitalist Economies', *Economic Journal*, Vol. 101, March, pp. 263–75.

Driscoll, R.E. & Wallender, H.W. (1981) 'Control and Incentives for Technology Transfer: A Multinational Perspective', in: Sagafi-nejad, T., Perlmutter, H.V. & Moxon, R.W. (eds.), *Controlling International Technology Transfer*, pp. 273–87, New York: Pergamon.

Dudley, J. (1998) 'Globalisation and Education Policy in Australia', in: Currie, J. & J. Vewson (eds.), *Universities and Globalisation*, London: Sage.

Dunning, J.H. (1979) 'Explaining Changing Patterns of International Production: In Defence of the Eclectic Theory', *Oxford Bulletin of Economics and Statistics*, Vol. 41, No. 4, pp. 269–95.

——— (1981) 'Alternative Channels and Modes of International Resource Transmission', in: Sagafi-nejad, T., Perlmutter, H.V. & Moxon, R.W. (eds.), *Controlling International Technology Transfer*, Chapter One, New York: Pergamon.

Easton, D. (1965) *A Systems Analysis of Political Life*, London: John Wiley.

——— (1975) 'Re-assessment of the Concept of Political Support', *British Journal of Political Science*, Vol. 5, October, pp. 435–57.

Eckaus, E.S. (1972) 'Absorptive Capacity', in: Bhagwati, J. & Eckaus, R.S. (eds.), *Development and Planning: Essays in Honour of Paul Rosenstein Rodan*, London: Allen & Unwin.

Eckaus, R.S. (1955) 'The Factor Proportions Problem in Underdeveloped Areas', *American Economic Review*, Vol. 45, No. 4, pp. 539–65.

Edge, D. (1995) 'The Social Shaping of Technology', in: Heap, N., Thomas, R., Einon, G., Mason, R. & Mackay, H. (eds.), *Information Technology and Society*, London: Sage.

Ekvall, G. & Arvonen, J. (1983) *Creative Organisational Climate: Construction and Validation of a Measuring Instrument*, Stockholm: Swedish Council for Management and Organisational Behaviour.

Ekvall, G. & Tangeberg-Anderson, Y. (1986) 'Working Climate and Creativity: A Study of an Innovative Newspaper Office', *Journal of Creative Behaviour*, Vol. 20, No. 2, pp. 215–24.

Elkington, J. (1986) 'The Sunrise Seven', in: Ekins, P. (ed.), *The Living Economy: A New Economics in the Making*, pp. 257–63, London: Routledge & Kegan Paul.

Elliot, K. (1985) 'Appropriate Technology', Introduction to the Special Issue of the *British Medical Journal*, pp. 1–2, London: British Medical Association.

Ellul, J. (1964) *The Technological Society*, New York: Knopf.

Emanuel, A. (1982) *Appropriate or Underdeveloped Technology?* London: John Wiley.

Emery, F.E. & Trist, E.L. (1965) 'The Causal Texture of Organisational Environments', *Human Relations*, Vol. 18, No. 2, pp. 21–32.

—— (1973) *Toward a Social Ecology*, London: Plenum.

Engelsman, E.C. & Raan, A.F.J. van (1994) 'A Patent-Based Cartography of Technology', *Research Policy*, Vol. 23, No. 1, pp. 1–26.

Enos, J. (1984) 'Government Intervention in the Transfer of Technology: The Case of South Korea', *IDS Bulletin*, Vol. 15, No. 2, pp. 26–31.

—— (1985) 'A Game-Theoretic Approach to Choice of Technology in Developing Countries', in: James, J. & Watanabe, S. (eds.), *Technology, Institutions and Government Policies*, pp. 47–80, London: Macmillan.

——, (ed.) (1991) *The Creation of Technological Capability in Developing Countries*, London & New York: Frances Pinter.

Enos, J. & Park, W. (1988) *The Adoption and Diffusion of Imported Technology: The Case of Korea*, London: Croom Helm.

Erber, F.S. (1985) 'The Development of the Electronics Complex and Government Policies in Brazil', *World Development*, Vol. 13, No. 3, pp. 293–310.

Erdilek, A. (1984) 'International Technology Transfer in the Middle East and North Africa', *Management Decision*, Vol. 22, No. 1, pp. 45–49.

Eres, B.K. (1981) 'Transfer of IT to Less Developed Countries: A Systems Approach', *Journal of the American Society for Information Science*, Vol. 32, No. 3, pp. 97–102.

Ergas, Henry (1987) 'The Importance of Technology Policy', in: Dasgupta, P. & Stoneman, P. (eds.), *Economic Policy and Technological Performance*, pp. 51–96, Cambridge: Cambridge University Press.

Ernst, D., (ed.) (1980) *The New International Division of Labour, Technology and Under-development: Consequences for the Third World*, New York: Campus Verlag.

Ettlie, J.E. (1973) 'Technology Transfer from Innovators to Users', *Industrial Engineering*, Vol. 5, No. 6, pp. 16–21.

Fagan, M.H. (2001) 'Global Information Technology Transfer: A Framework for Analysis', *Journal of Global Information Technology Management*, Vol. 4, No. 3, pp. 5–26.

Fagerberg, J. (1987) 'A Technology Gap Approach to Why Growth Rates Differ', *Research Policy*, Vol. 16, No. 2, pp. 87–99.

——— (1988) 'International Competitiveness', *Economic Journal*, Vol. 98, June, pp. 355–74.

Fan, W.S. (1991) 'The Effectiveness of Foreign Exchange Policy in Taiwan', unpublished M.B.A. thesis, Imperial College, University of London.

Fayerweather, J. & Kapoor, A. (1976) 'Strategy and Negotiation for the International Contracts in Less Developed Countries', Harvard University, Division of Research, Boston, Massachusetts.

Fayol, H. (1949) *General and Industrial Management*, New York: Pitman.

Fieldhouse, D.K. (1986) '*Black Africa 1945–1980: Economic Decolonisation and Arrested Development*, London: Allen & Unwin.

Fidel, J., Lucangeli, J. & Shepherd, P. (1978) 'The Argentine Cigarette Industry: Technological Profile and Behaviour', Working Paper No. 7, IDB/ECLA/UNDP Programme, Buenos Aires.

Findlay, R. (1978) 'Relative Backwardness, Direct Foreign Investment, and the Transfer of Technology: A Simple Dynamic Model', *Quarterly Journal of Economics*, Vol. 112, No. 1 (February), pp. 1–16.

——— (1984) 'Growth and Development in Trade Models', in: Jones, R.W. & Kenen, P.B. (eds.), *Handbook of International Economics*, Vol. 1, pp. 185–236, Amsterdam: North-Holland.

Fisher, W.A. (1976) 'Empirical Approaches to Understanding Technology Transfer', *R&D Management*, Special Issue on Technology Transfer, Vol. 6, No. 4, pp. 151–57.

Fitzgerald, E.V.K. (1978) 'The Public Sector in Latin America', Working Paper No. 18, Centre of Latin American Studies, Cambridge, UK.

——— (1983) 'The State and the Management of Accumulation in the Periphery', in: Tussies, D. (ed.), *Latin America in the World Economy and New Perspectives*, Aldershot: Gower.

Fleming, W. (1966) 'Authority, Efficiency and Role Stress: Problems in the Development of East-African Bureaucracies', *Administrative Science Quarterly*, Vol. 11, No. 3, pp. 386–404.

Fleury, A. (1999) 'The Changing Pattern of Operations Management in Developing Countries', *International Journal of Operations and Production Management*, Vol. 19, Nos. 5/6, pp. 552–64.

Fontes, M. (2001a) 'Contribution of New Technology-Based Firms to the Strengthening of Technological Capabilities in Intermediate Economies', *Research Policy*, Vol. 30, No. 1, pp. 79–91.

———— (2001b) 'Biotechnology Entrepreneurs and Technology Transfer in an Intermediate Economy', *Technological Forecasting and Social Change*, Vol. 6, No. 1, pp. 59–74.

Forbes, R. (1971) *The Conquest of Nature: Technology and Its Consequences*, London: Pall Mall (Issued to commemorate the 200th anniversary of the *Encyclopaedia Britannica*).

Forman, E.H., Saaty, T.L., Selly, M.A. & Waldom, R. (1992) *Expert Choice: Decision Support Software*, Pennsylvania: Expert Choice Inc.

Forsythe, D.J., McBain, N.S. & Solomon, R.F. (1980) 'Technical Rigidity and Appropriate Technology in Less Developed Countries', *World Development*, Vol. 8, Nos. 5/6, pp. 371–98.

Fortune International (1992) Special Issue on Total Quality Management, *Fortune International*, Vol. 19, September.

Frame, J.D. (1983) *International Business and Global Technology*, Lexington, Massachusetts: Lexington Books.

Fransman, M. (1985a) 'Conceptualising Technical Change in the Third World in the 1980s: An Interpretive Survey', *Journal of Development Studies*, Vol. 21, No. 2, pp. 572–652.

———— (1985b) 'A Biological Approach to New Technological Knowledge', Background Paper for ESRC Industry and Employment Committee Initiative in New Technology, Economic and Social Research Council, London.

———— (1986) *Technology and Economic Development*, Boulder, Colorado: Westview.

Freeman, C. (1974) *The Market for College Trained Manpower*, Cambridge, Massachusetts: Harvard University Press.

———— (1982) *The Economics of Industrial Innovation*, London: Frances Pinter.

———— (1986) 'The Diffusion of Innovations—Microelectronic Technology', in: Roy, R. & Wield, D. (eds.), *Product Design and Technical Innovation*, pp. 193–200, London: Open University Press.

———— (1988) 'Technology Gaps, International Trade and the Problems of Smaller and Less-Developed Economies', in: Freeman, C. & Lundvall, B. (eds.), *Small Countries Facing the Technological Revolution*, pp. 67–84, London: Pinter.

———— (1991) 'Catching up in World Growth and World Trade', in: Nissanke, M. (ed.), *Economic Crisis in Developing Countries: Policies for Recovery and Development*, London: Frances Pinter.

Freeman, C. & Perez, C. (1988) 'Structural Crisis of Adjustment: Business Cycles and Investment Behaviour', in: Dosi, G., Forsyth,

D.J.C., McBain, N.S. & Solomon, R.F. (eds.), *Technical Change and Economic Theory*, pp. 67–94, London: Pinter.

Freeman, D.M. (1974) *Technology and Society*, Chicago: Markham.

Fry, L.W. (1982) 'Technology-Structure Research: Three Critical Issues', *Academy of Management Journal*, Vol. 25, No. 3, pp. 532–55.

Fund for Multinational Education (FMME) (1978) *Public Policy and Technology Transfer: Viewpoints of U.S. Business*, New York: FMME.

Furtado, C. (1970) *The Economic Development of Latin America*, Cambridge: Cambridge University Press.

Fusfeld, H.I. (1986) *The Technical Enterprise: Present and Future Patterns*, Cambridge, Massachusetts: Ballinger.

Galbraith, J.K. (1967) *The New Industrial State*, Cambridge, Massachusetts: Harvard University Press.

Galbraith, J.K., Rostow, W.W. & Weintraub, S. (1988) 'Proposal for a High Level Report by an International Commission on the Future of the World Economy', University of Texas, Austin.

Gamman, J.K. (1994) *Overcoming Obstacles in Environmental Policymaking*, New York: State University of New York.

Gar-on, A. & Wu, F. (1999) 'The Transformation of the Urban Planning System in China from a Centrally-Planned to Transitional Economy', *Progress in Planning*, Vol. 51, No. 3, pp. 167–252.

Gaski, J.F. (1982) 'The Cause of Industrial Revolution: A Brief Single Factor Argument', *Journal of European Economic History*, Vol. 11, No. 1, pp. 227–34.

Gaskin, A. (1993) 'Training: Discussion', Proceedings of the Global Technology Partnership Conference, 23–25 March, Birmingham, UK.

Gee, S., (ed.) (1981) *Technology Transfer, Innovation, and International Competitiveness*, New York: John Wiley.

Geertz, C. (1963) *Agricultural Involution: The Process of Ecological Change in Indonesia*, Berkeley, California: University of California Press.

Gemmell, N. (1990) *Surveys in Development Economics*, Oxford: Basil Blackwell.

Gemmil, G. & Eicher, C. (1973) 'A Framework for Research on the Economics of Farm Mechanisation in Developing Countries', Rural Employment Paper No. 6, Department of Agricultural Economics, Michigan State University, East Lansing, Michigan.

Gendron, B. (1977) *Technology and the Human Condition*, New York: St. Martin's.

Georgantzas, N.C. & Madu, C.N. (1990) 'Cognitive Processes in Technology Management and Transfer', *Technological Forecasting and Social Change*, Vol. 38, No. 1, pp. 81–95.

Gerwin, D. (1981) 'Relationships between Structure and Technology', in: Nystrom, P.C. & Starbuck, W. (eds.), *Handbook of Organisational Design*, Vol. 2, pp. 3–38, Oxford: Oxford University Press.

Giese, A.S., Kahley, W.J. & Riefler, R.F. (1990) 'Foreign Direct Investment: Motivating Factors and Economic Impact', *Regional Science Perspectives*, Vol. 20, No. 1, pp. 105–27.

Gilfillan, S.C. (1935) *The Sociology of Invention*, London: Cambridge University Press & Chicago: Follet.

Gilpin, R., (ed.) (1975) *Technology, Economic Growth, and International Competitiveness*, Washington, D.C.: US Government Printing Office.

Glisson, C.A. (1978) 'Dependence of Technological Routinisation of Structure Variables in Human Service Organisations', *Administrative Science Quarterly*, Vol. 23, September, pp. 383–95.

Gocht, W.R. (1987) 'Government Functions in the Promotion of Technology Transfer', in: Daghestani, F., Gocht, W. & El-Mulky, H. (eds.), *Solar Energy Applications*, pp. 39–44, Amman: The Royal Scientific Society.

Godwin, P. (1993) 'Funding Technology Co-operation: The View from a Commercial Bank', Proceedings of the Global Technology Partnership Conference, 23–25 March, Birmingham, UK.

Goldin, I. & Winters, L.A. (1995) *The Economics of Sustainable Development*, Cambridge: Cambridge University Press.

Gomulka, S., (ed.) (1990) *The Theory of Technological Change and Economic Growth*, London: Routledge.

Gotsch, C.H. (1974) 'Economics, Institutions and Employment Generation in Rural Areas', in: Edwards, E.O. (ed.), *Employment in Developing Nations*, pp. 133–62, New York: Columbia University Press.

Gotsch, C.H. & McEachron, N.B. (1983) 'Technology Choice and Technological Change in Third World Agriculture', in: Lucas, B.A. & Freedman, S. (eds.), *Technology Choice and Change in Developing Countries: Internal and External Constraints*, pp. 29–63, Dublin: Tycooly International.

Goulet, H.G. (1977) *The Uncertain Promise: Value Conflicts in Technology Transfer*, Washington, D.C.: IDOC/North America, Inc.

Grant, A.A. (1991) 'The State of the Art of Infrastructure: The US Experience', Mexico Academy of Engineering Conference, Mexico City.

Green, D. (1999) 'Cross Cultural Technology Transfer of Sustainable Energy', *Renewable Energy*, Vol. 16, Nos. 1/2/3/4, pp. 1133–37.

Green, K.M. & Morphet, C., (eds.) (1977) *Research and Technology as Economic Activities*, London: Butterworth.

Greenfield, T.B. (1973) 'Organisations as Social Inventions: Rethinking Assumptions about Change', *Journal of Applied Behavioural Science*, Vol. 9, No. 5, pp. 551–74.

Greenpeace (1997) *WTO against Sustainable Development*, Amsterdam: Greenpeace.

Grimes, A.J. & Klein, S.M. (1973) 'The Technological Imperative: The Relative Impact of Task Unit, Model Technology and Hierarchy on Structure', *Academy of Management Journal*, Vol. 16, No. 4, pp. 583–97.

Grossman, G. & Helpman, E. (1990) 'Comparative Advantage and Long-Run Growth', *American Economic Review*, Vol. 80, No. 4, pp. 796–815.

Grubb, M. et al. (1992) *Emerging Energy Technologies: Impacts and Policy Implications*, Hants: Dartmouth Publishing.

Grubber, W.H. & Marquis, D.G. (1969) *Factors in the Transfer of Technology*, Cambridge, Massachusetts: MIT Press.

Grupp, G. (1992) *Dynamics of Science-Based Innovation*, Berlin/Heidelberg: Springer.

Gulhati, R. et al. (1986) 'Exchange Rate Policies in Africa: How Valid Is the Skepticism?' *Development and Change*, Vol. 17, pp. 399–423.

Gurley, J.G. & Shaw, E.S. (1960) *Money in a Theory of Finance*, Washington, D.C.: The Brookings Institute.

Gurr, K., Straker, L. & Moore, P. (1998) 'Cultural Hazards in the Transfer of Ergonomics Technology', *International Journal of Ergonomics*, Vol. 22, Nos. 4/5, pp. 397–404.

Hage, J.T. & Aiken, S.M. (1969) 'Routine Technology, Social Structure and Organisation Goals', *Administrative Science Quarterly*, Vol. 14, September, pp. 366–77.

Hague, M.M. (1991) 'Sustainable Development and Environment: A Challenge to Technology Choice Decision-Making', *Project Appraisal*, Vol. 6, No. 3, pp. 149–57.

Hales, M. (1991) 'A Human Resource Approach to Information Systems Development—The ISU (Information Systems Use) Design Model', *Journal of Information Technology*, Vol. 6, No. 3, pp. 140–61.

Hall, E.T. (1983) *The Dance of Life: The Other Dimension of Time*, New York: Anchor.

Hall, G.R. & Johnson, R.S. (1970) 'Transfers of U.S. Aerospace Technology to Japan', in: Vernon, R. (ed.), *The Technology Factor in International Trade*, pp. 305–58, New York: National Bureau of Economic Research.

Halle, M. (2000) 'Seattle and Sustainable Development', International Institute for Sustainable Development, Winnipeg, http://www.wcit.org/Halle_Seattle_and_sd.gtm.

Hannay, N.B. & McGinn, R. (1980) 'The Anatomy of Modern Technology: Prolegomenon to an Improved Public Policy for the Social Management of Technology', *Daedalus*, Vol. 109, Winter, pp. 25–53.

Hansen, S. (1990) 'Macroeconomic Policies and Sustainable Development in the Third World', *Journal of International Development*, Vol. 2, pp. 533–57.

Hanson, P. & Pavitt, K. (1987) *The Comparative Economics of Research, Development and Innovation in East and West: A Survey*, Chur, Switzerland: Harwood Academic.

Harrigan, K.R. (1985) *Strategies for Joint Ventures*, Lexington, Massachusetts: D.C. Heath, Lexington Books.

Harrison, P. (1980a) *Inside the Third World*, London: Pelican.

———— (1980b) *The Third World Tomorrow*, London: Penguin.

Harvey, E. (1968) 'Technology and the Structure of Organisations', *American Sociological Review*, Vol. 33, No. 2, pp. 247–59.

Havrylyshyn, O. & Civan, E. (1985) 'Intra-industry Trade among Developing Countries', *Journal of Development Economics*, Vol. 18, Nos. 2/3, pp. 253–72.

Hayashi, T. (1990) *The Japanese Experience in Technology: From Transfer to Self-reliance*, Tokyo: United Nations University Press.

Heaton, G., Repetto, R. & Sobin, R. (1991) *Transferring Technology: An Agenda for Environmentally Sustainable Growth in the 21st Century*, Washington, D.C: World Resources Institute.

Henderson, W.O. (1965) *Britain and Industrial Europe 1750–1870: Studies in British Influence on the Industrial Revolution in Western Europe*, Leicester: Leicester University Press.

Henry, R.J. (1995) 'Technology Transfer and Its Constraints: Early Warnings from Agricultural Development in Colonial India', in: MacLeod, R. & Kumar, D. (eds.), *Technology and the Raj*, New Delhi: Sage.

Herrick, B. & Kindleberger, C.P. (1983) *Economic Development* (Economics Handbook Series), New York: McGraw-Hill.

Hickson, D.J., Pugh, D.S. & Pheysey, D.C. (1969) 'Operations Technology and Organisation Structure: An Empirical Reappraisal', *Administrative Science Quarterly*, Vol. 14, No. 3 (September), pp. 378–97.

Hill, C.T. (1992) 'New Manufacturing Paradigms', *Technological Forecasting and Social Change*, Vol. 41, No. 4, pp. 351–63.

Hill, J.S. & Still, R.R. (1980) 'Cultural Effects of Technology Transfer by Multinational Corporations in Lesser Developed Countries', *Columbia Journal of World Business*, Vol. 15, Summer, pp. 40–51.

Hill, S. (1988) *The Tragedy of Technology*, London: Pluto.

Hirschman, A.O. (1967) *Development Projects Observed*, Washington, D.C.: The Brookings Institute.

Hodkinson, K. (1990) 'The Management of International Property Rights', in: Wild, R. (ed.), *Technology and Management*, pp. 42–57, London: Cassell.

Hoffman, K. (1990) 'Technical Change, Technology Transfer and Industrial Development in the Third World', in: Hoffman, K. & Girvan, N. (eds.), *Managing International Technology Transfer*, IDRC-MR259e, Ottawa: International Development Research Centre.

Hoffman, K. & Girvan, N., (eds.) (1990) *Managing International Technology Transfer*, IDRC-MR259e, Ottawa: International Development Research Centre.

Hoffman, L. (1985) 'The Transfer of Technology to Developing Countries', *Intereconomics*, Vol. 20, No. 3 (March/April), pp. 263–72.

Hofstede, G. (1980) *Culture's Consequences: International Differences in Work-Related Values*, Cross-cultural Research and Methodology, Vol. 5, Thousand Oaks, California: Sage.

———— (1998) 'Attitudes, Values and Organisational Culture', *Organisation Studies*, Vol. 19, No. 3, pp. 477–93.

Hollander, S. (1965) *The Sources of Increased Efficiency: A Study of DuPont Rayon Plants*, Cambridge, Massachusetts: MIT Press.

Holloman, J. (1966) 'Technology Transfer', Proceedings of the Conference on Technology Transfer and Innovation, National Science Foundation, US Government Printing Office, Washington, D.C.

Hrebiniak, L. (1974) 'Job Technology, Supervision and Work Group Structure', *Administrative Science Quarterly*, Vol. 19, September, pp. 395–410.

Hsiao, T.C. (1997) 'Capability Development and Management of R&D Professionals in a Developing Country', *Technovation*, Vol. 17, No. 10, pp. 569–81.

Huijiong, W. (1993) 'Technology Management in a Dual World', *International Journal of Technology Management*, Vol. 8, Nos. 1/2, pp. 108–20.

Hull, C.W. (1992) 'Macro-engineering in the 1980s', in: Davidson, F.P. & Meador, C.L. (eds.), *Macro-Engineering: Global Infrastructure Solutions*, London: Ellis Horwood.

Intarakumnerd, P., Chairatana, P. & Tangchitpiboon, T. (2002) 'National Innovation System in Less Successful Developing Countries: The Case of Thailand' , *Research Policy*, Vol. 31, Nos. 8/9, pp. 1445–57.

Ito, S. (1986) 'Technology Transfer from Japan to Asian Developing Countries', *The Developing Economies*, Vol. 24, No. 4, pp. 309–13.

Jafry, T. & O'Neill, D.H. (2000) 'The Application of Ergonomics in Rural Development', *Applied Ergonomics*, Vol. 30, No. 6, pp. 565–70.

James, J. (1979) 'The Economic Case for More Indigenous Scientific and Technological Research and Development in Less Developed Countries', in: Street, J.H. & James, D.D. (eds.), *Technological Progress in Latin America*, Boulder, Colorado: Westview.

James, J. & Bhalla, A. (1993) 'Flexible Specialisation, New Technologies and Future Industrialisation in Developing Countries', *Futures*, Vol. 25, No. 6 (July/August), pp. 713–32.

James, J. & Elgar, E. (2002) *Technology, Globalisation and Poverty*, Cheltenham, UK.

James, J. & Watanabe, S. (1985) *Technology, Institutions and Government Policies*, London: Macmillan.

Jansizewski, H.A. (1981) 'Technology-Importing: National Perspectives', in: Sagafi-nejad, T., Perlmutter, H.V. & Moxon, R.W. (eds.), *Controlling International Technology Transfer*, pp. 321–25, New York: Pergamon.

Jenkins, R. (1991) 'The Political Economy of Industrialisation: A Comparison of Latin America and East Asian Newly Industrialising Countries', *Development and Change*, Vol. 22, No. 2, pp. 197–231.

—— (1993) 'Industrialisation and Industrial Policy in Latin America and East Asia: The Case of the Motor Industry', Development Studies Discussion Paper, University of East Anglia, Norwich.

—— (1995) 'The Political Economy of Industrial Policy: Automobile Manufacture in the Newly Industrialising Countries', *Cambridge Journal of Economics*, Vol. 19, No. 5, pp. 625–45.

Jequier, N. & Walker, R. (1983) *The World of Appropriate Technology: A Quantitative Analysis*, Paris: OECD.

Jeremy, D.J. (1981) *Transatlantic Industrial Revolution: The Diffusion of Textile Technologies between Britain and America, 1790–1830s*, Oxford: Basil Blackwell.

Jimba, S.W. (2000) 'Information Technology and the Dialectics of Poverty in Africa', *New Library World*, Vol. 101, No. 1158, pp. 253–62.

Jin, J. & Zou, H. (2002) 'How Does Fiscal Decentralization Affect Aggregate, National and Subnational Government Size?' *Journal of Urban Economics*, Vol. 52, No. 2, pp. 270–93.

Johnson, B. (1988) 'An Institutional Approach to the Small-Country Problem', in: Freeman, C. & Lundvall, B. (eds.), *Small Countries Facing the Technological Revolution*, pp. 279–97, London: Pinter.

Johnson, C.R. (1980) 'Constructive Critique of a Hierarchical Prioritisation Scheme Employing Paired Comparisons', Proceedings of the International Conference of Cybernetics, Society of the Institute of Electrical Engineers (IEEE), Cambridge, Massachusetts.

Johnson, O. (1984) 'On Growth and Inflation in Developing Countries', *IMF Staff Papers*, No. 31, IMF, Washington D.C.

Jones, E.L. (1988) *Growth Recurring: Economic Change in World History*, Oxford: Clarendon.

Jones, H. & Twiss, B.C. (1978) *Forecasting Technology for Planning Decisions*, London: Macmillan.

Jones, J.V.S. (1985) 'Strategic Aspects of Technology and Science Policy in Africa', *Science and Public Policy*, Vol. 12, No. 4, pp. 175–90.

Jungnickel, R. (1993) 'Recent Trends in Foreign Direct Investment', *Intereconomics*, Vol. 28, May/June, pp. 118–25.

Kahen, Goel (1994) 'A Comprehensive and Strategic Model of Technology Transfer: Emphasising IT', IS UK Ph.D. Consortium, Cranfield, UK.

Kahen, Goel (1995a) 'Integrating Energy Planning and Techno-economic Development: A Solid Basis for the Assessment and Transfer of Energy Technology to Developing Countries', First Joint International Symposium on Energy Models for Policy and Planning, 18–20 July, London Business School, London.

—— (1995b) 'Institutionalising Technology Transfer within a Multi-dimensional Context: The Japanese Style', Proceedings of the International Conference on Japanese Information in S&T, pp. 184–95, University of Newcastle Upon Time, Newcastle.

—— (1995c) 'Assessment of Information Technology for Developing Countries: Appropriateness, Local Constraints, IT Characteristics and Impacts', *International Journal of Computer Applications in Technology*, Vol. 5, Nos. 5/6, pp. 325–33.

—— (1996a) 'Building a Framework for Successful Information Technology Transfer to Developing Countries: Requirements and Effective Integration to a Viable IT Transfer', *International Journal of Computer Applications in Technologies*, Vol. 6, No. 1, pp. 1–8.

—— (1996b) 'Strategic Development, Technology Transfer, and Strategic Technology Assessment in Changing Environments', Proceedings of the First International Conference on Dynamics of Strategy, 11–12 April, pp. 366–84, Surrey, UK.

—— (1996c) 'Disaster Prevention and Management: An Academic Challenge for Disaster Prone Developing Countries', in: Duggan, T.V. & Brebbia, C.A. (eds.), *Environmental Engineering, Education and Training*, pp. 251–60, Southampton: Computational Mechanics Pub.

—— (1997a) 'Energy Technology Transfer: A Proposal for the Strategic Assessment of Environmental Impacts within Developing Countries', *Energy & Environment*, Vol. 8, No. 2, pp. 115–31.

—— (1997b) 'Technology Transfer and a Conceptual Model for Technological Planning and Decision Making', *Journal of Technology Management: Strategies & Applications*, Vol. 3, No. 2, pp. 229–39.

—— (1997c) 'Devising the Convergence Manufacturing Strategy for Productivity Improvement: Effectiveness Based on the Human Element', *International Journal of Materials and Product Technology*, Vol. 12, No. 1, pp. 18–26.

—— (1999) 'The Japanese Management of Software Development Approach and Its Evolution', Proceedings of JOHO6 Conference, pp. 79–88, European Institute of Japanese Studies, Stockholm School of Economics, Stockholm.

—— (2001a) 'Managing Electronic Banking in Developing Countries: A New Dimension in Restructuring Banking Industry', National Workshop on Globalisation and Technology, 16–18 October, K.N. Toosi University of Technology, Tehran.

Kahen, Goel (2001b) 'Strategic Assessment of High-Technology Transfer: A Managerial Approach for Energy Technologies', Proceedings of the International Symposium on Environment Engineering, K.N. Toosi University of Technology, Tehran.

—— (2001c) 'Management of Clean-Energy Technology Transfer: Application of an Integrated Model for Environment Friendly Energy Systems', Proceedings of the International Symposium on Environment Engineering, Tehran.

Kahen, Goel & Griffiths, C. (1995) 'Human Factors, Technology Transfer, and Information Technology in the Socio-economic Development of the Third World', Proceedings of IT-DEV'95, pp. 188–206, University of Johannesburg, Johannesburg.

—— (1996) 'A Quantitative Model for Technological Risk Assessment in the Process of Information Technology Transfer', Proceedings of the Third European Conference on the Evaluation of Information Technology, University of Bath, UK.

Kahen, Goel & Sayers, B.McA. (1994) 'IT and National Development in the Third World', Fifth International Conference of the Information Resources Management Association, 22–25 May, Texas.

—— (1995a) 'Modelling Global-Oriented Energy Technology Transfer to DCs', Sixth Global Warming International Conference, 3–6 April, San Francisco.

—— (1995b) 'Modelling Optimal Allocation of Foreign Exchange for Technological Import Needs in DCs', Proceedings of the Fifth Conference on Monetary and Foreign Exchange Policies, 15–16 May, Tehran.

—— (1995c) 'The Context of Technological Change in Developing Countries', Proceedings of the (IAMOT) European Conference on Management of Technology, Birmingham, UK.

—— (1996a) 'Health Care Technology Transfer: Appropriateness and Evaluation of Expert and Information Systems for Developing Countries', Helina '96: International Conference on Informatics for Health in Africa, 12–17 April, Johannesburg.

—— (1996b) 'Energy Technology and Strategic Assessment of Environmental Impact for Developing Countries', Proceedings of the International Conference on Integrating Environmental Assessment and Socio-economic Appraisal in the Development Process, 24–25 May, Bradford, UK.

—— (1997) 'Health Care Technology Transfer: Expert and Information Systems for Developing Countries', *Methods of Information in Medicine*, Vol. 36, No. 2, pp. 69–78.

Kaldor, N. (1978) 'The Role of Industrialisation in Latin American Inflations', in: Kaldor, N. (ed.), *Further Essays in Applied Economics*, pp. 119–37, London: Duckworth.

Kalecki, M. (1976) 'The Problem of Financing Economic Development', in: Kalecki, M. (ed.), *Essays on Development Economics*, pp. 41–63, Sussex: Harvester.

Kalman, R. (1981) 'Eight Strategic Issues for Informatics', in: Bennet, J. & Kalman, R. (eds.), *Computers in Developing Nations*, pp. 87–102, Amsterdam: North Holland.

Kamien, M.I. & Schwartz, N. (1982) *Market Structures and Innovation*, Cambridge: Cambridge University Press.

Kanter, R.M. (1989) *When Giants Learn to Dance: Mastering the Challenge of Strategy, Management and Careers in the 1990's*, New York: Simon & Schuster.

Kanz, L.E. (1980) *The International Transfer of Commercial Technology: The Role of the Multinational Corporation*, New York: Arno.

Kaplinski, R. (1984) 'The International Context for Industrialisation in the Third World', *Journal of Development Studies*, Vol. 21, No. 1, pp. 75–96.

―――― (1990) *The Economies of Small: Appropriate Technology in a Changing World*, London: IT Publications.

Karani, P. (2001) 'Constraints for Activities Implemented Jointly: Technology Transfer in Africa', *Renewable Energy*, Vol. 22, Nos. 1/2/3, pp. 229–34.

Karshenas, M. (1990) *Oil, State and Industrialisation in Iran*, Cambridge: Cambridge University Press.

Kartiko, P., Stewart, D., Moore, G. & Diatmoko, R. (2003) 'Implementing a Technology Strategy in Developing Countries: The Experience of the Indonesian Rolling Stock Industry', *Technological Forecasting and Social Change*, Vol. 70, No. 2, pp. 163–76.

Kastner, J.K., Dawson, C.R., Weiss, S.M., Kern, K.B. & Kulikowski, C.A. (1984) 'An Expert Consultation System for Frontline Health Workers in Primary Eye Care', *Journal of Medical Systems*, Vol. 8, No. 5, pp. 389–97.

Katrak, H. (1985) 'Imported Technology, Enterprise Size and R&D in a Newly Industrialising Country: The Indian Experience', *Oxford Bulletin of Economics and Statistics*, Vol. 47, No. 3, pp. 213–29.

Katz, E., Levine, M.L. & Hamilton, H. (1963) 'Traditions of Research on the Diffusion of Innovations', *American Sociological Review*, Vol. 28, No. 2, pp. 237–52.

Katz, J. (1984) 'Domestic Technological Innovation and Dynamic Comparative Advantage', *Journal of Development Economics*, Vol. 16, Nos. 1/2, pp. 13–37.

―――― (1987) 'Domestic Technology Generation in LDCs: A Review of Research Findings', in: Katz, J. (ed.), *Technology Generation in Latin American Manufacturing Industries*, pp. 13–55, London: Macmillan.

Katz, J. et al. (1988) 'Productivity, Technology and Domestic Effort in R&D', Working Paper No. 13, Research Programme on Scientific and

Technological Development in Latin America, IDB/ECLA/UNDP Programme, Buenos Aires.

Kaul, M., Patel, N. & Shams, K. (1987) *Searching for a Paddle: Trends in IT Applications in Asian Government Systems*, Kuala Lumpur: Asian and Pacific Development Centre.

Kedia, B.L. & Bhagat, R.S. (1988) 'Cultural Constraints on Transfer of Technology across Nations: Implications for Research in International and Comparative Management', *Academy of Management Review*, Vol. 13, No. 4, pp. 559–71.

Keeney, R.L. & Raiffa, H. (1976) *Decisions with Multiple Objectives: Preferences and Value Tradeoffs*, New York: John Wiley.

Khor, M. (2000) 'The United Nations and Globalisation', published at http//www.corpwatch.org (article 613) in June 2003.

Kigada, M. (1991) *Directory of Telecommunications Services in Africa*, International Development and Research Centre (IDRC), Nairobi, Kenya.

Kiggundu, M.N. (1989) *Managing Organisations in Developing Countries: An Operational and Strategic Approach*, West Hartford, Connecticut: Kumarian.

Kiguel, M.A. & O'Connell, S.A. (1994) 'Parallel Exchange Rates in Developing Countries: Lessons from Eight Case Studies', Policy Research Working Paper Series, World Bank, Washington D.C.

Kilmann, H.C., Saxton, M.J. & Serpa, R. (1985) *Gaining Control of the Corporate Culture*, San Francisco: Jossey Bass.

Kim, J.B. & Kim, J.J. (2000) 'Reputation and International Technology Transfer', *International Business Review*, Vol. 9, No. 5, pp. 613–24.

Kim, L. (1980) 'Stages of Development of Industrial Technology in a Developing Country: A Model', *Research Policy*, Vol. 9, No. 3, pp. 254–77.

Kindleberger, C.P. (1978) *Economic Response: Comparative Studies in Trade, Finance and Growth*, Cambridge, Massachusetts: Harvard University Press.

King, K. (1984) 'Science, Technology and Education in the Development of Indigenous Technological Capability', in: Fransman, M. & King, K. (eds.), *Technological Capability in the Third World*, pp. 31–63, New York: St. Martin's.

——— (1992) 'Artificial Intelligence of Developing Countries: Promises and Possibilities', in: Odedra, M. & Bhatnagar, S.C. (eds.), *Social Implication of Computers in Developing Countries*, New Delhi: Tata McGraw-Hill.

King, K. & Beck, H. (1990) 'Medical AI Systems as Appropriate Technology for Developing Countries', *The Knowledge Engineering Review*, Vol. 5, No. 4, pp. 251–63.

Kleiman, H.S. & Jamieson, W.M. (1978) 'Two Faces of International Technology Transfer', *Battle Today*, No. 10, pp. 3–6.

Kleindorfer, P.R. & Partovi, F.Y. (1990) 'Integrating Manufacturing Strategy and Technology Choice', *European Journal of Operations Research*, Vol. 47, No. 2, pp. 214–24.

Kodama, F. (1990) 'Japanese Innovation in Mechatronics Technology', in: Sigurdson, J. (ed.), *Measuring the Dynamics of Technological Change*, London: Pinter.

Kogi, K. & Sen, R.N. (1987) 'Third World Ergonomics', in: Oborne, D.J. (ed.), *International Reviews of Ergonomics*, Vol. 1, pp. 77–118, London: Taylor & Francis.

Kolds, E. (1981) 'Comments', in: Sagafi-nejad, T., Perlmutter, H.V. & Moxon, R.W. (eds.), *Controlling International Technology Transfer*, New York: Pergamon.

Kosmo, M. (1987) *Money to Burn? The High Costs of Energy Subsidies*, Washington, D.C.: World Resources Institute.

Kotler, P. (1994) *Marketing Management: Analysis, Planning, and Control*, London: Prentice-Hall.

Kottenstlette, J. & Freeman, J. (1971) 'Project for the Analysis of Technology Transfer', *Annual Report*, Denver, Colorado: University of Denver Research Institute.

Kozmetsky, G. (1990) 'Challenges of Technology Innovation and Transfer', in: Williams, F. & Gibson, D.V. (eds.), *Technology Transfer*, pp. 21–42, Thousand Oaks, California: Sage.

Kozulj, R. (2003) 'People, Cities, Growth and Technological Change: From the Golden Age to Globalization', *Technological Forecasting and Social Change*, Vol. 70, No. 3, pp. 199–230.

Kroeber, A.L. (1934) 'Diffusionism', *Encyclopaedia of Social Sciences*, New York: Macmillan.

Kroemer, K.H.E. (1975) 'Muscle Strength as a Criterion in Control Design for Diverse Populations', in: Chapanis, A. (ed.), *Ethnic Variables in Human Factor Engineering*, Baltimore: Johns Hopkins University Press.

Krugman, P., (ed.) (1986) *Strategic Trade Policy and the New International Economics*, Cambridge, Massachusetts: MIT Press.

Kumar, N. (1987) 'Technology Imports and Local Research and Development in Indian Industry', *The Developing Economies*, Vol. 25, No. 3, pp. 220–33.

Kumar, N. & Siddharthan, N.S. (1994) 'Technology, Firm Size and Export Behaviour in Developing Countries: The Case of Indian Enterprises', *Journal of Development Studies*, Vol. 31, No. 2, pp. 289–309.

Kumar, V. & Jain, P.K. (2003) 'Commercialization of New Technologies in India: An Empirical Study of Perceptions of Technology Institutions', *Technovation*, Vol. 23, No. 2, pp. 113–20.

Kuznets, P.W. (1977) *Economic Growth and Structure in the Republic of Korea*, New Haven: Yale University Press.

Kuznets, S. (1966) *Modern Economic Growth: Rate, Structure and Spread*, New Haven: Yale University Press.

Kwon, Y.C. et al. (1987) 'Dynamic Competitive Position between Foreign Joint Venture and NICs' Indigenous Firms: A Case Study in South Korea', *Foreign Trade Review*, Vol. 22, July/September.

Lall, S. (1982) 'Technological Learning in the Third World: Some Implications of Technology Exports', in: Stewart, F. and James, J. (eds.), *The Economics of New Technology in Developing Countries*, pp. 157–79, London: Pinter.

—— (1984) 'Transnationals and the Third World: Changing Perceptions', *National Westminster Bank Quarterly Review*, May, pp. 2–16.

—— (1987) *Learning to Industrialise*, London: Macmillan.

Lall, S. & Mohammed, S. (1983) 'Foreign Ownership and Manufacturing Export Performance in the Large Corporate Sector of India', *Journal of Development Studies*, Vol. 20, No. 1 (October), pp. 56–67.

Lall, S. & Streeten, P. (1977) *Foreign Investment, Transnationals, and Developing Countries*, New York: Macmillan.

Lan, P. (1996) *Technology Transfer to China through Foreign Direct Investment*, Aldershot: Avebury.

Land, F. (1987) 'Social Aspects of Information Systems', in: Piercy, N. (ed.), *Management Information Systems: The Technological Challenge*, pp. 11–57, Beckenham: Croom Helm.

Landes, D.S. (1969) *The Unbound Prometheus: Technological Change and Industrial Development in Western Europe from 1750 to the Present*, Cambridge: Cambridge University Press.

Lands, D.S. (1989) 'Rich Country, Poor Country', *The New Republic*, Vol. 20, No. 1, pp. 23–27.

Lang, H. & Hines, C. (1993) *The New Protectionism: Protecting the Future against Free Trade*, London: Earthscan.

Lanza, G.R. (1985) 'Blind Technology Transfer: The Bhopal Example', *Environment Science Technology*, Vol. 19, No. 7, pp. 581–82.

Lash, S. & Urry, J. (1989) *The End of Organised Capitalism*, Cambridge: Polity.

Laurent, A. (1983) 'The Cultural Diversity of Western Conceptions of Management', *International Studies of Management and Organisation*, Vol. 13, Nos. 1/2, pp. 91–102.

—— (1986) 'The Cross-cultural Puzzle of International Human Resource Management', *Human Resource Management*, Vol. 25, No. 1, pp. 91–102.

—— (1991) 'A Cultural View of Organisational Change', in: Evans, P., Doz, Y. & Laurent, A. (eds.), *Human Resource Management in*

International Firms: Change, Globalization, Innovation, pp. 83–94, London: Macmillan.

Lauridsen, L. (2000) 'Industrial Policies, Political Institutions and Industrial Development in Thailand 1959–1991', Working Paper No. 21, International Development Studies, Roskilde University, Roskilde.

Lawrence, P.R. & Lorsch, J.W. (1967) *Organisation and Environment*, Cambridge, Massachusetts: Harvard University Press.

Layton, Edwin (1977) 'Conditions of Technological Development', in: Spiegel-Rosing & de Solla Price, D.J. (eds.), *Science, Technology and Society*, London: Sage.

Leader Williams, N. & Albon, S.D. (1988) 'Allocation of Resources for Conservation', *Nature*, Vol. 336, 6 December, pp. 533–35.

LeClair, M.S. (2002) 'Fighting the Tide: Alternative Trade Organisations in the Era of Global Free Trade', *World Development*, Vol. 30, No. 6, pp. 949–58.

Lecraw, D.J. (1977) 'Direct Investment by Firms from Less Developed Countries', *Oxford Economic Papers*, Vol. 29, No. 3, pp. 442–57.

Lee, J. (2000) 'Challenges of Korean Technology-Based Ventures and Governmental Policies in the Emergent-Technology Sectors', *Technovation*, Vol. 20, No. 9, pp. 489–95.

Lee, J.M., Bae, Z. & Choi, D. (1988) 'Technology Development Processes: A Model for a Developing Country with a Global Perspective', *R&D Management*, Vol. 18, No. 3, pp. 235–49.

Leontief, W.W. (1947) 'Introduction to a Theory of the Internal Structure of Functional Relationships', *Econometrica*, Vol. 15, No. 3, pp. 361–73.

Lerner, D. (1958) *Passing of Traditional Society*, New York: Free Press.
———— (1964) 'The Transformation of Institutions', in: Hamilton, W. (ed.), *The Transfer of Institutions*, Durham: Duke University Press.

Lewis, T. (2000) 'Technology Education and Developing Countries', *International Journal of Technology and Design Education*, Vol. 10, No. 2, pp. 163–79.

Leys, C. (1975) *Under-development in Kenya: The Political Economy of New Colonialism*, Berkeley, California: University of California Press.

Lie, M. (1991) *Technology as Masculinity*, Trondheim: SINTEF-IFIM.

Lin, C. (1988) 'East Asia and Latin America as Contrasting Models', *Economic Development and Cultural Change*, Vol. 36, No. 3, pp. S153–S197.

Lind, P. (1991) *Computerisation in Developing Countries*, London: Routledge.

Lindbeck, A. (1983) 'The Recent Slowdown of Productivity Growth', *Economic Journal*, Vol. 93, March, pp. 13–34.

Litter, D., (ed.) (1988) *Technological Development*, Oxford: Philip Allen.

Little, I.M.D. (1979) 'An Economic Reconnaissance', in: Galenson, W. (ed.), *Economic Growth and Structural Change in Taiwan: Post-war Experience of the Republic of China*, pp. 448–507, Ithaca: Cornell University Press.

Liu, H. & Jiang, Y. (2001) 'Technology Transfer from Higher Education Institutions to Industry in China: Nature and Implications', *Technovation*, Vol. 21, No. 3, pp. 175–88.

Liyanage, S. (1993) 'Changing Perspectives of Science and Technology Development in Developing Countries', *Science and Public Policy*, Vol. 20, No. 4, pp. 235–44.

Lucas, B.G. (1979) 'Working Note: Analysis of UNCSTD Developing Country National Papers', August, National Science Foundation, Vienna.

Lucas, B.G. & Freedman, S. (1983) *Technology Choice and Change in Developing Countries: Internal and External Constraints*, Dublin: Tycooly International.

Luckham, A. (1971) 'Institutional Transfer and Breakdown in a New Nation: The Nigerian Military', *Administrative Science Quarterly*, Vol. 16, No. 4, pp. 387–406.

MacCharles, D.C. (1987) *Trade among Multinationals: Intra-industry Trade and National Competitiveness*, London: Croom Helm.

MacDonald, S. (1983) 'Technology beyond Machines', in: MacDonald, S., Mandeville, T. & Lamberton, D. (eds.), *The Trouble with Technology*, pp. 26–36, London: Frances Pinter.

MacKenzie, D. & Wacjman, J. (1985) *The Social Shaping of Technology*, Milton Keynes, UK: Open University Press.

Maclaurin, W.R. (1953) 'The Sequence from Invention to Innovation and Its Relation to Economic Growth', *Quarterly Journal of Economics*, Vol. 67, No. 1, pp. 97–111.

MacLeod, R. & Kumar, D., (eds.) (1995) *Technology and the Raj*, New Delhi: Sage.

Madon, S. (1992) 'The Impact of Computer-Based Information Systems on Rural Development: A Case Study in India', Ph.D. dissertation, Imperial College of Science, Technology and Medicine, London.

Madu, C. (1989) 'Transferring Technology to Developing Countries: Critical Factors for Success', *Long Range Planning*, Vol. 22, No. 4, pp. 115–24.

Mahmood, I.P. & Singh, J. (2003) 'Technological Dynamism in Asia', *Research Policy*, Vol. 32, No. 6, pp. 1031–54.

Makhaya, G. & Roberts, S. (2003) 'Telecommunications in Developing Countries: Reflections from the South African Experience', *Telecommunications Policy*, Vol. 27, Nos. 1/2, pp. 41–59.

Malecki, E.J. (1990) 'Technological Innovation and Paths to Regional Economic Growth', in: Schmandt, J. & Wilson, R.W. (eds.), *Growth*

Policy in an Age of High Technology, pp. 97–126, Boston: Unwin Hyman.

——— (1991) *Technology and Economic Development,* London: Longman Scientific & Technical.

Mani, S. (1987) 'Small Sector Scores in In-house R and D', *Economic and Political Weekly,* 18 July, pp. 1174–76.

Manning, G. (1974) *Technology Transfer: Successes and Failures,* San Francisco: San Francisco Press.

Mansfield, E. (1968) *Industrial Research and Technological Innovation,* New York: Norton.

——— (1973) 'Determinants of the Speed of New Technology', in: Williams, B.R. (ed.), *Science and Technology in Economic Growth,* pp. 199–216, London: Macmillan.

——— (1977) *The Production and Application of New Industrial Technology,* New York: W.W. Norton.

——— (1989) *Economics: Principles, Problems, and Decisions,* New York: W.W. Norton.

Mansfield, E. & Romeo, A. (1984) 'Reverse Transfers of Technology from Overseas Subsidiaries to American Firms', *IEEE Transactions on Engineering Management,* Vol. EM-31, No. 3, pp. 122–27.

Mansfield, E., Teece, D. & Romeo, A. (1979) 'Overseas Research and Development by U.S.-Based Firms', *Economica,* Vol. 46, May, pp. 187–96.

Mansfield, E., Romeo, A., Schwartz, M., Teece, D., Wagner, S. & Brach, P. (1982) *Technology Transfer, Productivity and Economic Policy,* New York: W.W. Norton. (Reprinted 1994, New York: W.W. Norton.)

Mansour, M.B. (1981) 'Definitional Issues in Technology Transfer: Channels, Mechanisms and Sources', in: Hawkins, R.B. & Prasad, A.J. (eds.), *Technology Transfer and Economic Development,* Research in International Business and Finance, Vol. 2, pp. 1–9, Greenwich, Connecticut: Jai Press.

Marcotte, C. & Niosi, J. (2000) 'Technical and Organizational Learning: Canadian Technology Transfer to China', *Journal of Technology Transfer,* Vol. 25, No. 1, pp. 23–39.

Marris, R. (1970) 'Can We Measure the Need for Development Assistance?' *Economic Journal,* Vol. 80, No. 319, pp. 650–68.

——— (1982) 'How Much of the Slow-down was Catch-up?' in: Matthews, R.C.O. (ed.), *Slower Growth in the Western World,* London: Heinemann.

Marton, K. (1986) *Multinationals, Technology, and Industrialisation,* Lexington, Massachusetts: Lexington Books.

Mason, R.H. (1974) 'The Transfer of Technology and the Factor Proportions Problem: The Philippines and Mexico', United Nations Institute for Training and Research (UNITAR), Research Report No. 10.

Mason, R.H. (1981) 'Comments', in: Sagafi-nejad, T., Perlmutter, H.V. & Moxon, R.W. (eds.), *Controlling International Technology Transfer*, New York: Pergamon.

Mattelart, A., (ed.) (1983) *Transnationals and the Third World: The Struggle for Culture*, South Halley, Massachusetts: Bergin & Garvey.

Mayer-Stamer, J., Rauh, C., Riad, H., Schmitt, S. & Welte, T., (eds.) (1991) *Comprehensive Modernisation on the Shop Floor: A Case Study on the Brazilian Machinery Industry*, Berlin: German Development Institute.

McCarroll, T. (1991) 'What New Age?' *Time*, Vol. 138, 12 August, pp. 44–46.

Merhar, M. (1969) *Technological Dependence, Monopoly and Growth*, London: Pergamon.

Merrill, R. (1972) 'The Role of Technology in Cultural Evolution', *Social Biology*, Vol. 19, No. 3, pp. 219–23.

Meshkati, N. (1989a) 'An Etiological Investigation of Micro- and Macro-ergonomic Factors in the Bhopal Disaster: Lessons for Industries in Both Industrialised and Developing Countries', *International Journal of Industrial Ergonomics*, Vol. 4, No. 2, pp. 161–75.

———— (1989b) 'Technology Transfer to Developing Countries: A Tripartite Micro- and Macro-ergonomics Analysis of Human–Organisation–Technology Interfaces', *International Journal of Industrial Ergonomics*, Vol. 4, No. 2, pp. 101–15.

Meshkati, N. & Robertson, M.M. (1986) 'The Effects of Human Factors on the Success of Technology Transfer Projects to Industrially Developing Countries: A Review of Representative Case Studies', in: Brown, O. & Hendrick, H.W. (eds.), *Human Factors in Organisational Design and Management*, Vol. 2, pp. 343–49, Amsterdam: Elsevier.

Miller, W.H. (1979) 'Industry's Growing Space Harvest', *Industry Week*, 1 May, pp. 45–49.

Millman, A.F. (1990) 'Technology Strategy and the Inward Transfer of Foreign Technology in the UK Machine Tool Industry', Ph.D. dissertation, University of Warwick, UK.

Minami, R., (ed.) (1994) *The Economic Development of China*, London: Macmillan.

Miner, J.B., (ed.) (1982) *Theories of Organisational Structure and Process*, New York: Dryden.

Ming, W.X. & Xing, Z. (1999) 'A New Strategy of Technology Transfer to China', *International Journal of Operations and Production Management*, Vol. 19, Nos. 5/6, pp. 527–37.

Miranda Jr., C.V. (1991) 'Transnational Corporations in the Philippines', *Regional Development Dialogue*, Vol. 12, No. 1, pp. 139–61.

Mogavero, L.N. & Shane, R.S. (1982) *Technology Transfer and Innovation*, New York: Marcel Dekker.

Mohr, L.B. (1971) 'Organisational Technology and Organisational Structure', *Administrative Science Quarterly*, Vol. 16, No. 4, pp. 444–559.

Montealegre, R. (1998) 'Managing Information Technology in Modernising against the Odds: Lessons from an Organisation in a Less-Developed Country', *Information & Management*, Vol. 34, No. 2, pp. 103–16.

Moran, T.H. (1986) 'Investing in Development: New Roles for Private Capital?' US–Third World Policy Perspectives, No. 6, Overseas Development Council, Washington D.C.

Morishima, M., (ed.) (1976) *The Economic Theory of Modern Society*, Cambridge: Cambridge University Press.

Morisset, J. (1989) 'The Impact of Foreign Capital Inflows on Domestic Savings Re-examined: The Case of Argentina', *World Development*, Vol. 17, No. 11, pp. 1709–15.

Moroney, W.F. & Reising, J. (1992) 'Subjects in Human Factors: Just Who Are They?' Proceedings of the Human Factors Society, 36th Annual Meeting, pp. 1227–31, Santa Monica, California.

Morris, M.D. (1983) 'The Growth of Large Scale Industry to 1947', in: Kumar, D. (ed.), *The Cambridge History of India*, Cambridge: Cambridge University Press.

Morrow, D. & Rondinelli, D. (2002) 'Adopting Corporate Environmental Management Systems: Motivations and Results of ISO 14001 and EMAS Certification', *European Management Journal*, Vol. 20, No. 2, pp. 159–71.

Mostow, J., (ed.) (1995) Special Issue on 'Artificial Intelligence and Software Engineering', *IEEE Transactions on Software Engineering*, Vol. 11, No. 11.

Mowery, D. (1983a) 'Innovation, Market Structure, and Government Policy in the American Semiconductor Electronics Industry: A Survey', *Research Policy*, Vol. 12, No. 4, pp. 183–97.

——— (1983b) 'Economic Theory and Government Technology Policy', *Policy Sciences*, Vol. 16, No. 1, pp. 27–44.

Mowery, D. & Rosenberg, N. (1989) *Technology and the Pursuit of Economic Growth*, Cambridge: Cambridge University Press.

Murphy, J. (1967) 'Retrospect and Prospect', in: Spencer, D. & Woroniak, A. (eds.), *The Transfer of Technology to Developing Countries*, New York: Praeger.

——— (1985) 'A Modern View on the Transfer of Technology', *Science and Public Policy*, Vol. 12, No. 3, pp. 144–48.

Nabseth, L. & Ray, G.F. (1974) *The Diffusion of New Industrial Processes: An International Study*, Cambridge: Cambridge University Press.

Nafziger, E.W. (1990) *The Economics of Developing Countries*, New Jersey: Prentice-Hall.

Nakaoka, T. (1987) 'On Technological Leaps of Japan as a Developing Country', *Osaka City University Economic Review*, Vol. 22, No. 1, pp. 1–25.

Ndebbio, J.E.U. (1985) 'Growth Process and Economic Transformation through Technological Transfer in Africa', *Science and Public Policy*, Vol. 12, No. 4, pp. 211–22.

Nelson, R. (1993) *National Innovation Systems*, Oxford: Oxford University Press.

Nelson, R.N. (1959) 'The Economics of Invention', *Journal of Business*, Vol. 32, No. 2, pp. 101–27.

Nelson, R.R. & Winter, S.G. (1982) *An Evolutionary Theory of Economic Change*, Cambridge, Massachusetts: Harvard University Press.

Networks Group (1992) *Status of Networking in Africa*, Consortia Pisa Research, Italy.

Newman, K.L & Nollen, S.D. (1996) 'Culture and Congruence: The Fit between Management Practices and National Culture', *Journal of International Business Studies*, Vol. 27, No. 4, pp. 753–79.

Nickerson, R.S. (1981) 'Why Interactive Computer Systems Are Sometimes Not Used by People Who Might Benefit from Them', *International Journal of Man–Machine Studies*, Vol. 15, No. 4, pp. 469–83.

Noori, H. (1995) 'The Design of an Integrated Group Decision Support System for Technology Assessment', *R&D Management*, Vol. 25, No. 3, pp. 309–22.

Nordhaus, W.D. (1991) 'To Slow or Not to Slow: The Economics of the Greenhouse Effect', *Economic Journal*, Vol. 101, July, pp. 920–37.

Northcott, J., Fogarty, M. & Trevor, M. (1986) *Chips and Jobs: Acceptance of New Technology at Work*, London: Policy Studies Institute.

Odedra, M.R. (1990) 'The Transfer of Information Technology to Developing Countries: Case Studies from Kenya, Zambia, and Zimbabwe', Ph.D. dissertation, London School of Economics, London.

Okimoto, D.I. (1989) *Between MITI and the Market: Japanese Industrial Policy for High Technology*, Stanford, California: Stanford University Press.

O'Neill, D.H. (2000) 'Ergonomics in Industrially Developing Countries: Does Its Application Differ from That in Industrially Advanced Countries?' *Applied Ergonomics*, Vol. 31, No. 6, pp. 631–40.

Onn, F.C. (1989) 'Malaysia: In Pursuit of Newly Industrialising Economy', *Asian Development Review*, Vol. 7, No. 2, pp. 5–19.

Organisation for Economic Cooperation and Development (OECD) (1978) 'The Problems of Technology Transfer between Advanced and Developing Societies', Midway Through Inter-futures, February, OECD, Paris.

Organisation for Economic Cooperation and Development (OECD) (1981) *North/South Technology Transfer*, Paris: OECD.

——— (1987) *International Investment and Multinational Enterprises: Recent Trends in International Direct Investment*, Paris: OECD.

——— (1988) *New Technologies in the 1990s: A Socio-economic Strategy*, Paris: OECD.

——— (1997) *The World in 2020: Towards a New Global Age*, Paris: OECD.

Oshima, H.T. (1976) 'Development and Mass Communication: A Re-examination', in: Schramm W. & Lerner, D. (eds.), *Communication and Change*, Honolulu: University Press of Hawaii.

Osuntokun, B.O. (1991) 'Problems and Opportunities in the Absorption of Technology', HO Meeting of Regional Advisers on Technology Development, Assessment and Transfer, 17–21 June, Geneva.

Ouma-onyango, R. (1999) 'Information Resources and Technology Transfer Management in Developing Countries', *Journal of Asian Libraries*, Vol. 8, No. 5, pp. 182–83.

Oyomno, G.Z. (1995) 'Sustainability of Governmental Use of Microcomputer-Based Information Technology in Kenya: Critical Issues and Considerations', Proceedings of the International Federation for Information Processing International Conference, 3–5 January, Cairo.

Ozbekhan, H. (1969) 'Towards a General Theory of Planning', in: Jantsch, E. (ed.), *Perspectives of Planning*, pp. 47–155, Paris: OECD.

——— (1970) 'On Some of the Fundamental Problems of Planning', *Technological Forecasting and Social Sciences*, Vol. 1, No. 3, pp. 234–40.

Pack, H., (ed.) (1987) *Productivity, Technology and Industrial Development: A Case Study in Textiles*, New York: Oxford University Press.

Panerai, R.B. & Attinger, E.O. (1984) 'A Model of Technology Assessment and Resource Allocation for Prenatal Care in Developing Countries', Proceedings of the Conference on Appropriate Technology for Prenatal Care, 26–30 November, Pan-American Health Organisation, Washington, D.C.

——— (1985) 'A Quantitative Tool for Health Technology Decision-Making', Working Paper, American Hospital Association, Chicago, Illinois.

Panerai, R.B. & Pena Mohr, J. (1989) *Health Technology Assessment: Methodologies for Developing Countries*, Washington, D.C.: Pan-American Health Organisation.

Pang, E.F. & Hill, H. (1991) 'Technology Exports from a Small, Very Open NIC: The Case of Singapore', *World Development*, Vol. 19, No. 5, pp. 553–68.

Parvin, M. (1975) 'Technological Adaptation, Optimum Level of Backwardness and the Rate of Per Capita Income Growth: An Econometric Approach', *American Economist*, Vol. 19, No. 1, pp. 23–31.

Pascal, R.T. & Athos, A.G. (1981) *The Art of Japanese Management*, New York: Simon & Schuster.

Patarasuk, W. (1991) 'The Role of Transnational Corporations in Thailand's Manufacturing Industries', *Regional Development Dialogue* (UNCRD, Japan), Vol. 12, No. 1, pp. 92–112.

Patel, S.J. (1983) Foreword, in: Chudnovsky, D. & Nagao, M. (eds.), *Capital Goods Production in the Third World*, pp. xi–xvii, London: Frances Pinter.

Pavitt, K. (1980) 'Technical Innovation and Industrial Development', *Futures*, Vol. 12, No. 2, pp. 2–10.

Pavitt, K. & Patel, P. (1988) 'The International Distribution and Determinants of Technological Activities', *Oxford Review of Economic Policy*, Vol. 4, No. 4, pp. 35–55.

Pavitt, K. & Soete, L.G. (1982) 'International Differences in Economic Growth and the International Location of Innovation', in: Giersch, H. (ed.), *Emerging Technologies: Consequences for Economic Growth, Structural Change, and Employment*, pp. 105–33, Tubingen: J.C.B. Mohr (Paul Siebeck).

Pearce, D. & Turner, R. (1990) *Economics of Natural Resources and the Environment*, Hemel Hempstead: Harvester-Wheatsheaf.

Pearce, R.D. & Singh, S. (1992) *Globalizing Research and Development*, London: Macmillan.

Perez, C. (1988) 'New Technologies and Development', in: Freeman, C. & Lundvall, B. (eds.), *Small Countries Facing the Technological Revolution*, pp. 85–97, London: Pinter.

Perez, C. & Soete, L. (1988) 'Catching up in Technology: Entry Barriers and Windows of Opportunity', in: Dosi, G., Forsyth, D.J.C., McBain, N.S. & Solomon, R.F. (eds.), *Technical Change and Economic Theory*, pp. 458–79, London: Pinter.

Perlmutter, H.V. & Sagafi-nejad, T. (1981) *International Technology Transfer*, New York: Pergamon.

Perrow, C. (1965) 'Hospitals: Technology, Structure, and Goals', in: March, J.G. (ed.), *Handbook of Organisations*, pp. 910–71. Chicago: Rand McNally.

—— (1967) 'A Framework for the Comparative Analysis of Organisations', *American Sociological Review*, Vol. 32, No. 2, pp. 194–208.

—— (1970) *Organisational Analysis: A Sociological View*, Belmont, California: Wadsworth.

Pettigrew, A.M., (ed.) (1973) *The Politics of Organisational Decision Making*, London: Tavistock.

Pillai, P.M. (1979) 'Technology Transfer, Adaptation, and Assimilation', *Economic and Political Weekly*, November, pp. M121–M126.

Pinckney, T.C. et al. (1982) 'Microcomputers and Financial Management in Development Ministries: Experience from Kenya', Development Discussion Paper No. 137, Harvard Institute for International Development, Cambridge, Massachusetts.

Pohjola, Matti (2002) 'The New Economy: Facts, Impacts and Policies', *Information Economics and Policy*, Vol. 14, No. 2, pp. 133–44.

Porter, A.L., Roper, A.T., Mason, T.W., Rossini, F.A., Banks, J. & Wiederholt, B.J. (1980) *A Guidebook for Technology Assessment and Impact Analysis*, New York: North-Holland.

Porter, A.L. et al. (1991) *Forecasting and Management of Technology*, New York: John Wiley.

Porter, M. (1990) 'The Competitive Advantage of Nations', *Harvard Business Review*, Vol. 68, No. 2, pp. 73–93.

Posner, M.V. (1961) 'International Trade and Technical Change', *Oxford Economic Papers*, Vol. 13, No. 3, pp. 323–41.

Poznanski, K.Z. (1984) 'Technology Transfer: West–South Perspective', *World Policy*, Vol. 37, pp. 134–52.

Prasad, S.B. (1986) 'Technology Transfer: The Approach of a Dutch Multinational', *Technovation*, Vol. 4, No. 1, pp. 3–15.

Preece, D.A. (1990) *Managing the Adoption of New Technology*, London: Routledge.

Proff, H. (2001) 'Business Unit Strategies between Regionalisation and Globalisation', *International Business Review*, Vol. 11, No. 2, pp. 231–50.

Putranto, K., Stewart, D. & Moore, G. (2003a) 'International Technology Transfer and Distribution of Technology Capabilities: The Case of Railway Development in Indonesia', *Technology in Society*, Vol. 25, No. 1, pp. 43–53.

Putranto, K., Stewart, D., Moore, G. & Diatmoko, R. (2003b) 'Implementing a Technology Strategy in Developing Countries: The Experience of the Indonesian Rolling Stock Industry', *Technological Forecasting and Social Change*, Vol. 70, No. 2, pp. 163–76.

Quinn, J.B. (1969) 'Technology Transfer by Multinational Companies', *Harvard Business Review*, Vol. 47, No. 6 (November/December), pp. 147–61.

Rada, J.F. (1982) 'A Third World Perspective', in: Fredrichs, G. & Schaff, A. (eds.), *Microelectronics and Society: For Better or for Worse, A Report to the Club of Rome*, pp. 203–31, New York: Pergamon.

Radar, R.R. (1996) 'Intellectual Property Protection and Dispute Resolution', in: Liu, P.C. & Sun, A.Y. (eds.), *Intellectual Property Protection in the Asian-Pacific Region*, pp. 3–15, Occasional

Paper/Reprints Series in Contemporary Asian Studies, No. 4, University of Maryland Law School, Maryland.

Ramanathan, K. (1988) 'Technometric Model', *Science and Public Policy*, Vol. 15, No. 4, pp. 230–48.

Ramirez, D., Khanna, M. & Zilberman, D. (2001) 'Conservation Capital and Sustainable Economic Growth', 77th Annual Conference of Western Economic Associations, 4–8 July, San Francisco.

Ranis, G. (1984) 'Determinants and Consequences of Indigenous Technological Activity', in: Fransman, M. & King, K. (eds.), *Technological Capability in the Third World*, pp. 95–112, New York: St. Martin's.

——— (1985) 'Employment, Income Distribution and Growth in the East Asian Context: A Comparative Analysis', in: Corbo, V., Krueger, A., & Ossa, F. (eds.), *Export-Oriented Development Strategies: The Success of Five Newly Industrializing Countries*, Boulder, Colorado: Westview.

Rao, P.M. (2001) 'The ICT Revolution, Internationalisation of Technology Activity, and the Emerging Economies', *International Business Review*, Vol. 10, No. 5, pp. 571–96.

Reiko, Yamada (2001) 'University Reform in the Post-massification Era in Japan: Analysis of Government Education Policy for the 21st Century', *Higher Education Policy*, Vol. 14, No. 4, pp. 277–91.

Reuber, G.L. (1973) *Private Foreign Investment in Development*, Oxford: Clarendon.

Revermann, H. & Sonntag, A.P. (1989) *Key Technologies: Turbulent Changes in Industry as a Result of Innovative Dynamics*, Aldershot: Gower.

Reynolds, L.G. (1983) 'The Spread of Economic Growth to the Third World', *Journal of Economic Literature*, Vol. 21, No. 3, pp. 941–80.

Richard, M.D., Peck, M.J. & Kaluchek, E.D. (1967) *Technology, Economic Growth, and Public Policy*, Washington, D.C.: The Brookings Institute.

Robbins, M.D. & Milliken, J.G. (1976) 'Technology Transfer and the Process of Technological Innovation: New Concepts, New Models', *R&D Management*, Special Issue on Technology Transfer, Vol. 6, No. 4, pp. 165–70.

Robbins, S.P. (1987) *Organisation Theory*, New Jersey: Prentice-Hall.

Robertson, R. (1992) *Globalisation*, London: Sage.

Rodriguez, A.J. (1995) 'The East and Southern Africa Network: Technical and Management Perspectives', Proceedings of the International Federation for Information Processing International Conference, 9–11 January, Cairo.

Rodriguez, C.A. (1985) 'A Process for Innovators in Developing Countries to Implement New Technology', *Columbia Journal of World Business*, Vol. 20, No. 3, pp. 21–27.

Roe, T. (1993) 'Funding Technology Co-operation: The EC's View', Proceedings of the Global Technology Partnership Conference, 23–25 March, Birmingham, UK.

Roessner, J.D. & Porter, A.L. (1990) 'High Technology Capacity and Competition', in: Chatterji, M. (ed.), *Technology Transfer in the Developing Countries*, London: Macmillan.

Rogers, D.M.A. (1988) 'Toward a National Campaign for Competitive Technology Transfer', Paper presented at the AAAS Annual Meeting, 12–17 February, Boston.

Rogers, E. (1962) *Diffusion of Innovation*, New York: Free Press.

Rogers, E.M., Takegami, S. & Yin, J. (2001) 'Lessons Learned about Technology Transfer', *Technovation*, Vol. 21, No. 4, pp. 253–61.

Rolle, R. & Satin, M. (2002) 'Basic Requirements for the Transfer of Fermentation Technologies to Developing Countries', *International Journal of Food Microbiology*, Vol. 75, No. 3, pp. 181–87.

Romer, P. (1990) 'Indigenous Technological Change', *Journal of Political Economy*, Vol. 98, No. 5 (Part 2), pp. 71–102.

Ronstadt, R. (1984) 'R&D Abroad by US Multinationals', in: Stobaugh, R. & Wells, L.T. (eds.), *Technology Crossing Borders*, pp. 241–64, Boston, Massachusetts: Harvard Business School Press.

Roobeek, A.J.M. (1990) *Beyond the Technology Race*, Amsterdam: Elsevier.

Root, F.R. (1968) 'The Role of International Business in the Diffusion of Technological Innovation', *Economic and Business Bulletin*, Vol. 20, No. 4, pp. 17–24.

—— (1981) 'The Pricing of International Technology Transfers via Non-affiliate Licensing Arrangements', in: Sagafi-nejad, T., Perlmutter, H.V. & Moxon, R.W. (eds.), *Controlling International Technology Transfer*, pp. 5–10, New York: Pergamon.

Roper, G.C. & Sharp, J.A. (1990) 'The Analytic Hierarchy Process and Its Application to an Information Technology Decision', *Journal of Operations Research Society*, Vol. 41, No. 1, pp. 49–59.

Rosenberg, N. (1976) 'On Technological Expectations', *Economic Journal*, Vol. 86, September, pp. 523–35.

—— (1982) *Inside the Black Box: Technology and Economics*, Cambridge, Massachusetts: Cambridge University Press. (Reprinted 1990, New York: Cambridge University Press.)

Rosenberg, N. & Frischtak, C., (eds.) (1985) *International Technology Transfer*, New York: Praeger.

Ross, D.N. (1999) 'Culture as a Context for Multinational Business', *Multinational Business Review*, Vol. 7, No. 1, pp. 13–19.

Rostow, W.W. (1967) *The Stages of Economic Growth: A Non-communist Manifesto*, New York: Cambridge University Press.

Rothgeb, J.M. (1984) 'The Effects of Foreign Investment on Overall and Sectoral Growth in Third World States', *Journal of Peace Research*, Vol. 21, No. 1, pp. 5–15.

Rothwell, R. & Zegveld, W. (1981) *Industrial Innovation and Public Policy*, London: Frances Pinter.

Rothwell, S. (1984) 'Company Employment Policies and New Technology in Manufacturing and Service Sectors', in: Warner, M. (ed.), *Microprocessors, Manpower and Society: A Comparative, Cross-national Approach*, pp. 111–33, Aldershot: Gower.

Rousseau, D.M. & Cooke, R.A. (1984) 'Technology and Structure', *Journal of Management*, Vol. 10, No. 3, pp. 345–61.

Rubenstein, A.H. (1976) 'Technical Information, Technical Assistance and Technology Transfer: The Need for Synthesis', *R&D Management*, Vol. 6, No. 4, pp. 145–50.

Rubin, H., (ed.) (1995) *International Technology Transfers*, London: Graham & Trotman.

Rubin, H., Zepos, C.J. & Crocker, T.E. (1995) 'Structuring Alternatives for International Technology Transfer', in: Rubin, H. (ed.), *International Technology Transfer*, pp. 69–152, London: Graham & Trotman.

Rueschemeyer, D. & Evans, P. (1985) 'The State and Economic Transformation: Toward an Analysis of the Conditions Underlying Effective Intervention', in: Evans, P., Rueschemeyer, D. & Skocpol, T. (eds.), *Bringing the State Back In*, pp. 44–77, Cambridge: Cambridge University Press.

Rush, H. & Williams, R. (1984) 'Consultation and Change: New Technology and Manpower in the Electronics Industry,' in: Warner, M. (ed.), *Microprocessors, Manpower and Society: A Comparative, Cross-national Approach*, pp. 171–88, Aldershot: Gower.

Ruttan, V.W. (1978) 'Induced Institutional Innovation', in: Binswanger, H., Ruttan, V.W. & Ben-Zion, U. (eds.), *Induced Innovation*, Baltimore: Johns Hopkins University Press.

Ruttan, V. & Hayami, Y. (1973) 'Technology Transfer and Agricultural Development', *Technology and Culture*, Vol. 14, No. 2, pp. 119–50.

Sacerdoti, G. (1986) 'Crimping the Copiers', *Far Eastern Economic Review*, Vol. 134, No. 46 (November), p. 131.

Safarian, A.E. & Bertin, G.Y. (1989) *Multinationals, Governments and International Technology Transfer*, London: Croom Helm.

Sagafi-nejad, T. (1979) 'Developmental Impact of Technology Transfer: Theory, Determinants, and Verifications from Iran, 1954–74', Ph.D. dissertation, University of Pennsylvania, Philadelphia.

Sagafi-nejad, T., Perlmutter, H.V. & Moxon, R.W., (eds.) (1981) *Controlling International Technology Transfer*, New York: Pergamon.

Saggi, K. (2000) 'Trade, Foreign Direct Investment and International Technology Transfer: A Survey', WT/WGTI/W/88, World Trade Organisation, Dallas, Texas.

Saha, P.C. (2003) 'Sustainable Energy Development: A Challenge for Asia and the Pacific Region in the 21st Century', *Energy Policy*, Vol. 31, No. 11, pp. 1051–59.

Sakong, I. (1969) 'Factor Market Price Distortions and Choice of Production Techniques in Developing Countries', Ph.D. dissertation, Graduate School of Business Administration, University of California, Los Angeles.

Sakuma, A. (1995) 'The Dynamics of Innovation and Learning-by-Doing: The Case of Integrated Circuit Industry', in: Minami, R., Makine, H. & Soe, J. (eds.), *Acquiring, Adapting and Developing Technologies*, pp. 165–90, London: St. Martin's.

Salam, A. & Kidwai, A. (1991) 'A Blueprint for Science and Technology in the Developing World', *Technology in Society*, Vol. 13, No. 4, pp. 389–404.

Salas, Rafael M. (1986) *Reflections on Population*, New York: Pergamon.

Saltzman, C. & Duggal, V.G. (1995) 'Financial Deepening and the Technological Constraint: A Look at Korea', *Journal of Developing Areas*, Vol. 29, July, pp. 341–54.

Sankar, Y. (1991) *Management of Technological Change*, New York: John Wiley.

Saveri, Andrea (1999) 'Shifts in the Global Business Landscape: Opportunities and Threats for 21st Century Organisations', Proceedings of the Globalisation Management Strategies Conference, 17–18 May, California.

Sayers, B.McA. (1995) 'Engineering in the Health Sciences: The Impact of Scientific Advances on Future Health', Report of a WHO–CIOMS Colloquium, 20–24 June, Charlottesville, Virginia.

Scarbrough, H. & Corbett, J.M. (1992) *Technology and Organisation*, London: Routledge.

Schechter, J. (1982) 'Technology Transfer to Developing Countries Using an Applied Research and Development Institute', in: Mogavero, L.N. & Shane, R.S. (eds.), *Technology Transfer and Innovation*, New York: Marcel Dekker.

Scherer, F.M., (ed.) (1986) *Innovation and Growth*, Cambridge, Massachusetts: MIT Press.

Schoenecker, T.S., Myers, D.D. & Schmidt, P. (1989) 'Technology Transfer at Land-Grant Universities', *Journal of Technology Transfer*, Vol. 14, No. 2, pp. 28–32.

Schon, D.A. (1967) *Technology and Change: The New Heraclitus*, New York: Delacorte.

Schramm, W. (1964) *Mass Media and National Development*, Stanford, California: Stanford University Press.

Schumacher, E.F. (1973) *Small Is Beautiful: A Study of Economics as if People Mattered*, London: Blond & Briggs.

Schumpeter, J.A. (1934) *The Theory of Economic Development*, Cambridge, Massachusetts: Harvard University Press (Reprinted 1974, Oxford University Press, Oxford).

―――― (1939) *Business Cycles: A Theoretical, Historical and Statistical Analysis of the Capitalist Process*, New York: McGraw-Hill.

―――― (1947) *Capitalism, Socialism and Democracy*, London & New York: Harper & Row.

Scott, B.R. & Lodge, G.C. (1985) *US Competitiveness in the World Economy*, Boston, Massachusetts: Harvard Business School Press.

Scott, M. (1995) 'What Sustains Economic Development?' in: Goldin, I. & Winters, L.A. (eds.), *The Economics of Sustainable Development*, pp. 83–110, Cambridge: Cambridge University Press.

Scott-Kemmis, D. & Bell, M. (1988) 'Technological Dynamism and the Technological Content of Collaboration: Are Indian Firms Missing Opportunities?' in: Desai, A. (ed.), *Technology Absorption in Indian Industry*, pp. 71–86, New Delhi: Wiley Eastern.

Sebastian, I. & Alicbusan, A. (1989) 'Sustainable Development', Environment Department Divisional Working Papers 1989–96, World Bank, Washington, D.C.

Sedaitis, J. (2000) 'Technology Transfer in Transitional Economies: A Test of Market, State and Organisational Models', *Research Policy*, Vol. 29, No. 2, pp. 135–47.

Seers, D. (1962) 'A Theory of Inflation and Growth', *Oxford Economic Papers*, Vol. 14, June, pp. 174–97.

Segal, A. (1986) 'From Technology Transfer to Science and Technology Utilisation', in: McIntyre, J.R. & Papp, D.S. (eds.), *The Political Economy of International Technology Transfer*, Westport, Connecticut: Quorum Books.

Segal, M.W. (1978) 'Effective Technology Transfer from Laboratory to Production Line', *Mechanical Engineering*, Vol. 100, No. 4, pp. 32–35.

Sen, A.K. (1960) *Choice of Techniques*, Oxford: Blackwell.

Sen, R.N. (1984) 'Application of Ergonomics to Industrially Developing Countries', *Ergonomics*, Vol. 27, No. 1, pp. 1021–32.

Senker, P. (1995) 'Technological Change and the Future of Work', in: Heap, N. et al. (eds.), *Information Technology and Society*, London: Sage.

Shahnavaz, H. (1992) 'Ergonomics and Industrial Development', *Impact of Science on Society*, Serial No. 165: Vol. 42, No. 1, pp. 99–108.

Sharif, M.N. (1986) *Technology Policy Formulation and Planning,* Bangalore: APCTT.

―――― (1988) 'Basis for Techno-economic Policy', *Science and Public Policy,* Vol. 15, No. 4, pp. 217–29.

Sharif, N. (1992) 'Technological Dimensions of International Cooperation and Sustainable Development', *Technological Forecasting and Social Change,* Vol. 42, No. 4, pp. 367–83.

―――― (1994a) 'Integrating Business and Technology Strategies in Developing Countries', *Technological Forecasting and Social Change,* Vol. 45, No. 2, pp. 151–67.

―――― (1994b) 'Technology Change Management', *Technological Forecasting and Social Change,* Vol. 47, No. 1, pp. 103–14.

―――― (1999) 'Strategic Role of Technological Self-reliance in Development Management', *Technological Forecasting and Social Change,* Vol. 62, No. 3, pp. 219–38.

Shaw, E.S. (1973) *Financial Deepening in Economic Development,* New York: Oxford University Press.

Siddharthan, N.S. (1999) 'Technology Transfer, WTO and Emerging Issues', National Seminar on Economy, Society and Policy in South Asia, 16–17 November, Institute of Economic Growth, Delhi.

Simon, D. (1991) 'International and the Trans-border Movement of Technology: A Dialectical Perspective', in: Agmon, T. & Glinow, von M. (eds.), *Technology Transfer in International Business,* pp. 5–29, Oxford: Oxford University Press.

Simon, H. (1960) *The New Science of Management Decisions,* New York: Harper & Row.

Slaybaugh, C.W. (1981) 'Factors in Technology Transfer: A Multinational Firm Perspective', in: Hawkins, R.G. & Prasad, A.K. (eds.), *Technology Transfer and Economic Development,* Research in International Business and Finance, Vol. 2, pp. 289–305, Greenwich, Connecticut: Jai Press.

Soete, L. (1981) 'A General Test of Technological Gap Trade Theory', *Weltwirtschaftliches Archive,* Vol. 117, No. 4, pp. 639–59.

Solow, R.M. (1957) 'Technical Change in the Aggregate Production Function', *Review of Economics and Statistics,* Vol. 39, No. 3, pp. 312–20.

Soon, C. (1994) *The Dynamics of Korean Economic Development,* Washington, D.C: Institute for International Economics.

Souder, W.E. (1980) *Management Decision Methods for Managers of Engineering and Research,* New York: Van Nostrand Reinhold.

―――― (1989a) *Managing New Product Innovations,* Lexington, Massachusetts: Lexington Books.

―――― (1989b) 'Improving Productivity through Technology Push', *Research-Technology Management,* Vol. 32, No. 2, pp. 19–24.

Souder, W.E. & Padmanabhan, V. (1989) 'Transferring New Technologies from R&D to Manufacturing', *Research-Technology Management*, Vol. 32, No. 5, pp. 38–43.

——— (1990) 'A Role Interaction Model for Implementing CIMS', in: Parsaei, H.R., Ward, T.L. & Karwowski, W. (eds.), *Justification Methods for Computer Integrated Manufacturing Systems*, Amsterdam: Elsevier.

Souder, W.E., Nashar, A.S. & Padmanabhan, V. (1990) 'A Guide to the Best Technology-Transfer Practices', *Journal of Technology Transfer*, Vol. 15, Winter–Spring, pp. 5–16.

Spencer, R. (1993) 'Technology Transfer by Information Exchange', Proceedings of the Global Technology Partnership Conference, 23–25 March, Birmingham, UK.

Stankiewicz, R. (1990) 'Basic Technologies and the Innovation Process', in: Sigurdson, J. (ed.), *Measuring the Dynamics of Technological Change*, London: Pinter.

Steele, Lowell W. (1975) Proceedings of the UN/ECE Seminar on Management of the Transfer of Technology within Industrial Co-operation, 14–17 July, Geneva.

Stern, N.H. (1993) 'The World Bank as an Intellectual Actor', STICERD, London: London School of Economics.

Stewart, F. (1977) *Technology and Under-development*, London: Macmillan.

——— (1978) *Technology and Development* (Second edition), London: Macmillan.

——— (1981) 'Taxation and Technology Transfer', in: Sagafi-nejad, T., Perlmutter, H.V. & Moxon, R.W. (eds.), *Controlling Technology Transfer*, Chapter Six, New York: Pergamon.

——— (1984) 'Facilitating Indigenous Technical Change in Third World Countries', in: Fransman, M. & King, K. (eds.), *Technological Capability in the Third World*, pp. 81–94, New York: St. Martin's.

——— (1987) *Macro-Policies for Appropriate Technology*, Boulder, Colorado: Westview.

——— (1990) 'Technology Transfer for Development', in: Evenson, R.E. & Rains, G. (eds.), *Science and Technology: Lessons for Development*, pp. 301–24, Boulder & San Francisco: Westview.

——— (1992) *North–South and South–South*, London: Macmillan.

Stewart, F. & Ranis, G. (1990) 'Macro-Policies for Appropriate Technology: A Synthesis of Findings', in: Stewart, F., Thomas, H. & de Wilde, T. (eds.), *The Other Policy*, pp. 3–43, London: IT Publications.

Stiglitz, J. & Dasgupta, P. (1977) 'Market Structure and the Nature of Innovative Activity', IEA Conference on Economic Growth and Resources, August, Tokyo.

Stobaugh, R. & Wells, L.T., (eds.) (1984) *Technology Crossing Borders*, Boston, Massachusetts: Harvard Business School Press.

Stock, G.N. & Tatikonda, M.V. (2000) 'A Typology of Project-Level Technology Transfer Processes', *Journal of Operations Management*, Vol. 18, No. 6, pp. 719–37.

Storper, M. & Walker, R. (1989) *The Capitalist Imperative: Territory, Technology, and Industrial Growth*, Oxford: Basil Blackwell.

Strassmann, W.P. (1968) *Technological Change and Economic Development: The Manufacturing Experience of Mexico and Puerto Rico*, Ithaca: Cornell University Press.

Subrahmanian, K.K. (1987) 'Towards Technological Self-reliance', in: Brahmananda, P.R. & Panchamukhi, V.R. (eds.), *The Development Process of the Indian Economy*, pp. 420–46, Bombay: Himalaya.

Sullivan, N.F. (1995) *Technology Transfer: Making the Most of Your Intellectual Property*, Cambridge: Cambridge University Press.

Summers, R. & Heston, A. (1988) 'A New Set of International Comparisons of Real Products and Price Levels: Estimates for 130 Countries, 1960–85', *Review of Income and Wealth*, Vol. 34, No. 1, pp. 1–25.

Sun, Y. (2000) 'Spatial Distribution of Patents in China', *Regional Studies*, Vol. 34, No. 5, pp. 441–54.

Sung, T.K., Gibson, D.V. & Kang, B. (2003) 'Characteristics of Technology Transfer in Business Ventures: The Case of Daejeon, Korea', *Technological Forecasting and Social Change*, Vol. 70, No. 5, pp. 449–66.

Symons, V. (1990) 'Evaluation of Information Systems: IS Development in the Processing Company', *Journal of Information Technology*, Vol. 5, No. 4, pp. 194–204.

Szyliowicz, J.S. (1981) *Technology and International Affairs*, New York: Praeger.

Tambunlertchai, S. (1989) 'Economic Prospects and External Economic Relations of Thailand', *Asian Development Review*, Vol. 7, No. 2, pp. 20–31.

Tang, J.C.S. & Nam, I.S. (1993) 'Sector Priority and Technology Choice in the Korean Machinery Industry', *International Journal of Technology Management*, Vol. 8, Nos. 3/4/5, pp. 333–41.

Tapscott, D. (1982) *Office Automation: A User Driven Method*, New York: Plenum.

Tarjanne, P. (1999) 'Preparing for the Next Revolution in Telecommunications: Implementing the WTO Agreement', *Telecommunications Policy*, Vol. 23, No. 1, pp. 51–63.

Tata, R.J. & Schultz, R.R. (1988) 'World Variation in Human Welfare: A New Index of Development Status', *Annals of the Association of American Geographers*, Vol. 78, No. 4, pp. 580–93.

Taylor, L. (1983) *Structuralist Macroeconomics: Applicable Models for the Third World*, New York: Basic Books.

Teece, D.J. (1977) *Technology Transfer by Multinational Firms: The Resource of International Technology Transfer*, Cambridge, Massachusetts: Ballinger.

Teramoto, Y., Richter, F.J. & Iwasaki, N. (1993) 'Learning to Succeed: What European Firms Can Learn from Japanese Approaches to Strategic Alliances', *Creativity and Innovation Management*, Vol. 2, No. 2, pp. 114–21.

Tharakan, P.K.M. (1984) 'Intra-industry Trade between the Industrial Countries and the Developing World', *European Economic Review*, Vol. 26, Nos. 1/2, pp. 213–27.

The Technology Atlas Team (1987a) 'Components of Technology for Resources Transformation', *Technological Forecasting and Social Change*, Vol. 32, No. 1, pp. 19–35.

—— (1987b) 'Assessment of Technology Climate in Two Countries', *Technological Forecasting and Social Change*, Vol. 32, No. 1, pp. 85–109.

Thomas, R. (1982) *India's Emergence as an Industrial Power*, New Delhi: Vikas.

Thompson, J. (1967) *Organisations in Action*, New York: McGraw-Hill.

Thomson, R. (1993) *Learning and Technological Change*, London: St. Martin's.

Tisdell, C. (1988) 'Technology: A Factor in Developing Socio-economic and Environmental Change', in: Tisdell, C. & Maitra, P. (eds.), *Technological Change, Development and the Environment*, pp. 1–7, London: Routledge.

—— (1999) 'Conditions for Sustainable Development: Weak and Strong', in: Dragun, A.K. & Tisdell, C. (eds.), *Sustainable Agriculture and Environment: Globalisation and the Impact of Trade Liberalisation*, pp. 23–36, Cheltenham: Edward Elgar.

—— (2001) 'Globalisation and Sustainability: Environmental Kuznets Curve and the WTO', *Ecological Economics*, Vol. 39, No. 2, pp. 185–96.

Tisdell, C. & Maitra, P. (1988) *Technological Change, Development and the Environment*, London: Routledge.

Todaro, M.P. (1981) *Economic Development in the Third World*, New York: The Book Press.

—— (1983) *The Struggle for Economic Development: Readings in Problems and Policies*, New York: Longman.

—— (1994) *Economic Development*, New York: Longman.

Todd, D. & Simpson, J.A. (1983) 'The Appropriate Technology Question in a Regional Context', *Growth and Change*, Vol. 14, No. 4, pp. 46–52.

Todo, Y. (2003) 'Empirically Consistent Scale Effects: An Endogenous Growth Model with Technology Transfer to Developing Countries', *Journal of Macroeconomics*, Vol. 25, No. 1, pp. 25–46.

Tolba, M.K. (1992) *Saving Our Planet*, London: Chapman & Hall.

Tolba, M.K. et al., (eds.) (1993) *The World Environment 1972–1992*, London: Chapman & Hall.

Tolentino, P.E. (1993) *Technological Innovation and Third World Multinationals*, London: Routledge.

Tonn, B.E. (2003) 'The Future of Futures Decision Making', *Futures*, Vol. 35, No. 6, pp. 673–88.

Touche Ross (1991) 'Global Climate Change: The Role of Technology Transfer', Report prepared for the UK Department of Trade and Industry and the Overseas Development Administration, Touche Ross Management Consultants, London.

Trajtenberg, M. (2001) 'Innovation in Israel 1968–1997', *Research Policy*, Vol. 30, No. 3, pp. 363–89.

Turnipseed, D. (1994) 'The Relationship between the Social Environment of Organisations and the Climate for Innovation and Creativity', *Creativity and Innovation Management*, Vol. 3, No. 3, pp. 184–95.

Ulrich, R.A. & Weiland, G.F. (1980) *Organisation Design and Theory*, Homewood, Illinois: Irwin.

Unger, K. (1988) 'Industrial Structure, Technical Change and Microeconomic Behaviour in LDCs', in: Dosi, G., Forsyth, D.J.C., McBain, N.S. & Solomon, R.F. (eds.), *Technical Change and Economic Theory*, London: Pinter.

United Nations (UN) (1972) General Assembly Resolution, 2997 (XXVII), 15 December, Stockholm Conference on the Human Environment, Stockholm, Sweden.

—— (1978) 'Transnational Corporations in World Development: A Re-examination', Sales No. E78 II A.5, New York: UN Economic and Social Council.

—— (1980) The International Code of Conduct on the Transfer of Technology, UN TD/CODE TOT/25, Geneva.

United Nations Centre on Transnational Corporations (UNCTC) (1987) *Transnational Corporations and Technology Transfer: Effects and Policy Issues*, New York: UNCTC.

United Nations Conference on Trade and Development (UNCTAD) (1975) Draft Outline for Preparation of an International Code of Conduct on Technology Transfer Submitted by the Expert from Brazil on Behalf of the Experts of the Group of 77, and Draft Outline for Preparation of an International Code of Conduct on Technology Transfer Submitted by the Expert from Japan on Behalf of the Experts from Group B, 28 November, UNCTAD, Geneva.

United Nations Conference on Trade and Development (UNCTAD) (1979) The International Code of Conduct on the Transfer of Technology, TD/COD TOT/C.1/CRP.3, February, UNCTAD, Geneva.

——— (1982) 'Report and Recommendations of the Asian Regional Workshop on Policies and Planning for Technological Transformation', UNCTAD/TT/50, UNCTAD & Regional Centre for Transfer of Technology, Bangalore.

——— (1983) 'Technology Issues in the Capital Goods Sector: A Case Study of Leading Machinery Producers in India', UNCTAD, Geneva.

——— (1997) Promoting the Transfer and Use of Environmentally Sound Technologies: A Review of Policies, New York: UNCTAD.

United Nations Educational, Scientific and Cultural Organisation (UNESCO) (1992) UNESCO Statistical Yearbook 1991, Paris: UNESCO.

United Nations Environment Programme (UNEP) (1981) In Defence of the Earth: The Basic Texts on Environment, Founex, Stockholm & Cocoyoc, Nairobi: UNEP.

——— (1987) Environmental Perspective to the Year 2000 and Beyond, Nairobi: UNEP.

——— (1992) Status of Desertification and Implementation of the United Nations Plan of Action to Combat Desertification, UNEP, Nairobi.

——— (2002) Environmental Impact Assessment Issues, Trends and Practice, New York: Earth Print, UNEP.

United Nations International Development Organisation (UNIDO) (1979) 'World Industry since 1960: Progress and Prospects', Special Issue of the Industrial Development Survey for the Third General Conference of UNIDO, New York.

Usher, D. (1981) The Economic Prerequisites to Democracy, Oxford: Basil Blackwell.

van de Ven, A.H. & Delbecq, A.A. (1974) 'A Task Contingent Model of Work Unit Structure', Administrative Science Quarterly, Vol. 19, No. 2, pp. 183–97.

van Gigch, J.P. (1978) Applied General Systems Theory, New York: Harper & Row.

Veblen, T., (ed.) (1966) Imperial Germany and Industrial Revolution, Ann Arbor: University of Michigan Press.

Vincent, T.C. et al. (1985) Environmental Impact Assessment, Technology Assessment, and Risk Analysis: Contributions from the Psychological and Decision Sciences, Berlin: Springer-Verlag.

Vitelli, G. (1978) 'Competition, Oligopoly and Technological Change in the Construction Industry: The Argentine Case', Working Paper No. 3, Research Programme in Science and Technology, IDB/ECLA/UNDP Programme, Buenos Aires.

Vongpanitlerd, S. (1992) *The Development of Thailand's Technological Capability in Industry*, Bangkok: Thailand Development Research Institute.

Voss, C.A. (1984) 'Production, Operation Management: A Key Discipline for Research', *Omega*, Vol. 12, No. 3, pp. 309–19.

Wade, R. (1990) 'Industrial Policy in East Asia: Does It Lead or Follow the Market?' in: Gereffi, G. & Wyman, D. (eds.), *Manufacturing Miracles*, pp. 231–66, Princeton, New Jersey: Princeton University Press.

Walker, A.E. (1988) 'The Transfer of Technology: A Study of United Kingdom Cook-Chill Catering Operation', Ph.D. dissertation, Dorset Institute of Higher Education, UK.

Wallace, J., (ed.) (1990) *Foreign Direct Investment in the 1990s: A New Climate in the Third World*, Dordrecht: Martinus Nijhoff.

Wallender, H. (1979) *Technology Transfer and Management in Developing Countries*, Cambridge Massachusetts: Ballinger.

Walsham, G. (1993) 'Decentralisation of IS in Developing Countries: Power to the People?' *Journal of Information Technology*, Vol. 8, No. 2, pp. 74–81.

Walsham, G., Symons, V. & Waema, T. (1990) 'Information Systems as Social Systems: Implications for Developing Countries', in: Bhatnagar, S.C. & Bjorn-Anderson (eds.), *Information Technology in Developing Countries*, pp. 51–61, Amsterdam: North-Holland.

Wang, Z. (2003) 'The Impact of China's WTO Accession on Patterns of World Trade', *Journal of Policy Modeling*, Vol. 25, No. 1, pp. 1–41.

Weaver, J.H. & Jameson, K. (1978) *Economic Development: Competing Paradigm—Competing Parable*, Washington, D.C.: Development Studies Programme, Agency for International Development.

Wells, J.P. & Malan, P.S. (1984) 'Structural Models of Inflation and Balance of Payments Disequilibria in Semi-industrialized Economies: Some Implications for Stabilisation and Growth Policies', in: Csikos, N., Hague, D. & Hall, G. (eds.), *The Economics of Relative Prices: Proceedings of a Conference held by the International Economic Association in Athens, Greece*, pp. 391–408, New York: St. Martin's.

Wells, L.T. (1973) 'Economic Man and Engineering Man: Choice of Technology in a Low-Wage Country', *Public Policy*, Vol. 21, Summer, pp. 219–42.

———— (1984) 'Economic Man and Engineering Man', in: Stobaugh, R. & Wells, L.T. (eds.), *Technology Crossing Borders*, Boston, Massachusetts: Harvard Business School Press.

Wen, G.J. (2000) 'New Frontier of Economic Globalisation: The Significance of China's Accession to WTO', *China Economic Review*, Vol. 11, No. 4, pp. 432–36.

Wenk, E. & Kuehn, T.J. (1977) 'International Networks in Technological Delivery Systems', in: Haberer, J. (ed.), *Science and Technology Policy*, pp. 153–57, Lexington, Massachusetts: Lexington Books.

Westphal, L.E., Kim, L. & Dahlman, C.J. (1985) 'Reflections on the Republic of Korea's Acquisition of Technological Capability', in: Rosenberg, N. & Frischtak, C. (eds.), *International Technology Transfer*, pp.167–221, New York: Praeger.

Westphal, L.E., Rhee, Y.W., Kim, L. & Amsden, A.H. (1984) 'Exports of Capital Goods and Related Services from the Republic of Korea', World Bank Staff Working Paper No. 629, World Bank, Washington, D.C.

Westphal, L.E., Kritayakirana, K., Petchsuwan, K., Sutabutr, H. & Yuthavong, Y. (1990) 'The Development of Technological Capability in Manufacturing: A Macroscopic Approach to Policy Research', in: Evenson, R.E. & Ranis, G. (eds.), *Science and Technology*, Boulder, Colorado: Westview.

White, G. & Wade, R. (1988) 'Developmental States and Markets in East Asia: An Introduction', in: White, G. (ed.), *Development States in East Asia*, pp. 1–26, London: Macmillan.

Williams, D. (1976) 'National Planning and the Choice of Technology: The Case of Textiles in Tanzania', D.B.A. dissertation, Harvard Business School, Boston, Massachusetts.

Williams, F. & Gibson, D.V. (1990) *Technology Transfer: A Communication Perspective*, Sage.

Wilmot, P.D. (1977) 'Technology Transfer in a Multinational Firm', in: Cetron, M.J. & Davidson, H.F. (eds.), *Industrial Technology Transfer*, pp. 355–61, Leiden: Noordhoff.

Winner, L. (1986) *The Whale and the Reactor*, Chicago: University of Chicago Press.

Wisner, A. (1980) 'Action at National Level in Framing Education and Training Policies and Programmes in Occupational Safety and Health and Working Conditions', Asia-Pacific Tripartite Regional Seminar on Education and Training Policies and Programmes in the Field of Working Conditions and Environment, ILO, Bangkok.

—— (1984) 'Organisations Transfer towards Industrially Developing Countries', in: Hendrick, H.W. & Brown, O.J. (eds.), *Human Factors in Organisational Design Management*, pp. 83–95, Amsterdam: Elsevier.

Withey, M., Daft, R.L. & Cooper, W.H. (1983) 'Measures of Perrow's Work Unit Technology: An Empirical Assessment and a New Scale', *Academy of Management Journal*, Vol. 26, No. 1, pp. 45–63.

Wong, J. & Khan, H. (1991) 'Transnational Corporations and Industrialisation in Singapore', *Regional Development Dialogue* (UNCRD, Japan), Vol. 12, No. 1, pp. 67–88.

Woodward, J. (1965) *Industrial Organisations: Theory and Practice*, London: Oxford University Press.

—— (1970) *Industrial Organisations: Behaviour and Control*, London: Oxford University Press.

——, (ed.) (1958) *Management and Technology*, London: Her Majesty's Stationery Office.

World Bank (1979) *World Development Report*, Washington, D.C.: World Bank.

—— (1997) *World Development Report*, Washington, D.C.: World Bank.

World Trade Organisation (WTO) (2001a) WTO Capacity Building and Development, http//www.wto.orgenlishres.

—— (2001b) Doha Ministerial Declaration, WT/MIN(01)/DEC/1, November, WTO, Doha.

—— (2001c) 'Towards Free Market Access for Least-Developed Countries', Doha WTO Ministerial Conference, Briefing Notes, WTO, Doha.

World Wide Fund for Nature (WWF) (1999) 'Initiating an Environmental Assessment of Trade Liberalisation in the WTO', WWF International, Amsterdam.

Xu, B. (2000) 'Multinational Enterprises: Technology Diffusion and Host Country Productivity Growth', *Journal of Development Economics*, Vol. 62, No. 2, pp. 477–93.

Yam, Joseph (2001) 'The WTO: China's Future and Hong Kong's Opportunity', *Cato Journal*, Vol. 21, No. 1, pp. 1–11.

Yang, G. (2001) 'Intellectual Property Rights, Licensing, and Innovation in an Endogenous Product-Cycle Model', *Journal of International Economics*, Vol. 53, No. 1, pp. 169–81.

Yankey, G. (1986) 'The Role of the International Patent System in the Transfer of Technology to West Africa', Ph.D. dissertation, University of Warwick, UK.

Yapa, L.S. (1977) 'The Green Revolution: A Diffusion Model', *Annals of the Association of American Geographers*, Vol. 67, pp. 350–59.

Yin, J.Z. (1992) 'Technological Capabilities as Determinants of the Success of Technology Transfer Projects', *Technological Forecasting and Social Change*, Vol. 42, No. 1, pp. 17–29.

Zadeh, L.A. (1965) 'Fuzzy Sets', *Information and Control*, Vol. 8, No. 3, pp. 338–58.

—— (1975) 'The Concept of a Linguistic Variable and Its Application to Approximate Reasoning', *Information Science*, Vol. 8, No. 3, pp. 199–249.

—— (1976) 'The Concept of a Linguistic Variable and Its Application to Approximate Reasoning', *Information Science*, Vol. 9, No. 1, pp. 43–80.

Zhang, Q. (1996) *International Technology Transfer: Disputes and Prevention with Case Studies*, Shanxi: Economic Publishing.

INDEX

About the Author

Goel Cohen is currently Visiting Professor at the Imperial College of Science, Technology and Medicine, University of London, and faculty member at Teheran University, Iran. He began his career in 1976 with the Arya-Mehr (Sharif) University of Technology, Iran. Subsequently, he joined the faculty of Management and Environment, University of Teheran, as Senior Lecturer, before enrolling as an Honorary Research Associate at the Imperial College, London, to pursue research in technology management and decision-making. Professor Cohen has been the recipient of as many as 19 awards in Iran in recognition of his teaching and research publications. He has authored numerous books in Persian on the topics of engineering management, organisational theory and management, strategic management, sustainable development and communications. Professor Goel Cohen has also jointly authored more than 30 papers and journal articles in English and has undertaken consultancy work for a number of private and public sector organisations. He has a PhD from the Imperial College of Science, Technology and Medicine, University of London.